The Mexican Revolution began in 1910 with high hopes and a multitude of spokesmen clamoring for a better life for ordinary Mexicans. This anthology examines how the revolution brought change and often progress. Women, the landless, the poor, the country folk are among those receiving consideration in the twenty-seven readings, which range from political and economic to social and intellectual history.

Combining the best new scholarship by modern historians; outstanding work by distinguished Mexicanists of the past; excerpts from Mexico's finest fiction, poetry, and commentary; reminiscence; cartoons; and illustrations, *Twentieth-Century Mexico* brilliantly illuminates the Mexican experience from Porfirio Díaz to petrodollars. A concluding essay ties together the strands of twentieth-century Mexican culture to help U.S. readers understand not only Mexico's present situation but also its relations with the Colossus of the North. Like its predecessor, *Mexico: From Independence to Revolution* (UNP, 1982), this book includes suggestions for further reading and an index.

W. Dirk Raat, professor of history at the State University of New York at Fredonia, was the editor of *Mexico: From Independence to Revolution*. Among his other works is *The Mexican Revolution: An Annotated Guide to Recent Scholarship* (1982). William H. Beezley, professor of history at North Carolina State University, is the author of *Insurgent Governor: Abraham Gonzalez and the Mexican Revolution in Chihuahua* (UNP, 1973) and other works.

TWENTIETH-CENTURY MEXICO

Edited, with commentary, by
W. Dirk Raat and William H. Beezley

University of Nebraska Press
Lincoln and London

Library of Congress Cataloging-in-Publication Data
Main entry under title:

Twentieth-century Mexico.

Bibliography: p.
Includes index.
1. Mexico—History—20th century—Addresses, essays,
lectures. 2. Mexico—Social conditions—Addresses,
essays, lectures. I. Raat, W. Dirk (William Dirk),
1939–   . II. Beezley, William H. III. Title: 20th
century Mexico.
F1234.T975   1986   972.08   85-14109
ISBN 0-8032-3868-1

Second printing: 1988

Dedicated to the memory of
David C. Bailey and Roger M. Haigh

CONTENTS

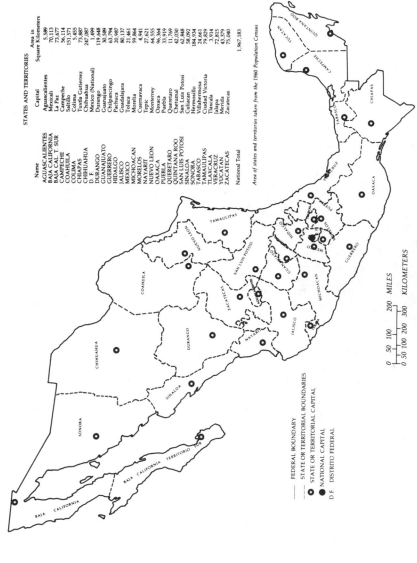

STATES AND TERRITORIES

Name	Capital	Area in Square Kilometers
AGUASCALIENTES	Aguascalientes	5,589
BAJA CALIFORNIA	Mexicali	70,113
BAJA CAL. T. SUR	La Paz	73,677
CAMPECHE	Campeche	56,114
COAHUILA	Saltillo	151,571
COLIMA	Colima	5,455
CHIAPAS	Tuxtla Gutierrez	73,887
CHIHUAHUA	Chihuahua	247,087
D. F.	Mexico (National)	1,499
DURANGO	Durango	119,648
GUANAJUATO	Guanajuato	30,589
GUERRERO	Chilpancingo	63,794
HIDALGO	Pachuca	20,987
JALISCO	Guadalajara	80,137
MEXICO	Toluca	21,461
MICHOACAN	Morelia	59,864
MORELOS	Cuernavaca	4,941
NAYARIT	Tepic	27,621
NUEVO LEON	Monterrey	64,555
OAXACA	Oaxaca	96,364
PUEBLA	Puebla	33,919
QUERETARO	Queretaro	11,769
QUINTANA ROO	Chetumal	42,030
SAN LUIS POTOSI	San Luis Potosi	62,848
SINALOA	Culiacan	58,092
SONORA	Hermosillo	184,934
TABASCO	Villahermosa	24,661
TAMAULIPAS	Ciudad Victoria	79,829
TLAXCALA	Tlaxcala	3,914
VERACRUZ	Jalapa	72,815
YUCATAN	Merida	43,379
ZACATECAS	Zacatecas	75,040
National Total		1,967,183

Area of states and territories taken from the 1960 Population Census

Map 1. STATES AND TERRITORIES OF MEXICO. Reprinted from *Atlas of Mexico* (1970), p. 4, by permission of the Bureau of Business Research, University of Texas at Austin.

Map 2. PHYSIOGRAPHY OF MEXICO. Reprinted from *Atlas of Mexico* (1970), p. 5, by permission of the Bureau of Business Research, University of Texas at Austin.

PREFACE

Mexico's twentieth century has been one of dramatic upheaval, violence, chaos, growth, and change, inexplicably acted out against a backdrop of frozen, traditional values and ancient American history. The contradictory worlds of ancient and modern Mexico are often expressed through seemingly endless conflicting forces. Thus it is that the peasant confronts the landlord; subsistence agriculture loses out to commercial farming; traditionalism struggles with modernism in art and politics; the indigenous East does battle with the modern West; communalism faces capitalism; rural Mexico undergoes urbanization; and *Mexicanos* love and hate the gringo Colossus of the North. These contradictions and conflicts are expressed daily by Mexicans. On the one hand, Marxist pundits speak of repression, pharaohism, corruption, pollution, and poverty. They call for revolution. On the other hand, bureaucrats speak of justice, democracy, honesty, cleanliness, and the "economic miracle." A contemporary style of doublespeak is officially adopted, and the call is for a continuation of the "institutionalized revolution."

So it is that Mexico's so-called revolutionary tradition embraces past and future. The PRI—that is, the Partido Revolucionario Institucional, which dominates Mexico's political landscape—is the modernizing agency that has left Mexico both traditional and modern, a PRI-modern nation. Contemporary Mexico reflects the many strains of a people in transition—what historians view as a struggle and dialogue between past and present. While these contradictions may seem abstract to outsiders, they can be understood in concrete and human terms. For example, nine basic foodstuffs, including meat and beans, underwent a 100-percent price increase in only twelve days in January 1984. Tortillas, then at the official price of 15.5 pesos, were selling in the *tortillerías* for more than 36 pesos. This kind of inflation forced Jaime Delgado (the Mexican counterpart of John Doe), a small *ranchero* from Puebla, to substitute milk for tea, rough brown *piloncillo* (unrefined sugar) for sugar, and beans for meat. Yet as bad as conditions were, Delgado's pesos bought even less a month later, when the leaders of the Banco de México affirmed that a daily 13-centavo slippage of the Mexican peso against the United States dollar would continue throughout 1984. When Jaime tried to make sense of all this, he was told by the bankers that devaluation, while resulting in increases in price levels, would in the long run stabilize the currency and start a downward trend of deflation. Meanwhile, Jaime's wife, Alicia, returned home with less food and more bad news: the price of eggs had risen from 95 pesos a kilo to 130.

The editors hope that this one-volume anthology will assist English-speaking readers, especially North Americans, to understand better the plight of Jaime, Alicia, and their neighbors to our south. For this reason the anthology, a sequel to *Mexico: From Independence to Revolution, 1810–1910* (Lincoln: University of Nebraska Press, 1982), begins and ends with the themes of agrarian reform, Mexico's food problems, and the images that Mexicans have of the United States. Michael C. Meyer's concluding essay should enable the reader to understand today's Mexico and some of the essential differences between the two cultures and societies of Mexico and the United States. We hope that this essay will assist the reader in reversing his or her vision and see the United States from a Mexican point of view, and that the first and last essays taken together will help readers understand Mexico and themselves better.

Overall the readings in this collection have been organized into four groups, with three pictorial sections that represent eras and themes in the contemporary history of Mexico. The first section is a general twentieth-century grouping, containing articles on agrarian reform and change, women's history, popular culture, folklore, and diplomacy. The other groupings are "The Great Rebellion, 1900–1923" (taken from the title of Ramón Ruíz's recent book and reflecting the editors' belief that Mexico in this period underwent more of a political rebellion and bureaucratic change than a broadranging social revolution; "Mexico under Calles and Cárdenas, 1923–40"; and the last era, "Mexico since Cárdenas, 1940 to the 1980s." This organization is a modest departure from traditional periodization and again reflects the editors' view that continuity characterizes Mexico's history from the late Porfiriato (1890s) to the 1920s and after.

The essays in Part I introduce the reader to general themes that run throughout Mexico's twentieth-century history. All of these themes are repeated in later sections. For example, Part I contains an article on women in Mexico as well as a pictorial collection on the same theme. In Part II the essay and pictorial section on Posada's Mexico examines the role of women at work. Part III includes a description by diplomat Josephus Daniels of the reaction of some of Mexico's women to the oil expropriation of 1938. Finally, Part IV contains an eyewitness account of the Tlatelolco massacre of 1968, a revealing view of the relationship of men to women in the radical movement.

With the exception of Part I, the first essay in each part is an introduction designed to acquaint the reader with general historical themes and problems of interpretation for the period. Each of these contains primary as well as secondary materials. Some of the primary materials consist of important literary documents, such as selections from the novels of Mariano Azuela and Gregorio López y Fuentes or the poem "Tarahumara Herbs" by Alfonso Reyes. Some nonliterary sources are included as well. These are the ballad or *corrido* "De Madero," the illustrations by José Guadalupe Posada, the urban legends and tales reproduced in the article on folklore, Diego Rivera's artwork, the cartoons by Abel Quezada, and the photographs of Mexican women. Other primary selections are contemporary accounts or descriptions of Mexico. Examples of this type include ambassador Henry Lane Wilson's account of the Décena Trágica, the Ten Tragic Days of February 1913 (reproduced here for the first time), Carleton Beals's travel account, diplomat Josephus Daniels's description of the oil expropriation, the interview by labor leader Vicente Lombardo Toledano (presented here in English for the first time), and the anonymous eyewitness accounts of the Tlatelolco massacre.

A wide range of interpretive essays have been included as well. Most of these represent recent scholarship, many of which are original works that appear here for the first time. Original essays include John Hart's study on agrarian reform, William Beezley on popular culture, W. Dirk Raat on folklore, Mark T. Gilderhus on United States–Mexican relations, Lyle Brown on Calles and

Cárdenas, David LaFrance on recent Mexico, Judith Hellman on social control, and the study of the church in Mexico by the late David Bailey.

Other essays were selected because of their worth in terms of content and interpretation. These are previously published works. An important contribution is John Womack's essay on the Mexican economy during the revolution. It is a challenging example of revisionist thinking. The same is true of Ramón Ruiz's profile of rebels and the excerpt on the *cristeros* by Luis González. Both of these come from prizewinning books. Shirlene Soto's perspective challenges the traditional view of women in Mexico. For variety, and to demonstrate the historian's dependence on auxiliary studies, we have included some important articles by nonhistorians. These are by anthropologist Paul Friedrich on agrarian revolt, political scientist Judith Hellman on social control, and writer Thomas Sanders on food problems.

The compilers have also collected works that demonstrate the diversity of Mexico's history and the variety of approaches that historians use in reconstructing Mexico's past. Excerpts include Marxist and non-Marxist accounts. Herein the reader can find examples of traditional narrative history (including the recent revival of narrative history referred to as "the new old history"), as well as the so-called new social history. Topics range from political, diplomatic, and religious history to intellectual, social, and economic history. Comparative history and analysis is reflected in the work by Michael Meyer. Luis González's contribution is an excellent example of regional history, while Paul Friedrich's study is a kind of ethnic history. The use of nonliterary sources by historians is illustrated in William Beezley's account of popular culture and W. Dirk Raat's study of folklore.

Of the various approaches contained here, the greatest emphasis is on social history. The compilers desire that the everyday concerns of Jaime and Alicia Delgado not be out of sight and mind. "People's history" is revealed in the *corrido,* Jas Reuter's essay on José Guadalupe Posada, and the several nonliterary sources found in this anthology. Novels and poems can also be important sources for the social historian who is willing to read between the lines. Many of the essays are in the *Annales* tradition of social history, including the works on popular culture, folklore, the Mexican cartoon tradition, women's history, indigenism, demography, and geography.

We hope that the reader of this volume will take away from his or her experience a new awareness and sensitivity to Mexico and things Mexican. Perhaps it is appropriate that we leave that reader with a final hint: When your Mexican friend blocks your view in the local Cuernavaca cinema, don't shout, "You'd make a better door than window!" Just say in a strong, firm voice, *"La carne de burro no es transparente"* (donkey meat is not transparent). You see, an awareness of Mexican history and cultural differences can have many wonderful practical results.

Special thanks go to the people who made original contributions to the volume. They are John M. Hart, Mark T. Gilderhus, Lyle Brown, David LaFrance, the late David C. Bailey, Judith Hellman, and Michael Meyer. Professor Meyer also served as general editor for this project. Also helpful were John Womack, Jr., Shirlene Soto, Jas Reuter, and Paul Friedrich, all of whom allowed us to reproduce their previously published articles. Vera Waller assisted in preparation of the final draft.

The political and topographical maps of Mexico that precede this preface were reproduced from Michael E. Bonine et al., *Atlas of Mexico* (Austin: Bureau of Business Research, University of Texas, 1970), pp. 4–5.

A NOTE ON THE EDITING

Reprinted pieces were reproduced with editorial deletions. Ellipses indicate those deletions. Source citations have been omitted from the reprinted essays. Readers who wish to follow up on the sources can consult the original articles; complete citations for them can be found at the beginning of each essay. The contributors of the original essays were instructed by the compilers to exclude endnotes and footnotes. The purpose has been to provide the beginning student of Mexico with essays unadorned with complicated and overwhelming references. Writers' preferences have been followed concerning whether to include bibliographical essays at the end of their essays. The articles by Hart, Raat, Gilderhus, LaFrance, and Meyer include some bibliography. All writers contributed to the "For Further Study" section at the end of the book, a guide to important printed materials on contemporary Mexico.

If they [government officials] would come down off their pedestals to share the lives of their countrymen and see their misery, I believe that out of their own pockets they would install electricity, sewage, and do something to help.

Manuel Sanchez in *The Children of Sanchez,* by Oscar Lewis

PART I
MEXICO IN THE TWENTIETH CENTURY

Mexicans have endured a past that has seemed to lurch from cataclysm to cataclysm. This has never been more true than in the present century, as upheavals reflect the sudden, often violent movements of modernization. Revolution, industrialization, and urbanization have effected political, economic, and population changes that together have been praised as progress. Yet twentieth-century Mexico retains constraints and limits despite its superficial changes. For everyday Mexicans, the crucial questions, as always, remain land, men and women, culture, and the presence of the United States.

The most pressing and enduring aspect of Mexican life has been the land. Since the restoration of Benito Juárez's Liberal regime in 1867, which signaled the birth of modern Mexico, land-tenure questions have bedeviled every presidential regime. The dictator Porfirio Díaz pushed a policy of distribution of lands that resulted in the creation of privately owned estates of vast size at the expense of Church and village institutional owners. Sporadic agrarian resistance challenging his policy reached its zenith in the Revolution, securing a promise of agrarian reform that revolutionary regimes have attempted, with varying degrees of success, to redeem. (See Reading 1.) Redistribution, credit, and extension programs cannot escape the limits of existing arable land (see Reading 26), no matter how great the political commitment.

The appearance of governments with increasingly strident revolutionary rhetoric cannot obscure the fundamental role of the nation's people. Mexico has gained human potential but faces expanded demands on scarce resources that come with its zooming population. Claims of modernism by the current regime aside, the population growth rate, the predominance of young people, and the overwhelming urban distribution — especially in the capital city — reflect premodern patterns of demography.

Women have been an ignored segment of this population. Until this century, with only a handful of brilliant exceptions, they have been shunted aside into roles of resignation and passivity. In the twentieth century, *Mexicanas* have struggled for their rights. Until the 1950s, the women's movement was primarily concerned with voting and holding office. This campaign had its first stirrings in the years of the Revolution, scored its initial success in 1925 when Chiapas became the first state to permit female voters and elected officials, gained momentum with the 1935 creation of the United

Front for Woman's Rights, obtained the national law allowing women to vote in municipal elections in 1947, and triumphed in 1955 with complete suffrage. In the 1970s, feminists challenged statutes and attitudes that denigrated the Mexican woman; in 1974 they secured laws, much like the Equal Rights Amendment languishing in the United States, for equal job opportunities, salaries, and legal standing. Feminists have raised other economic, social, and family questions only occasionally since the 1880s. Reading 2 traces the women's movement from the 1880s to the 1940s, with emphasis on the Cárdenas years (1934–40).

While land and people impose restraints on Mexico, the rise of mass culture (see Reading 3) has raised new interests, if not possibilities. Old problems give the nation a traditional character, while the popular culture gives Mexico the "feel" of modernity. Movies, sport, *fotonovelas,* cartoons, music, radio, and television have the mass quality of western Europe and the United States. Peculiarly, North American mass media and popular culture have fostered a modern kind of folk culture and folklore. (See Reading 4.) Nevertheless, these forms, even those copied from foreign examples, have been stamped with a Mexican character.

In popular culture and elsewhere, the United States leaves an indelible imprint on Mexico. The Revolution represents the essence of Mexico's twentieth-century nationalism, yet even this political upheaval was pushed and shoved by United States policies. (See Reading 5.) President Woodrow Wilson wanted to control the Revolution in Mexico. He could not, but he and his successors found ways to contain and influence its direction.

In the eighth decade of the twentieth century, Mexico remains a land of contrasts. The contradictions today reveal a nation not yet modern, but no longer traditional. The rhetoric turned out by the political bureaucracy ignores natural limits and exaggerates modernity. The label *PRI-modern* portrays this disparity. Meanwhile national identity, *lo Mexicanidad,* must reflect in an authentic way the land, the men and women, and the culture that includes its history. The absence of authenticity more than anything else contributes to the malaise of contemporary Mexico. The movement that began as a revolution of small things — a corn patch, a school, a vote, a village pump — has become a modern enterprise that charts progress in industrial statistics, balance of payments, and international loans. The heady atmosphere of economic growth until recently allowed the regime to ignore the misery endured by Manuel Sanchez and hundreds of thousands of others who are suffering because they lack the small things. Until the leaders of today recognize the limits of progress, Mexico's repressive past of the Porfirian dictatorship can only lead to the oppressive future of the PRI-modern state, and finally to another cataclysm.

1

AGRARIAN REFORM

John M. Hart

John Hart, professor of history at the University of Houston, began his study of los de abajo, Mexico's lower classes, when he published Anarchism and the Mexican Working Class, 1860–1931. *His book went beyond anarchism and the labor movement to examine agrarian unrest, resistance, and reform. In the following essay, he takes up this theme again, tracing the agrarian problem as a cause of the Mexican Revolution and agrarian reform as a goal of the victorious revolutionaries. He follows the twisting government policies that favor first private ownership, then communal (the* ejido*), then back again; charts presidential commitment measured by the amount of land distributed; and explains the success of the heirs of the Revolution in using land programs to bind the Mexican* campesino *to the emergent state. His account of the Otomi recalls the most persistent theme in Mexico's past: the conflict between the "progressive" townsmen and "backward" villagers. For today's Mexico, this essay raises two urgent concerns: How long will the increasingly desperate, increasingly numerous rural poor remain loyal to the regime? What new strategies will the state devise to offer land to a nation with more landless people today than at the outbreak of the Revolution?*

The Mexican land reform, initiated during the Revolution of 1910 and elaborated by successive governments since 1915, has been recognized by all observers as one of the nation's most significant political, social, and economic programs in the twentieth century. It grew out of public demand for a redress of grievances resulting from competition over increasingly valuable agricultural resources during the nineteenth century. That competition had resulted in a polarization of land ownership, which displaced masses of the peasantry, who in 1910 constituted some 80 percent of the nation's populace.

During the last half of the nineteenth century, a massive land-tenure transformation took place. It began in the late 1850s when Liberals took control of the national government. Dominated by *hacendados* (great landowners) and provincial and local elites (including middle-sized landowners and professionals), the Liberals passed constitutional and enabling legislation that nullified the rights of peasant communities and the Church to their massive tracts of land. The Church's share of property at that time was estimated to constitute one-half of the nation's arable total. Outlawed village communes and cooperatives held a significant portion of the remainder.

A tremendous wave of peasant unrest accompanied the commercialization of agriculture. Uprisings swept the country for twenty-five years; the recurring alliances of resisting peasants with the mutually hostile Conservatives and Liberals ended after 1883 with the establishment of the Porfirian "peace." During the course of those struggles, agrarian ideas developed and proclamations and plans were issued that delineated in detail the fundamentals of the later twentieth-century agrarian reform program.

Peasant unrest continued in isolated regions for the next twenty-seven years. In 1906, shortly before the *maderista* revolution began, the anarchist Mexican Liberal Party, headed by Ricardo Flores Magón, issued its own revolutionary plan, which anticipated the agrarian reform that followed. That plan called for the restoration of village communes and *ejidos*.

By 1910 almost all of Mexico's land had been placed in the hands of commercial agriculturalists, creating totals of some 45,000 *rancheros* or middle-sized holders and 7,500 *hacendados* in a nation of 15 million. But an even smaller group of self-perpetuating political officials installed by Porfirio Díaz, who had ruled Mexico as dictator-president for thirty-five years, controlled the economy and politics of the nation. Most of the high-ranking government officials at the national and state levels owned large agricultural estates. In some cases their holdings totaled millions of acres. In addition to the properties of the Mexican elites, the government sold tens of millions of acres to American businesses, including the Hearst, Guggenheim, Rockefeller, and Texas Oil Company interests. Those sales helped create a nationalistic reaction among the Mexican people. The failure of the Porfirian agricultural program to allocate sufficient acreage for domestic consumption resulted in

massive food shortages throughout central and northern Mexico
between 1908 and 1910. Endemic famine forced the emergency
importation of 35 million pesos worth of corn from South Africa,
Australia, Argentina, and the United States to alleviate urban
rioting.

The original dispute between Madero's supporters and the
government was articulated in narrow political terms, around his
1910 candidacy against Díaz for the presidency and the issues of one
man–one vote and an end to boss rule. During the campaign
Madero attracted some peasant support, but not a great deal. After
his defeat in the discredited election of 1910 he fled to San Antonio,
where he published the Plan of San Luis Potosí. That proclamation
was interpreted by many Mexicans as specifically promising to
return the land to all those who had been despoiled. Article 3 of the
plan declared:

> Through unfair advantages taken under the Law of Untitled
> Lands, numerous proprietors of small holdings, for the most part
> Indians, have been dispossessed of their lands—either by
> rulings of the Ministry of Public Works or by decisions of the
> nation's courts. It being full justice to restore arbitrarily dis-
> possessed lands to the former owners, the dispositions and
> decisions are declared subject to review. Those who acquired
> them immorally, or their heirs, will be required to return them to
> the original owners, to whom they will also pay an indemnity for
> the damages suffered. In cases where the lands already have
> passed to third parties before the promulgation of this plan, the
> original owners will receive indemnification from those who
> profited through the dispossession.

Madero had in mind the establishment of a reservation system
in Sonora and Sinaloa for Yaqui and Mayo Indians, who had
suffered terribly in fighting with the Díaz government's forces to
defend their homelands. He also thought in terms of the small and
middle-sized proprietors who had lost out in the push and shove of
agribusiness expansion and the reorganization of land tenure. He
definitely did not want the villages to return to the self-supporting
subsistence agriculture that he and other upper-class progressives
regarded as archaic and unproductive. He felt that village communal agriculture was not conducive to industrialization or
urbanization.

Misreading Madero's intentions, the *zapatistas* (followers of Emiliano Zapata) in south central Mexico—mainly in the states of Morelos, Guerrero, the southeastern and southwestern areas of the state of México, and western Puebla—supported the Revolution. When Madero came to power and failed to satisfy their demands for the immediate restoration of village lands, they revolted against him and issued their own revolutionary Plan de Ayala. The *zapatista* agrarian plan was rooted in the peasant unrest of the past and the revolutionary present. Its demands echoed those of the radical Ley del Pueblo issued by Manuel Serdan and Alberto Santa Fe in the state of Puebla in 1879. Article 6 of the Plan de Ayala declared: "The pueblos or citizens who have the titles corresponding to those properties, fields, timber and water which the landlords, *científicos* [scientific ones] or bosses have usurped will immediately enter into possession of that real estate of which they have been despoiled by the bad faith of our oppressors, maintaining at any cost with arms in hand said possessions; the usurpers who consider themselves with rights to them will prove it before special tribunals that will be established upon the triumph of the revolution."

Article 7 continued to outline the program: "There will be expropriated the third part of those monopolies of the powerful proprietors with prior indemnification in order that the pueblos and citizens of Mexico may obtain *ejidos*, colonies and foundations for pueblos, and fields to plan and work."

The Plan de Ayala conflicted with Madero in advocating reallocation of the properties of the great estates to the village communes and cooperatives that claimed them. It differed with the proposals of competing factions later in the Revolution because it insisted upon local village and pueblo control over land adjudication rather than the outside intrusion of state and national government.

On January 6, 1915, the victorious Constitutionalist faction issued its famous agrarian law establishing the National Agrarian Commission, now known as the Secretariat of Agrarian Reform. The law empowered the commission, acting for the national government, to restore improperly seized *campesino* lands. Article 3 of the Decreto de Seis de Enero, in competition with its *zapatista* counterpart, provided that "the pueblos that lack *ejidos*, need them, or unable to achieve their restitution for lack of titles, through the impossibility of identifying them, or because they were legally alienated, will be able to receive land donations sufficient to reconstitute them in conformity with the needs of their populations by expropriations, under the auspices of the national government, of those lands indispensable to this end which are encountered immediately adjacent to the pueblos concerned."

The Law of January 6, 1915, became the legal basis for land distributions by the Constitutionalist army. Throughout 1915 the army staged property reallocation ceremonies, granting lands to *campesinos* and villagers in the newly occupied areas of central Mexico, especially in those zones formerly held by the *zapatistas*. Beginning as a strategem to oppose the agrarians, the Ley Seis de Enero (Law of January 6) became the legal precedent for the agrarian reform provision, Article 27 of the Constitution of 1917. During the revolutionary fighting and lower-class upheaval, it served as a "legal" method of land distribution in the midst of hundreds of localized violent seizures of properties carried out by peasants in the name of *zapatismo*.

In the north the *villistas* (the followers of Pancho Villa) soon promulgated their own agrarian law. It called for agrarian communities protected and held by civic militias along a model similar to that suggested by nineteenth-century French socialist Charles Fourier. The bodies of government judged best fit to rule society were the respective sovereign and free states. The *villistas* nationalized idle *haciendas* and those owned by their opponents. They seized cattle, timber, and mineral assets, attempting to use them to purchase materials needed in their war effort. In the meantime, the *campesinos* in the north carried out numerous land occupations, which the *villista* authorities did nothing about. One of the largest properties affected by these lower-class initiatives was the American-owned 830,000-acre Corralitos Hacienda in western Chihuahua.

Given the widespread *campesino* and village land seizures extending from the south to the north of the country, there was a powerful desire to resolve the "agrarian question" when the representatives of the victorious forces in the Mexican Revolution met in Querétaro late in 1916. On February 4, 1917, President Carranza promulgated the new Constitution. The agrarian plank, Article 27, supplemented by other provisions, offered a comprehensive program to the impoverished and restless countryside masses. It placed the rights of the community over those of private interests. Great estates could be expropriated much like eminent domain for the creation of small private holdings and village communes and collectives. The declared aim was "an equitable distribution of wealth." The government would issue 5 percent twenty-five-year bonds to the former owners. The national government now also claimed ultimate ownership of all subsoil resources and bodies of water. The rational use of hydraulic resources was recognized by the Constitution's framers as an essential part of any program that attempted to achieve rural prosperity and a democratic land tenure system.

Despite the seemingly good intentions of the committee that drafted the agrarian proviso, the *zapatistas* and *villistas* denounced it and the Constitution. They argued that it was written by enemies of the villages and *campesinos*, that it removed the power over the land from what should have been autonomous municipalities and the states, and that it placed all authority in the hands of a corrupt national government and great landholders. They continued to fight for another two years until the death of Zapata in 1919 and the surrender of an isolated Villa in 1920. Indeed, the *zapatista-villista* charges of corruption and collusion with the great landowners looked valid to many observers. Between 1916 and 1920, *carrancista* generals (followers of Venustiano Carranza) occupied landed estates and claimed them as their own. They lived the lives of winners enjoying their war prizes.

Then, in 1920, Alvaro Obregón seized power, backed by most of the army and an alliance of agrarian reformers, organized labor, and middle-class functionaries. The *carrancista* generals were forced out of some of their more notorious excesses, especially in those places where agrarian elements had supported Obregón's movement. A victorious general, Obregón had created one of Mexico's largest *latifundia* (great rural estate) complexes for himself in his home state of Sonora. His profits came largely from commercial crop exports to the nearby United States. His plan of Agua Prieta espoused the virtue of "small private properties" as a principal aspect of Article 27 and of the government's future agrarian reform program.

The Obregón government moved very slowly on behalf of the agrarian masses. Few land donations were made in response to a growing welter of demands from the villages and pueblos of the nation. But he did allow the National Agrarian Commission to continue its work. He provided the operating funds that it required in order to continue an ambitious program of countryside research preliminary to any land grants.

Between 1916 and 1924, during the reigns of Carranza and Obregón, teams of half-trained but enthusiastic investigators studied hundreds of remote pueblos, compiling data on their population size, ethnic and linguistic composition, age groupings, gender balance, labor and intellectual skills, land and water resources, economic potential, access to markets, and customs and practices. They also compiled assessments of neighboring commercial estate land titles and reported on the nationality and politics of their owners. The information obtained became the basis of the agrarian reform program carried out between 1934 and 1940 by President Lázaro Cárdenas. The reports served as guides in determining what lands and how many acres were needed by the rural centers involved. The National Agrarian Commission's investigative reporting on the countryside diminished significantly during the presidency of Plutarco Elías Calles, 1924–28, and the years of his hegemony, 1928–34.

These *hacendado* presidents—Carranza, Obregón, and Calles—shared Madero's lack of enthusiasm regarding the restoration of village communes and cooperatives as the basis of agrarian reform. They all favored private holdings but recognized the need for village *dotaciónes* (grants of land) as a means of social control. Both Obregón and Calles rewarded their progovernment agrarian organizations with *ejidal* and communal land grants.

Under Carranza, despite massive unrest and the tactic of legitimizing peasant land seizures in order to buy village loyalties, only 290,000 acres were approved as *ejidal* or communal holdings. Most of those actions merely recognized earlier land occupations by revolutionary peasants. The politics of the Obregón and Calles administrations rested upon a wider, more popular social base. Both presidents moved to satisfy the demands of their supporters and to forestall rural political instability. Between 1920 and 1924 Obregón approved land donations to the pueblos and villages totaling 2,136,200 acres; they were awarded in a manner inexplicable on the basis of the relative legitimacy of the claims. The nationality and politics of the affected neighboring landowners, the political loyalties of the petitioners, and the relative need for political order seem to have been major considerations in the adjudications.

Under Calles between 1924 and 1928, presidential land donations continued to operate with the same criteria. They increased to 7,630,448 acres. Land grants could be blocked by combinations of local elites or rival village interest groups that enjoyed favorable relations with the government. After the assassination of Obregón in 1928, mounting resistance to continued land allocations from foreigners and provincial and local elites combined with Calles's conservatism to cause a slowdown and then a virtual standstill in the agrarian reform program. Calles openly declared the effort ended. Three short-term presidents who served under his hegemony obliged him for the most part. Then, between 1934 and 1940, the Cárdenas government dispensed 44 million acres to more than 1,200 pueblos, creating a new balance between the large commercial estates, the middle-sized *ranchos,* and the village and pueblo collectives and communes. The formation of the government-controlled National Confederation of Campesinos (CNC) played a major part in a new land tenure regime and closer state-dominated political and economic relations with the peasantry.

The motives behind the Cárdenas-era reforms are hotly disputed. One view points to the great strength of the president's adversaries as he seized their properties and dispensed them to the poor and needy. His reallocation of property attacked some of the largest landholdings in the nation, including those of the Chihuahua oligarchy, the Creel-Terrazas interests. He also nationalized the oil company holdings and parceled out to the *campesinaje* many of their nonpetroleum-bearing properties in Tamaulipas, Veracruz, and the Isthmus of Tehuantepec. Historians who hold this view assert that Cárdenas's commitment to social democracy, his deep sense of nationalism, and the overwhelming needs of the people explain his "revolutionary" program.

A more critical perspective points out Cárdenas's long affiliation and loyalty to the ruling procapitalist elite that governed the country and ran its economy. That loyalty included his status as an affluent *hacendado* in Michoacán and his failure to include the *latifundia* complex in Sonora owned by his old chief, Alvaro Obregón, in his agrarian reform package. His agrarian reforms came in the wake of the long and violent Cristero War, in which a grassroots peasantry, politically intertwined with the Church hierarchy, fought the government's efforts to intrude upon the established regimes of the countryside. His social program included support for government-dominated unions and the growth of corporate organizations affiliated with the government for all social classes. These elements are seen as part of a far-reaching effort to save Mexican capitalism and the ruling elite from incipient lower-class unrest rooted in the economic hardships of the Great Depression.

When Cárdenas left office, he yielded to right-wing threats of a counterrevolution and supported a compromise presidential candidate who represented business interests — General Manuel Avila Camacho — in lieu of a leading reformist candidate within his own clique. The result was an eighteen-year hiatus in the agrarian reform effort. Critically, the government educational and material aid programs that were developed under Cárdenas for the *campesinaje* were allowed to fall apart. The presidency of right-wing businessman Miguel Alemán, 1946–52, marked the nadir in agrarian ideology and politics. The president imposed a law forbidding the creation of new communes. All village-pueblo lands had to be donated in the form of *ejidos,* the land of which is owned by the applying municipalities but held and worked by individuals independent of local controls.

During the period 1940–58 a conviction grew within the governing elite that the agrarian reform program had gone too far. But an explosive population growth rate forced yet more reforms. Between 1940 and 1960 the number of Mexicans increased from 20 million to more than 35 million. Most of the newborn were in the countryside. The pressures for new land donations to the peasantry mounted. Between 1958 and 1964 the government of President Adolfo López Mateos enjoyed great popularity despite the suppression of a railroad workers' strike and the arrest of strike leaders. His regime parceled out more than 30 million acres. But the lands involved composed most of the last great acreages of arable properties, except those of the most powerful within the "revolutionary" elite. The ensuing twenty years witnessed a population expansion in which the number of Mexicans doubled. By 1970 there were more landless *campesinos* than at the inception of the Revolution.

For almost forty years the Mexican agrarian reform program

forestalled a rush of the nation's burgeoning rural population from the countryside to the cities. The program is no longer capable of maintaining these restraints. During the same era the agrarian reform served as an exemplary mechanism of social control. For most of half a century, peasants who had formerly taken up arms litigated in the courts, appealed CNC committee decisions, and researched with their lawyers among the three million bundles of village-pueblo papers held in the archives of the Secretariat of Agrarian Reform.

The Mexican state at the upper levels has clearly been cynical in its use of the agrarian reform program to defuse lower-class unrest. Little effort was made, after the first waves of idealistic zeal, to help the peasants improve their education, their economic lives, or their hygiene. Only the regime of Luis Echeverría Alvarez in the middle 1970s, which encountered tremendous opposition, attempted to reverse this dominant trend. The zeal of lower- and middle-level functionaries in the agrarian reform program has been blunted by underfunding in the agency and heavily documented discrimination by the Ejidal Bank, which is supposed to underwrite land and community improvement projects.

In the mid-1970s Otomi villagers near San Miguel de Allende were flooded out of their best lands and their village habitational zone by the lake that was formed by one of the many new dams constructed by the government in its effort to increase hydraulic capacities. Despite the proximity of the village and its lands to the lake waters, state and national government officials stringently deny them their use in favor of large commercial farms located twenty miles to the south in the valley near Celaya. The Otomi cannot subsist on the dry hillside lands that remain for them. This case is typical of land-water relationships throughout the nation.

The Mexican state, like the French revolutionaries between 1789 and 1792, carried out an agrarian reform program that forged a strong but imperfect bond of loyalty between it and a previously revolutionary peasantry. Today the lands available for distribution are minimal, the rural citizenry still constitute 43 percent of the nation's populace, and the economic condition of the *campesinaje* is desperate. Two questions arise: How long can Mexican *campesino* political loyalties endure declining services and economic collapse? What new strategies will the state devise?

BIBLIOGRAPHICAL NOTE

The archival basis of this article, the Archivo Seis de Enero, Secretariat of Agrarian Reform, Mexico City, has now been dispersed. The Archivo Seis de Enero contained more than 80,000 bundles of documents related to land tenure and conflicting pueblo-*hacendado* land claims. The materials refer to original titles, nineteenth-century "usurpations," twentieth-century land allocations, assessments of village resources, and a variety of contemporary economic and social data. Since the decentralization of the archive in 1980 and 1981, the materials have been sent to regional centers such as San Luis Potosí, Chilpancingo, Oaxaca, and others. Now in the hands of provincial bureaucracies and elites, the materials are frequently described as "misplaced," "lost," or "inaccessible."

2

WOMEN IN THE REVOLUTION

Shirlene Soto

Shirlene Soto, assistant vice-president at California State University, Northridge, provides an introduction to the feminist movement in Mexico by examining the status of women from the era of the dictator Porfirio Díaz until 1940. Her article surveys the struggle for women's rights, especially the vote, as one of the reforms of the Mexican Revolution by which the leaders attempted to incorporate the disenfranchised into Mexican life. This selection reviews women's participation in the early phases of the Revolution, then concentrates on the presidency of Lázaro Cárdenas, when the feminist movement reached a crescendo in its drive for suffrage. This discussion should be compared with other selections in Part III that deal with the administration of Cárdenas.

Although Soto emphasizes the suffrage movement, her essay reveals other themes about modern Mexico as well. She demonstrates clearly the persistence of regionalism after the Revolution's destructive stage had ended in 1920. The women's movement achieved its first successes in Yucatán as a result of the governorships of Salvador Alvarado and Felipe Carrillo Puerto, while it languished elsewhere in the nation. The suffrage campaign demonstrates the impact of foreign events on Mexican reformers. In this instance legislators reacted against female voting when they learned that Spanish women had voted heavily against the Liberal administration in their first trip to the ballot box just prior to the Spanish Civil War. The author raises the issue of the Mexican male's intense machismo as an almost insurmountable obstacle to women's rights. Finally, Soto identifies several women whose leadership in the struggle for female rights entitles them to a place in Mexican history, yet who had been ignored until she prepared this study. Each of these themes warrants discussion and further exploration.

Reprinted from *The Mexican Woman: A Study of Her Participation in the Revolution*, by Shirlene Ann Soto (Palo Alto, CA: R&E Research Associates, Inc., 1978), pp. 92–97, 106–107. Used by permission of the author. Copyright © 1979 by Shirlene Ann Soto.

The Mexican Revolution had a profound effect on the lives of women. Two significant factors basic to this achievement were expanded: industrialization, which provided a host of new jobs for Mexican women, and the activities of feminists in the United States and Europe, which encouraged Mexican women to demand full participation in national affairs. Consequently, during the Revolution, women were able to undertake new kinds of social responsibilities and occupations, were able to travel throughout the Republic, and were able to become more self-aware. Paradoxically, their sacrifices and contributions were almost ignored. Historian Ernest Gruening observed that "the Revolution has done little, purposefully, toward the emancipation of women." Women participated in the fighting, the planning, and attempts to implement the ideological goals of the Revolution; but afterward they were neither recognized adequately for their efforts nor granted the political equality promised to them. Some were awarded pensions and commissioned with rank, but most lived poverty-stricken and died unknown. Their failure to obtain suffrage under the Constitution of 1917 was a bitter disappointment for women. Ironically, the conservatives favored allowing women to vote because they thought it would ensure conservative control over Mexico. The radicals, however, remained vehemently opposed, because they feared that women would merely serve conservative interests. Both factions expressed more concern with manipulation of Mexico's political future than with women's rights, democratic government, or fulfillment of the Revolution's goals of justice and social equality.

For Mexican women the first major break with discriminatory laws, customs, and traditions took place during the Porfiriato (1876–1911). The most dramatic changes occurred in education. Middle-class women attended schools and universities, and many entered the labor market as teachers, nurses, and government employees. Politically they organized labor and anti-Díaz groups. Several women wrote extensively, publishing books and magazines. No longer confining themselves to the traditionally "feminine" subjects of music and religion, they wrote revolutionary poetry, criticized the Díaz regime, and questioned women's submissive role in society. The lower-class women's situation remained dismal; they worked for a pittance as domestics or factory hands or turned to prostitution. So many were driven into prostitution that Mexico City had more registered prostitutes than Paris, a much larger metropolis. Despite the advances during the Porfiriato, women, irrespective of social class, suffered heavy legal discrimination. Their lives were severely circumscribed by laws prohibiting them from professions and locking them into marriage and family life. In addition, the Catholic Church reinforced institutionalized sexism by encouraging women to confine their existence to family and home.

From the outset of the Revolution, women undertook new occupational and social roles and faced political challenges. Accordingly, they recognized the need for political organization. During the post-Porfiriato era, increased numbers of upper-class women worked for health and charitable organizations, middle-class women served in a wide variety of revolutionary support roles, and many lower-class women served as *soldaderas*. Such involvement by women of all classes reinforced their general awareness of the need for organization as a means to achieve their goals. During this era, women achieved some legal gains: divorce was permitted for the first time, and the 1917 Constitution guaranteed certain rights for working women. However, equal political rights for women remained outside their grasp because of their close relationship with the Church, which revolutionaries believed must be destroyed if the Revolution were to succeed.

While the Revolution raged, the immediate effects of the fighting—rape and pillage, death and the breakup of the family—were also devastating to women. Everyday living was disrupted by separations, deaths, and new liaisons. Unprotected women were pressed into service, kidnapped, and often abused. Under these circumstances, women organized to correct injustices and to demand their rights.

Between 1915 and 1924 the most intense struggle for women's rights in Mexico centered in the state of Yucatán. Site of the first two Feminist Congresses, Yucatán was the scene of the most active political participation of women in Mexico. Yucatán's leadership in the women's movement resulted from the support of its socialist governors, the progressive ideas of its women, and wealth from its henequen production. In addition, it was one of the first Mexican states to provide education for women. Governor Salvador Alvarado expanded educational opportunities and improved working conditions in an attempt to incorporate women into the society. These programs were broadened further under the next governor, Felipe Carrillo Puerto. Women were granted suffrage, allowed to run for office, and provided access to birth control information and educational benefits. Elvia Carrillo Puerto, Felipe's younger sister, organized women into Feminist Leagues, which sponsored meetings, conducted night schools, and launched campaigns against illiteracy and superstition, alcoholism, poor hygiene, and improper child care.

The assassination of Carrillo Puerto by the opposition forces in 1924 abruptly halted nine years of social reforms. The new administration dissolved the Feminist Leagues, removed women from their positions in municipal and state government, cancelled suffrage, and stopped all social programs supported by the leagues. After 1924 the women's movement centered in Mexico City, where feminists in the 1920s and 1930s organized on a massive scale.

Women achieved only limited success during the 1920s. After helping to win the Revolution and to carry out its earlier reforms, especially in education and health, women received few of its benefits. There were several reasons for this: The ruling "Sonora dynasty" did not view women's rights as an integral part of the goals of the Revolution; national and international crises preempted attention; and women's continued support of the Church against the government embittered revolutionary leaders, who felt they must protect their control of the Revolution against this feminist "fifth column." The arguments of those favoring women's rights were weakened by women's open sympathy for the de la Huerta revolt against the government in 1923, by the Cristero rebellion in 1926, by the assassination of President-elect Obregón in 1928, and by women's resistance to the government's program of socialist education. Finally, their disorganization and political divisiveness, so evident in the 1925 Congreso de Mujeres de la Raza, damaged their image. Nevertheless, women organized on a broader scale and sponsored and attended many conferences. A few educated women assumed prominent positions in government and in the universities. By the end of the decade, the PRM (the official government party) recognized women's political potential and acted to incorporate them into the party. However, women were still not full participatory members of society, because the key ingredients for acquisition of political equality—a supportive president and strongly organized women's associations—were absent until after 1934.

During the six-year presidency of Lázaro Cárdenas (1934–40), women worked concertedly towards winning the right to vote. For Mexican women this was an era of enormous hope. President Cárdenas was receptive and supportive, and women in all social classes were well-organized. Unlike many revolutionary leaders, Cárdenas viewed the incorporation of women into the political structure as an essential goal of the Revolution. He stated, "A sound basis for social revolution will not be achieved until the Constitution is reformed to grant equal rights." As governor of Michoacán, in 1928, he organized women to combat alcoholism and religious fanaticism. In undertaking his agrarian reform program, he encouraged women to guard the fields with guns while their husbands worked. During his presidency he affirmed his support for women's suffrage. The basis for his views, however, was not feminism, but socialism and revolutionary logic. Not surprisingly, several members of the Cárdenas cabinet were also strong supporters of women's rights. The ministries of agriculture (under Tomás Garrido Canabal), communications (under Francisco Múgica), and public education worked closely with women's associations and had women serving on their staffs. Unlike many other politicians, Cárdenas was also honest. What he stated publicly he did privately. He did not attack the Church and send his children to convents or publicly support women's rights and lock his wife in at night. Betty Kirk, an American reporter who interviewed First Lady Amalia Solórzano de Cárdenas in October 1940, found her to be her husband's equal. She was modern and progressive.

Church and state both viewed women as a potential force as yet untapped and undertook vigorous campaigns to compete for their loyalties. In 1934 the Church began publishing the monthly *El Boletín Católico*, aimed at the organization of Catholic women in "defense of the family" and more specifically at preventing the acceptance of the new socialistic education. In every diocese in Mexico, Catholic women formed committees to promote traditional values and to fight against the encroachment of the state. Clubhouses with sewing machines and hand irons were established to attract lower-class women. Upper- and middle-class women ran the clubhouses and worked to gain community support.

In the tug-of-war between the Church and state, Cárdenas offered women participation in politics and suffrage in exchange for their backing in the 1934 election. To support his candidacy and to counteract the influence of the Church, he attempted to organize women more extensively than ever before. The Feminine Sector, later called Feminine Action of the National Revolutionary Party, sponsored delegates and subcommittees throughout the republic. Ligas Femeniles were organized from the Laguna district in Coahuila, where Cárdenas was politically weak, to Quintana Roo. Young girls were incorporated into Brigadas Juveniles. Women in the PNR tackled a variety of problems, from health, alcoholism, drugs, and illiteracy to recruitment. They also formed vigilante groups to check consumer prices. Committees monitored price fluctuations on articles of prime necessity and denounced any infractions. Another program involved determining how much women paid for indispensable items. In addition, several members in the Cárdenas cabinet were supportive of women's rights. The Ministry of Agriculture under Tomás Garrido Canabel, the Ministry of Communications directed by Francisco Múgica, and the Ministry of Public Education all had women's associations and women serving on their staffs.

With increased communication, Mexican women in the 1930s were more aware and integrated into the worldwide feminist movement than ever before. Mexican feminists were sensitive that their sisters in neighboring countries were winning suffrage. In Latin America women were beginning to exercise their political rights: in Ecuador in 1929, Brazil and Cuba in 1934, Puerto Rico in 1935, Uruguay in 1938, El Salvador in 1939, and Chile in 1940. Several new organizations begun in Mexico attracted women of all social classes. The Ejército de Defensa de la Mujer, organized in 1934 to protect and defend Mexican women, the Ateneo Mexicano de Mujeres begun in 1936 by Amalia Castillo de Ledón, the Liga de Acción Femenina led by Elvia Carrillo Puerto, and the Acción Femenina of the PNR all served important roles in uniting Mexican women. The centralizing organization was the Frente Unico Pro Derechos de la Mujer, begun in 1935. Its main strength lay in its broad cultural appeal. Many new organizations were internationally oriented, such as the Club Internacional de Mujeres, formed in June 1933 by women of all nationalities; the Unión de Mujeres Americanas, organized by Margarita Robles de Mendoza the following year; and the Unión Femenina Ibero-Americana (UFIA), begun by Palma Guillén in February 1936. Mexican women also attended and participated in several international conferences held in the United States, Mexico, Europe, and Latin America.

Women demonstrated increasing interest in their own social betterment. In February 1937 the First National Congress of Industrial Hygiene was held in Mexico City with 576 delegates attending. Hundreds of resolutions were adopted and referred to the proper government departments. On June 21 a significant breakthrough occurred when a Child Welfare Bureau was established as a department of government to supervise all social welfare work for mothers and children in both public and private institutions. The welfare of women and children was also aided by the founding of the Asociación de Médicas by Dr. Methilde Rodríguez Cabo in 1938. The same year a League of Mental Hygiene was begun in the capital. These institutions were reinforced in July 1939 when the National Committee for Mother and Child was established in Mexico City.

Dr. Esther Chapa noted with dismay in her book *Woman's Right to Vote* that the law excluding women from voting automatically placed them "in the same category as vagabonds, inmates of insane asylums, owners of houses of prostitution, ex-convicts, gamblers, fugitives from justice and other public charges to whom the vote is also denied." To alter their status and to acquire what they considered to be an indispensable legal weapon, women decided to concentrate all their efforts on suffrage. Immediately preceding Cárdenas's administration, delegates to the Seventh Congress for the Women's International League for Peace and Freedom in July 1930 accepted suffrage as one of their major goals. In 1931 the PNR, realizing women's enormous political potential, called the first officially sponsored meeting to deal exclusively with their rights, problems, and needs. It was at this meeting that Cuca García boldly accused former President Calles and President Pascual Ortíz Rubio, both present, of murdering *campesinos*. She was immediately arrested and imprisoned. Within a few hours, as word of the event spread, thousands of women converged on the jail. Police, fearing a riot, were forced to release her. In January 1932 Florinda Lazos León, Elvia Carrillo Puerto, Edelmira R. Vda. de Escudero, Guadalupe Joseph, and María Ríos Cárdenas decided to go directly to Congress to demand women's suffrage. Amid the congressmen's laughter, Elvia protested, "We [women] need to live. Women ought to go to the Cámaras, because the nation is not made up of men only." Even under the pressure of repeated requests for suffrage, Congress decided that it was not a propitious time to allow women to vote.

Women participated to a greater degree than ever before in the 1934 presidential campaign. Edelmira R. Vda. de Escudero organized the Feminist Revolutionary Party, which worked with the PNR in support of Cárdenas. In return for feminine assistance, Cárdenas agreed to support a nationwide drive for woman suffrage. For the first time, it appeared that a president was serious about keeping his promise. On December 19, 1934, at the request of Margarita Robles de Mendoza, Mexican delegate to the Inter-American Commission of Women, Cárdenas announced Mexico's adherence to the Convention on the Neutrality of Women, signed by nineteen American republics. He also appointed Palma Guillén as Mexican minister to Colombia. This made Mexico the first Latin American country to designate a woman diplomat. In his presidential message to Congress on September 1, 1935, Cárdenas pledged to create youth and feminine sectors for the party. He also stated that "the working woman has the right to take part in the elections, since the constitution puts her on an equal footing with man." Shortly after his congressional speech, the president approved the organization of a Feminine Action section of the PNR. With this approval came the pledge for the incorporation of women into the civic and political life of the nation; equal rights for women to develop themselves to the extent of their capabilities; campaigns against alcoholism, illiteracy, and religious fanaticism; and equal rights for women under the civil, social, economic, and political laws of Mexico.

These events encouraged women to escalate their activities. In this promising atmosphere, the most powerful women's organization in the 1930s was founded in 1935. In an attempt to provide organizational and pragmatic coherence, which the women's movement lacked, Cuca García organized the Frente Unico Pro Derechos de la Mujer (FUPDM) and served as its first Secretary General. The Frente served as an umbrella organization and had great strength because of its broad cultural appeal. García was described as "a short, round little woman of forty with a serene face, an inexhaustible wealth of physical energy, and the utter simplicity of all those who have dedicated their lives to a cause that is beyond all thought of self." From the middle to the late 1930s she increasingly came to be associated with Mexico's radical Left, led by General Francisco Múgica and Senator Ernesto Soto Reyes. Former President Emilio Portes Gil identified her with the Communist women, headed by Dr. Mathilde Rodríguez Cabo, who were directing a campaign to discredit him as president of the National Executive Committee of the party. The object was to put Múgica in the presidency in 1940.

The women working in close collaboration with Cuca on the Frente were mostly leftists. They included Consuelo Uranga, René Rodríguez, Esther Chapa, Soledad Orozco Avila (who had participated in the Red Battalions during the Revolution), and Frieda Khalo (Diego Rivera's wife). The Communists' goal was to reach beyond the demand for suffrage and to establish a basis for collective solidarity from which to press for the advancement of women. The Frente, in attempting to incorporate women from all social classes and backgrounds, presented a comprehensive program with the following objectives: the unrestricted right to vote and be elected to office; equalization of legal rights between the sexes through alteration of the Civil Code; modification of the Federal Labor Law to allow for the special maternity needs of women; amendment of the Agrarian Code to allow women who fulfilled the same qualifications as men to receive land; legislation to protect women government employees; integration of indigenous women into the social and political life of Mexico; organization of work centers for unemployed women; special programs for treatment of children's problems and protection of infants; and establishment of a broad program of cultural education for women. The success of the Frente was reflected in both the composition of its constituency and its numbers. By 1939 it had consolidated hundreds of women's groups and encompassed eight hundred organizations with more than fifty thousand women.

The Six-Year Plan presented in 1934 by the PNR recommended organizing a cooperative of women under the Ministry of Labor. Little was done to implement this provision during 1935 when Cárdenas was struggling to eliminate the Calles faction, but in January 1936 he proposed to Congress that an Oficina Investigadora be established to report on the working conditions of women and minors within the Ministry of Labor. This investigatory body was organized, although it was empowered only to make suggestions and to publicize its findings. The report was to include data not only on working conditions but also on the relationship of work to the role of the woman as mother and family head.

In the spring of 1936 the PNR granted women the right to vote in party primaries. Women voted as members of labor unions, peasant organizations, and women's sections of the party. The Pan American Union reported that 2,750 women participated in these primaries in the Federal District, where women's political activity was the greatest. At about the same time, Mexico's states began to grant women political rights. Guanajuato had allowed limited suffrage in 1934. Puebla followed in 1936, and later Veracruz, Durango, Tamaulipas, and Hidalgo. . . .

In the PNR primary elections, held early in April 1937, women participated in large numbers all over the nation for the first time. Cuca García and Soledad Orozco Avila were selected as candidates for the Chamber of Deputies in Uruapán, Michoacán, and Guanajuato, although the national election law still restricted eligibility to male voters. These women planned to run in the regular elections held in June and appealed to the Supreme Court to overrule the Constitution's Article 37 on electoral laws because it conflicted with Articles 34 and 35, which conferred citizenship upon all Mexicans. Although she was opposed by four PNR-supported candidates, the consensus at the time was that Cuca had won in Uruapán. Orozco, a widow with six children, was also rumored to have won. This forced a decision upon the National Executive Committee of the party. They ruled that a constitutional amendment would be needed before women could vote or stand as candidates in national elections. The electoral committee awarded the seats to their male opponents.

Because of the PNR electoral committee's decision in 1937, women demanded to know the president's position. They occupied his residence but did not find him there. The women then launched an intensive search in the capital, intending to hold him to his campaign promise. Frustrated in their attempts, in late August they undertook their most radical action: They staged a hunger strike outside the president's home. This strike continued for two weeks until Cárdenas, under pressure and unwilling to create any female martyrs, promised in a speech before a women's conference in the port of Veracruz to introduce a bill in the next congressional session that would establish equal political and civil rights for women.

Following the president's public pledge came an outpouring of mail that flooded the government palace in Mexico City urging that the bill be passed. Both individual women and women's organizations requested that Cárdenas amend the suffrage articles. Elvia Carrillo Puerto, Margarita Robles de Mendoza, Cuca García, Mathilde Rodríguez Cabo, and even Hermila Galindo, who had been in retirement since Carranza's death, sent messages encouraging suffrage. Telegrams streamed in from all over the world. Women in the United States expressed a special interest in their neighbors' fate. Anna Kelton Wiley, representing the National Women's Party, visited Mexico in May 1937 and met with members of the Frente. Cuca gave her a message for American women. She asserted that the Mexican government had "taken advantage of services, [and] sent us [women] back home," but "we are not discouraged by the indifference of our Government in denying us our rights." Of her own attempt for a place in the Chamber of Deputies, she stated that she had been nominated for Congress with a 10,000-vote margin but had not been allowed to take her seat. Cuca frankly admitted that she was displeased with the decision of the PNR Board because it "does not represent the will of the people." She defiantly vowed to run again and pledged to continue the fight for women's equality.

Cárdenas, keeping his promise, sent his proposed amendment of Article 34 to include women as citizens to the Senate on November 23, 1937. When the committee recommended changes, the president, pressured by the powerful CTM (the national labor union) and feminist organizations, sent it back. On December 18 the committee recommended passage of the original amendment, and the Senate approved the measure by unanimous vote on December 21, 1937. Two days later the amendment went to the Chamber of Deputies. Here it was referred to committee, but the members adjourned without acting on it. Even though passage of the amendment was thus postponed, women were still optimistic. This was the closest they had ever come to political equality. With no intention of letting the opportunity slip away, they undertook efforts for increased activity. . . .

In June 1938 Cárdenas called a special congressional session for early July. On July 6 the proposed amendment to Article 34 came up for consideration by the Chamber of Deputies. There was some opposition, but it was easily quelled. Since no one was willing to defy the president openly, the amendment was unanimously approved the same day and referred to state legislatures for ratification. . . .

By the end of 1938 a majority of Mexican states had ratified Cárdenas's proposal. In May 1939, however, with the session almost over, no action had been taken on the amendment, even though all twenty-eight states had ratified it. . . . Congress adjourned without completing the formal ratification process, and the amendment never became law. A major stumbling block for Mexican women in their quest for equal political rights was their inability to sever their traditional connection with the Church. The overwhelming support from women for the conservative candidate in the 1940 presidential race confirmed suspicions about their disloyalty to the revolutionary government. In addition, internal distractions — conflict with the Church, political intrigue, and succession — as well as outside influences such as the Spanish Civil War and the foreign oil expropriations embittered leaders and stole the focus from the women's struggle.

Despite their efforts and the support they marshaled, women in 1940 remained disenfranchised. Nevertheless, they were organized and acquired the experience of working together. However, much of this energy dissipated in the 1940s as problems of industrialization and World War II diverted attention from their concerns. In the postwar period, when women in the United States suffered severe reversals, Mexican women won the legal battle for political equality. On December 31, 1946, they officially received the municipal vote. Seven years later, on December 31, 1953, after the Church and state had arrived at a modus vivendi, and the official party, now called the PRI, was firmly in control, they were granted complete suffrage. In 1958 Mexican women had the privilege of voting in their first presidential election, and since then several women have served in Congress and the legal rights of Mexican women as equal citizens are firmly established.

MEXICAN WOMEN IN THE EARLY
TWENTIETH CENTURY

Turn-of-the-century tortilla factory. From Thomas Unett Brockle-
hurst, *Mexico To-Day: A Country with a Great Future* (London, 1883).

Women revolutionists, September 1911. Prints and Photographs Division, Library of Congress, Washington, D.C.

Plow and Woman. Archivo General de la Nación, Mexico.

The Water Carrier. Early twentieth century. Archivo General de la
Nación, Mexico.

3

POPULAR CULTURE

William H. Beezley

In the following essay, William H. Beezley, one of the editors of this volume, professor of history at North Carolina State University, and author of Insurgent Mexico: Abraham González *and the* Mexican Revolution in Chihuahua, *introduces Mexican popular culture by examining five of its components: movies, fotonovelas, political cartoons, music, and sport. He argues that in spite of tremendous foreign influence, especially from the United States, popular culture south of the Rio Grande has a distinctive Mexican character that reflects the vitality of the country's nationalism. Modern popular culture emerged in the post – World War II years along with the rise of industrialism and the increased bureaucracy of the Institutionalized Revolutionary Party (the PRI). This mass culture reveals new characteristics in the caricatures of political cartoons, the forms (such as the fotonovelas), the nostalgia, the themes of the cinema, and the rise in the number of spectators at sporting events. Earlier, in the 1920s, the Revolution's leaders attempted to promote* indigenismo, *the traditional village Indian way of life; but this support has been overwhelmed by today's urban mass culture. So recently have scholars begun to study popular culture that there are many more questions than answers about the degree of imitation of foreign cultures, about the way Mexicans refashion cultural forms to give them a Mexican character, and about the preferences for music, cartoons, films, and sports by different social classes. On these and other questions, the journal* Studies in Latin American Popular Culture *provides the latest scholarship.*

A major emphasis of the Mexican Revolution in the 1920s was the promotion of indigenism. This campaign to reinvigorate Indian arts and traditions while creating a national appreciation for them has withered since World War II as *indianismo* has degenerated into little more than museum artifacts or government-funded enterprises such as the Fondo Nacional de Artesanías. Village life and traditions fell victim to the twentieth-century Western urban society that has emerged in Mexico with its mass component called popular culture.

As in other parts of the world, this popular culture has been derived from cinema, radio, television, music, comic books, jokes, and sport. Unique to the Latin world are the cartoon-like magazines of romantic stories called *fotonovelas*, which combine movie photographs and comic-strip dialogue. As one would expect, Mexico's popular culture reveals the influence of western Europe and the United States. Nevertheless, despite the cultural flood that washes across the border, each of these mass traditions is distinctly Mexican.

Mass culture in Mexico sprang largely from the communications developments of this century. Radio, since stations CYL and CYB (now the powerful XEB) first began broadcasting in 1923, spread quickly throughout the country. By 1970 more than 680 stations beamed music, news, and "La Hora Nacional" ("The National Hour," featuring traditional music, folklore, and patriotic stories) to listeners in every nook of the country. Television arrived September 1, 1950, when Mexico City's XHTV, channel 4, telecast Miguel Alemán's presidential message. By 1970 Mexicans were enjoying three networks: channel 2 (thirty-six stations in twenty states), channel 4 (fourteen affiliates in ten states), and channel 8 (fifteen stations in ten states). Today satellite and cable offer United States programming, especially the Dallas Cowboys. Popular and powerful as these communications media are, it was motion pictures that first captured public interest and remains the most significant of these media.

Today Mexico has the largest and most influential film industry in the Spanish-speaking world. Mexican domination has been the case since 1940, and these films represent in practice the kind of cultural imperialism usually attributed exclusively to Hollywood. Mexican actors such as Ricardo Montalbán, Dolores del Río, Rodolfo Acosta, and Cantinflas have achieved international reputations. The industry represents an important source of foreign income, as films ranked sixteenth in exports in 1961.

Motion pictures first arrived with an exhibition of the Edison kinetoscope from the United States in 1895. Within months films appeared from Paris, and the first Mexican film was made in 1897. The first era of Mexican cinema extends from this early production until 1929; it encompasses the rise and decline of the silent film. The father of the Mexican film industry was Salvador Toscano Barrabán. In the 1890s he opened a movie salon, obtained a camera, and began filming political and sensational events (short pieces compiled by his daughter into the film *Memorias de un Mexicano*) and made the first fiction movie, *Don Juan Tenorio*. Toscano and other filmmakers during the last decades of the Díaz dictatorship concentrated on documentaries of the president's political appearances, civic celebrations, and historic documentaries such as *Grito de Dolores*. The silent film industry reached its zenith from 1915 to 1923. Enrique Rosas scored the greatest success of the era in 1919 with *La Banda del Automóbil Gris* (*The Grey Car Gang*). The boom days withered in the face of competition from the industry in the United States. One Mexican successfully switched to Hollywood and became a star using the stage name Dolores del Río.

From 1929 to 1959, the cinema went through another growth, boom, and decline cycle. This era began July 1, 1929, with the Mexico City premiere of *The Jazz Singer*. Talkies revitalized Mexican filmmaking as Hollywood proved inept at Spanish-language production and attempts at dubbing ended in a cacophony of accents that destroyed any sense of reality in the picture. The growth of the Mexican industry was boosted by three events in the 1930s: the 1931 remake of Federico Gamboa's novel and silent picture *Santa*, which demonstrated the possibilities of genuine Spanish-language talkies; the 1930 arrival in Mexico of the eminent Soviet director Serge Eisenstein, whose epic ¡*Que Viva Mexico!* was never released, but whose techniques and vision had tremendous influence on Mexican directors; and the 1936 release of Fernando de Fuentes's *Allá en el Rancho Grande*, which discovered what both Mexican and other Latin American audiences wanted, thus launching the enduring ranch comedy.

During this period, the goal of the cinema was not to educate, but to entertain the public; not to reflect social attitudes, but to relieve viewers briefly from their concerns. Yet the popularity of certain films revealed the interests, the yearnings, of everyday Mexicans. *Allá en el Rancho Grande*, the era's most popular film, reflected the nation's growing conservatism as it brought to the screen an idealized vision of the traditional rural hierarchy. The desire to reduce the pace of revolutionary policies apparently made those films popular that pictured a traditional, stable society. This movement climaxed in Juan Bustillo Oro's 1939 production *En Tiempos de don Porfirio Díaz.*

The industry grew to unprecedented proportions during World War II. The Spanish-American market boomed as Latin Americans ignored the Hollywood films made as wartime propaganda. The Mexicans benefited when the government created the Banco Cinematográfico, offering credit for both production and distribution. Besides the enthusiasm for *ranchera* films, audiences applauded the nationalistic and pro-Indian school that debuted with Emilio "El Indio" Fernández's 1943 classic *María Candelaria,* starring Dolores del Río. Wartime profits thrust the nation into a postwar boom and the film industry into its golden age. The star system during these years salvaged formula films and even overcame the problems that followed the unionization of the industry's workers. Packaged films included family melodramas, *comedias rancheras,* typical comedies, and a new form, the cabaret film. The latter stories, often built around the tragic life of a bar girl, dramatized the breakdown of values in Alemán's Mexico. On occasion these films offered a savage indictment of development in the nation. The best of these is Luis Buñel's *Los Olvidados* (*The Young and the Damned*), released in 1950. The golden age of entertainment films tarnished rapidly after 1955 with general artistic stagnation as the union blocked filmmaking by young experimental producers and actors, and with the lapse into titillating eroticism to defeat the challenge of television.

From the trough of mediocre to worse films in the second half of the 1950s, the Mexican cinema has begun another cycle that reflects a new rise of commercial popularity. With the industry in its darkest days of artistic and financial bankruptcy, encouragement to young producers outside the union came from Carmen Toscano, who organized the first film archive in 1963. Today the Cinemateca has government sponsorship and provides the filmic heritage that can be used by aspiring directors to learn their craft. The tragic events of the 1968 Tlatelolco demonstration and massacre had the ironic effect of opening Mexican society to greater freedom of expression. Independent producers launched Mexico's version of the Cinema Nova, and even union producers took on more controversial political and social themes. The leader of these films was Luis Alcoriza's *Mecánica Nacional* (1971), until the 1975 appearance of what is destined to become the classic of both the 1968 riots and the hostility between city and countryside Mexico: Felipe Cazals's superb *Canoa*. President Luis Echeverría shaped this regenerated film production of the 1970s. He nationalized the industry, then threw open the ranks to new talented directors and encouraged the widest possible themes for pictures. His identification with the Third World led to many films being coproduced with artists from Castro's Cuba. Echeverría's policies were in the main reversed when new president José López Portillo appointed his sister Margarita as head of the new Directorate of Radio, Television, and Cinema, an agency that coordinates government production in these media. López Portillo's goal was to reverse nationalization and return moviemaking to private enterprise. Since 1977, moviemakers have achieved renewed commercial success with traditional topics and soft-core pornography. Their financial condition has been strengthened by Televisa's production of made-for-television films broadcast in Mexico and elsewhere. Throughout these twists and turns, the one constant has been the entertainment aspect of Mexican cinema. Mexican films are deeply embedded in the popular culture; their subjects, their overacting, and their language are undeniably Mexican.

Second in popularity only to the movies are the *fotonovelas*. The photonovel was first developed by French and Italian publishers before World War II. It consists of still photographs with balloon captions that take into consideration the lower literacy levels prevalent in Latin America, including Mexico. *Fotonovelas* have passed through three stages. The *fotonovela rosa*, which specialized in Cinderella romances of the poor but pure heroine meeting the rich but racy hero, dominated the field from the time Mexican publishers took over production in 1950. Mexicans drew on the nation's strong comic book (*historieta*) heritage for inspiration. Elsewhere in the hemisphere, especially in Brazil and Argentina, *fotonovelas* grew out of the national film industry. In 1970 the second type of photonovel appeared: the *suave* or soft novel. This genre had more realistic plot devices, with men of lower social-class origins for heroes, revealing that social barriers were often artificial. This type of novel attracted new readers, including many men. The *suaves* remained the dominant form until 1978, when the *fotonovela roja* appeared. These stories rely on more explicit sex and violence. The red photonovel tells morality parables, using photographs that reach the level of soft pornography. This form has dominated publishing to the present. A random survey found that readers believe these *fotonovelas* portray life in the *barriadas* in a more realistic fashion.

As *fotonovelas* have become more realistic, some scholars have suspected that they present a form of gender stereotyping that reinforces Mexican *machismo*. Recent studies have found, however, that the behavior they portray does not correspond to rigid roles for men and women. This is probably because the *fotonovelas* are less about gender than other social issues. Such questions as class and urbanization receive specific treatment; the theme of migration from the countryside to the city, for example, appears in realistic detail. The role of the adult in the workplace also gets realistic treatment, but the most common and perhaps the most important theme in the photonovels is class. Lower-class characters are good and their upper-class counterparts are evil, but the novels end unhappily for those from the lower strata and happily for their upper-class characters. This suggests that the readers, the literate population of Mexico, will accept a wide range of activities by men and women but hold rigid views of class roles and relations.

Photonovels reflect society, while the political cartoons satirize its politics. The best known of these comic critics in Mexico is the comic book author Eduardo del Río, known to his readers throughout the hemisphere as Ríus. He has created three well-known series: *Los Supermachos, Los Agachados,* and *For Beginners* (for example, *Cuba for Beginners*). He has gained fame for his cast of characters, which reappear from series to series, although often with different names. Ríus developed these characters for his fictional San Garabato, Cucuzcán, hometown of *Los Supermachos,* and they include Calzontzín, the barefoot Indian sage; the local political boss, Don Perpetuo, with ten-gallon hat, red nose, and moustache; and the *beata,* Doña Emerrenciana, always wrapped in a rebozo and armed with her rosary, the typical churchgoing woman. Ríus draws on a rich Mexican tradition; Fernández de Lizardi chose the satirical picaresque form to poke fun at the newly independent political leaders in the 1820s and José Guadalupe Posada's *calaveras* (skull and madcap skeletal sketches), which caricature the social problems of the Porfirio Díaz regime. Ríus also reveals familiarity with international satire, such as Walt Kelly's classic North American comic strip, *Pogo.*

Although Ríus is today the best-known of the new Mexican cartoonists, the first break with the turn-of-the-century form created by José Guadalupe Posada came in 1950. Abel Quezada introduced a new style when he replaced the *charro*, priest, general, and skeleton (the *calavera*) with the caricature of the new rich and the Mexican macho. His sketches show the rich with large diamond rings in their noses, and the Charro Matías wears a sombrero with slogans on its brim that always contradict his actions. His purpose has been to make Mexicans aware of the abuses of the rich and the arrogance of their own *machismo*. (See Reading 22.)

The landmark year for Mexico's political cartooning was 1966, when Ríus began to publish his first comic book, *Los Supermachos*. This publication, which he wrote and illustrated for a hundred issues before being forced by the publishers to abandon it, both expanded and deserted Mexico's traditional cartoons. It remained squarely in the heritage of biting satire carried forward by Quesada. But it abandoned the comic book tradition that grew from foreign examples such as Walt Disney. Ríus's comics were not for escapist entertainment but were intended as cultural guerrilla warfare, attempting to shame the middle-class Mexican into an awareness of his society and its glaring inequities and hypocrisies. *Los Supermachos* was followed by *Los Agachados* and a number of books that explained Cuba and Marxism to beginners.

This brings Ríus to an irony that extends as well to the other prominent political cartoonists of the present, such as José Polomo. These satirists combat the creeping influence of the United States in the language and culture in Mexico, yet at the same time try to promote universal interests over the authentic Mexican culture. Polomo, a refugee from Allende's Chile, demonstrates this more clearly in his cartoons than does Ríus. Polomo's work is entitled "The Fourth Reich"; his style belongs to the same genre as "Doonesbury" from the United States and "Malfalda" from Argentina. Appearing in *Uno Más Uno* since 1977, his cartoons attempt to present a pan–Latin American perspective by aiming their barbs at universal problems — authoritarianism, economic disaster, and the class structure — within the context of foreign imperialism. Polomo, though, never allows his readers to forget that Latin Americans, not foreigners, torture, exploit, and repress their own people. His goal is to expand his readership outside of Mexico to English-speaking readers. He concedes that most of his readers probably share his views about the hemisphere and did so before they began reading the comic strip.

Mexicans also have their middle-class spokesman, Gabriel Vargas, the creator of the forty-five-year-old comic strip of domestic life, "La Familia Burrón." From the same category as "Blondie" and others in the United States, "The Burrón Family" differs in its portrayal of status distinctions. Class is recognized and affirmed. Authority figures are distrusted and disliked. Leaders are portrayed as men of ignorance, depravity, dishonesty, and greed, yet they are never challenged directly, let alone confronted. They are only endured. The women are degraded or ignored unless they conform to the role of the woman in middle-class Mexican homes. Unlike the other two popular cartoonists, Ríus and Polomo, Vargas has no interest in educating his readers about social problems or universal concerns; he prefers to give a reflection of reality that reveals traditional values under stress, but he does not parody them. His concerns are the universal aspects of family life, not the concerns of the politically motivated.

Curiously, in response to universal themes identified by cartoonists and the foreign challenges to the nation's culture, there has been a return to regional roots in popular music. Guy Bensusan has charted the merging of Mexico's regional music into a general national sound and then a redivision into its regional and stylistic components in recent years. This trend can be seen through the career of one of the most important and popular singers, Refugio (Cuco) Sánchez. From remote Tamaulipas, Cuco achieved his first national hit in 1939, and since then he has produced more than two hundred commercial successful songs, usually in the *ranchera* style. Early in his career, Sánchez recorded "Rancheras de la Época de Oro," an album that demonstrates the variety and quality of regional music. These *rancheras* were the most popular trend in Mexican music in the late 1930s, but radio, recordings, motion pictures, and finally television broke through the barriers that had sustained regionalism. A montage of regional music emerged, for example with mariachi versions of coastal Caribbean songs. And soon the old songs were being done in the swing style and other big band arrangements. This was the popular music of the golden years of radio, from 1920 to 1945.

After World War II, several broad trends of development

occurred in popular music. First among these was a nostalgic revival that stressed regional distinctions and the return of the *ranchera* sound. Emblematic of this trend was the 1974 reissuance of Sánchez's album with a new cover and liner notes stressing regional differences. This significant feeling of nostalgia represents a reaction to the shallow national culture foisted by urbanization and the mass media on those who still feel some longing for the days when Veracruz meant a cultural subregion rather than simply a port city. It represents a mild but genuine reaction against the schmalz of revolutionary rhetoric that abounds today, or the tawdry imitations of foreign music that constitute a second trend in popular music. Although foreign influence has been both inspiring and destructive, Los Yakis and the Folkloristas have gained from this influence, while those groups making unfortunate Spanish versions of the Beatles and the Rolling Stones have not. Perhaps a better example is the *música tropicál,* the regional music of Veracruz, which was originally derived from Cuban sources and continues to draw on Cuba for inspiration, retaining its popularity. This form has gained in strength since World War II as part of the regional revival in reaction to the Mexican version of modern music.

Other significant emerging aspects of popular music after World War II include Mexican *roncanrol,* which is distinct from the ersatz rerecordings of North American and British tunes. Northern border music, with many fans in the southwestern United States, and protest songs have emerged since the 1960s and often include bands affecting Andean instrumentation and dress styles.

There seems to be some correlation presently between class and musical preference, with the lower classes in both urban and rural regions choosing indigenous popular music — *rancheras,* for example — while the middle and upper classes in the cities seem more susceptible to foreign musical fashions, especially from the United States. Why this should be so is a complex question, but the reasons must include a desire to appear chic among those who can afford imported foreign music and the nostalgic longing of those in the mushrooming squatter settlements for home. The traditional music provides these urban migrants a tenuous but real link to the *patria chica* ("little homeland").

Mass sport developed in Mexico only shortly after the rise of these events in the United States and western Europe. Today the country's most popular sport is soccer, which has a tremendous youth following in the United States but has proved unable to establish itself as a professional attraction north of the Rio Grande. Mexican sport draws millions of spectators, and several of the most popular clubs are now the property of government institutions, such as the Social Security Institute, which owns Atlante, and corporate enterprises such as Cruz Azul, named for the cement company that owns it. Mexico's soccer federation has given the nation international recognition by hosting the World Cup Games in 1972 and by the fact that Mexico has been selected host again for 1986. Mexico remains the strongest nation in this sport in the North American and Caribbean region.

Mexicans have also demonstrated a great affinity for baseball. This game has been played in Mexico since the 1880s, with Mexicans achieving their greatest success in the 1950s by twice winning the Little League World Series. (The team from Monterrey captured the title both times.) The Mexican League was organized in the 1920s and drew visiting players from the United States in the off-season. Large numbers of players from the segregated black leagues supplemented their incomes by playing during the winter season in Mexico. The capital city promoters, the Pasquel brothers, made a strong push to create a Mexican major league during the years immediately after World War II. Their plan included raiding teams in the United States, and they scored their greatest success when they tempted Mickey Owens, Max Lanier, and Sal Maglie to make a collective jump into the Mexican League. Rumors were that the Pasquels had even begun negotiations with Ted Williams. The National and American Leagues reacted by banning any of the "jumpers" from the majors. This campaign by the Pasquels had the effect of seeing the Mexican League given official status alongside the International League (which included Havana and Montreal) with a AAA ranking. The Mexican League retains its status as a top minor league today. It is known primarily as a hitter's league, partly no doubt because of the high elevations of the towns in the circuit. More than Mexican teams or the league, the major attraction of baseball has been the Mexican players who have reached the major leagues in the United States. No Mexican has done that with quite the splash and glitter and glamour of Fernando Valenzuela of the Los Angeles Dodgers. Valenzuela—El Toro to his countrymen— has become an instant hero in Mexico and the southwestern United States.

American sports have some following in Mexico. There was a

major effort to introduce basketball across the country in the 1930s; countless backboards and rims stand in remote villages in testimony to this campaign. American football also has some followers, but mostly as fans. Shortly after television arrived in Mexico, the Dallas Cowboys' games were beamed into the country. The Cowboys, who claim to be America's team, most certainly have become Mexico City's team. National Football League doubleheaders today, with Dallas and another game, are common on Sunday afternoon television. For those with the peso equivalent of $1,800 to $2,300, Super Bowl trips, which feature excursions to Disneyland and Sea World, have become popular attractions.

Bullfights remain popular in Mexico, but they would probably not survive without the patronage of tourists who go to be repelled by the bloody attraction. Those interested in traditional sport in Mexico more often turn to *charrería,* the equestrian event that involves a display of men and women in *charro* and *poblana* costumes in rodeo-like performances.

Mexicans have participated in the Olympic Games since the 1920s and continue to support the international Olympic movement in the face of boycotts by the United States in 1980 and the Soviet Union in 1984. Mexicans have achieved their greatest success in these international contests in bicycling and racewalking events. Mexico received recognition from industrial nations that it had achieved a level of modernization when it was chosen as host of the 1968 Olympic Games. The tragic Tlatelolco massacre, when the army shot more than three hundred students to death on the eve of the games, marred the event, but the games themselves were organized, financed, and carried out with great skill and verve before an international television audience.

In each of the forms of popular culture — movies, *fotonovelas,* cartoons, music, and sport — a Mexican quality exists. Nationalists quite rightly work against the increased penetration of foreign influence in the language, the mass media, and other facets of culture. Nevertheless, their major fear that a sombrero version of United States culture will emerge seems unfounded. Mexico's mass culture reveals a nationalistic resiliency that absorbs foreign influence, reshapes it, and gives it a Mexican stamp. The movie industry has been the most successful in achieving an authenticity that makes Mexican movies easily identifiable throughout the hemisphere. Popular culture in Mexico is indeed Mexican popular culture.

4

THE MEXICAN PET AND OTHER STORIES: FOLKLORE AND HISTORY

W. Dirk Raat

W. Dirk Raat, one of the coeditors of and commentators in this book, teaches Latin American history at the State University of New York at Fredonia. He is the author of several articles in English and Spanish on Mexican intellectual history, Mexican historiography, and the Mexican Revolution. His books include El positivismo durante el Porfiriato; Revoltosos! Mexico's Rebels in the United States, 1903–1923; Mexico: From Independence to Revolution, 1810– 1910; *and* The Mexican Revolution: An Annotated Guide to Recent Scholarship.

In the following essay Raat distinguishes folklore from popular culture, and folklore from "fakelore." He argues that the historian of Mexico, often trained to distrust oral traditions and nonliterary sources, should be open to the new opportunities that research and fieldwork in folklore provide. After describing three types of folkloric sources —material, customary, and oral—he focuses on oral folklore, which includes simple names, phrases, and proverbs, as well as more elaborate ballads, myths, legends, and folktales. Urban legends and urban tales, products of modern cities, are a recent form of folklore. The historian, through a careful study of the sociological and historical context of oral narratives (legends, tales, anecdotes, jokes, and the like), can derive keys that unlock many mysteries of today's Mexico.

In a speech before an academic group in San Antonio in 1970, the well-known folklorist Américo Paredes called folklore "the unofficial heritage of a people." The definition was developed further by folklore scholar Jan Harold Brunvand, who described folklore as an unofficial and traditional, noninstitutional part of culture. It encompasses all knowledge, values, attitudes, and beliefs transmitted in traditional form by word of mouth, customary behavior, or material forms (for example, artifacts). Although many of these habits of thought are part of the common experience of people, they take place in cultural and historical contexts that make them specific to particular groups, places, and times. Both Paredes and Brunvand characterize folklore as historical in some aspects, and Brunvand called legends (one subtype of narrative lore) folk history.

Social historians usually distinguish between elite (or academic) traditions and popular (or mass) culture on the one hand, and folklore on the other. One distinction concerns origins. The authorship of elite and popular culture can usually be determined, whereas folklore often has anonymous beginnings. In general, the elite and popular traditions are transmitted in print or by other formal means like television serials, Hollywood films, and radio talk shows. Elites have their own oral, customary, and material traditions, and their culture reflects the values and attitudes of highly educated middle and upper classes. Popular culture is more widespread, can include all socioeconomic groups (especially urban ones), and is transmitted through the mass media. The culture of the "folk" is nonliterate and conservative, the product of peasants, workers, and middle-class urban groups. These definitions are not precise, however; some writers speak of the folklore of the elites, and others use the coined term *elitelore* to refer to the oral traditions of the upper class.

Further complications often blur distinctions between popular culture and folklore, in part because ideas can move back and forth among elite, popular, and folk groups. For example, the ballad and legend of Gregorio Cortez, a Mexican hero, was for years a part of the oral traditions of the Mexican-American community of the lower Rio Grande Valley of Texas. When Américo Paredes, the foremost scholar of border folklore, published his work on this *corrido* (ballad) entitled *With His Pistol in His Hand* (1958), the legend in its printed form became a kind of elitelore. By the 1980s, when the legend was retold in cinematic form as "The Ballad of Gregorio Cortez," it had become a hybrid of popular and elite art.

If ideas, customs, and material forms can move from one level of society to another, so too can they stay or "march" in place. Many barn types of the folk have remained with the folk. Movies as popular art maintain a continuity in themes and form throughout the years. For example, during World War I publisher William

Randolph Hearst produced a film called *Patria,* a "preparedness" film that told the story of the heroine, Patria, and her Secret Service lover, who, along with an army of patriots, were able to save America (or southern California, which was the same thing for Hearst) by defeating a combined invasion force of Japanese and Mexican soldiers. The same appeals to nativism can be seen in Hollywood's 1984 release of *Red Dawn,* a salute to Reagan's America, in which a group of spunky teenagers takes to the hills of Colorado to defend the country from a Communist occupation. In *Red Dawn* we are told that the Communist invasion began with illegal Mexican aliens blowing up a Strategic Air Command base.

Any supposed folklore that is the product of professionals and is transmitted by print, broadcasting, or other commercial means is sometimes referred to by folklorists as *fakelore.* Again, it is not always easy to distinguish fakelore from folklore, as another example from the border illustrates. Shortly after the assassination of John F. Kennedy in Dallas in 1963, *corridos* were heard in cantinas, over the radio, and on jukeboxes throughout the Southwest. These ballads expressed the Mexican Americans' sorrow over Kennedy's death. One *corrido,* for instance, stated, "All the world is in mourning; we weep with feeling. Kennedy, you were so good to all Mexicans."

Because the Kennedy *corridos* were not composed anonymously, were transmitted through mass media (radio and phonograph records), and were not variants of one *corrido,* a few critics branded them "fakelore" and assigned to them the same lowly status as other Kennedy memorabilia that appeared and disappeared overnight. Yet the authors of these *corridos* were amateurs, the content of the ballads was traditional in a fixed and standard form, and the songs circulated throughout members of a particular ethnic group. More important, they were not foisted on the public by professionals for commercial purposes, even though they were exploited commercially. Whether fakelore (in this example a form of popular culture) or folklore, or both, these *corridos* reflect a historical truth: The ballads about Kennedy, so well received by the Mexican-American community, made of Kennedy a symbol that embodied the Mexican Americans' aspiration for equal rights, racial justice, and full citizenship.

Students of Mexican history have often used certain kinds of folkloric sources in reconstructing the past. Material folk traditions include folk architecture like the adobe houses of Mexico and the Southwest, Indian crafts and arts such as pottery-making and basketry, and folk costumes like the traditional dress of the Tarascans or other indigenous groups. Folk foods like corn tortillas, refried beans, and peppers are another material tradition. Such staples are not only primary sources of calories and nutrients; they are also "soul food" that convey a sense of psychological security. These foods are closely tied up with Mexican religion, mythology, and history.

Scholars who study Mexico also make use of customary folklore. Mexico is a land of tradition in which superstitions are acted out with frequency. Festivals and fiestas celebrate everything and everyone from Hidalgo's cry for independence to the *angelitos* (little children) of the Day of the Dead. As Mexican essayist and poet Octavio Paz has noted, for the Mexican the fiesta is a moment of true joy, an intoxication, a "whirlwind." Other folk customs include dances and dramas. Having their origins as religious or political rituals, they are now acted out as forms of entertainment in villages and towns. Even gestures have meaning, whether a warm *abrazo* (embrace) of greeting or an obscene lifting of the arm.

Equally important for the historian of Mexico is the development and historical meaning of oral folklore. Oral traditions range from the simple to the complex, from short phrases, names, and proverbs to more elaborate ballads, myths, legends, and folktales. These sources are especially helpful for understanding the group values and attitudes that often shape relationships between people — families, ethnic minorities, classes and occupational groups, men and women, and national groups. Students of intercultural relations can benefit from an understanding of such oral traditions.

North American folk speech contains many examples of ethnic slurs. Residents of the western United States may speak of a "Mexican credit card," that is, a hose for stealing gasoline. In my teenage days in Utah during the mid-1950s I was often instructed by older boys to shove the gearshift level into "Mexican overdrive" (coast down a hill in neutral in order to conserve gasoline). These and similar usages testify to the Anglo folk belief that Mexicans (and Mexican Americans) are criminal, reckless, unsophisticated (especially in relationship to technological matters), and impoverished (another reason for their being a criminal class). Such racial and class biases have historical antecedents, and it is the historian's job to locate and trace them.

The kinds of oral folklore that have received the most attention by Mexicanists are proverbs, ballads, and myths. The use of *dichos,* or proverbial sayings, is extremely old, dating in Mexico back to Toltec and Aztec times. "The fewer donkeys, the more corncobs," the Mexican will say, and in so doing expresses traditional values and the collective wisdom of the people. Investigating the social and historical context of such proverbs provides an understanding not only of the meaning of the words but also of the social circumstance that gave rise to the saying (in this case the economic condition of scarcity and want).

Studies of *corridos,* or ballads, by Merle E. Simmons, Américo Paredes, Manuel H. Peña, and others show that *corridos* function as barometers of the Mexican's attitudes towards events. The *corrido* is a kind of collective diary, an ethnohistorical document containing facts about society and history. Most *corridos* depict the Mexican as either victim or hero and often have themes of intercultural conflict. Many express frustration and anger over Anglo and North American dominance, and are, at times, a call to action. On those occasions when the *corrido* is represented in printed or pictorial form, such as the graphic art of José Guadalupe Posada (see Reading 7), it can be considered popular culture.

Of the various myths and legends that permeate Mexico, the apparition of the Virgin of Guadalupe has to be the central symbol of Mexican history. Having its origins in early colonial times, "Our Lady of Guadalupe" is an Indian fertility goddess (Tonantzin) in medieval Christian garb ("The Most Holy Virgin Mary, Mother of Orphans"). The Virgin of Guadalupe affects all aspects of Mexican folk belief and custom. She is celebrated and worshiped in the folk fair, fiesta, and festival to Guadalupe (December 12); depicted in statues, altars, and relics of the Church; spoken of in countless ballads (see Reading 8) and folktales (including erotic jokes about nuns and virgins*); and reflected in folk foods like *pulque* (known as

---

*A bishop is waiting to see the Mother Superior in the reception room of a convent. A nun is telling him the names of the virgins whose pictures hang on the walls:

"This is the Virgin of Fátima, and this is the Virgin of los Remidos. This is the Virgin of Guadalupe—"

"And this virgin, who is she?" asks the bishop.

"Oh, that is no virgin, that's the Mother Superior."

"Virgin's milk"). Adopted by Father Hidalgo as a national symbol of independence in 1810, she has maintained her vitality throughout the revolutionary decades of the twentieth century. It is not an exaggeration to say that it is almost impossible to describe contemporary Mexico and its history except by reference to her.

Although much Mexican folklore is rural in its origins, urbanization has made the modern city and its suburbs the social setting of many of today's legends and folktales. Because United States popular culture penetrates Mexico City directly via cable television and other mass media, Mexico City has replaced the border as a launching pad of modern lore. Of special importance for scholars of contemporary Mexico and relations between Mexico and the United States are urban legends and urban tales, two types of lore overlooked by most historians.

Like myths, legends are traditional prose narratives considered to be truthful accounts of the past. Unlike myths, legends are secular, set in the recent past, and deal with the activities of normal human beings rather than ancient gods and demigods. Tales and jokes differ from legends in being purely fictional and not believable; however, they still contain hints as to social attitudes and prevailing historical conditions.

One example of an urban legend recently circulating in the United States is the story of "The Mexican Pet." Published here for the first time, it was told to folklorist Brunvand by three independent witnesses, two in California and one in Texas, and variations of it are known even beyond border towns. The place names differ in Brunvand's three versions (Mexico City, Acapulco, Tijuana), but the story is the same. A composite account goes like this:

> A woman who lives on Sutton Place in New York City took a trip to Mexico. While touring Mexico City she spotted a lost Mexican Chihuahua dog standing in an alley. It looked emaciated and hungry. The woman impulsively scooped the little animal up and took it back to her hotel room. For the rest of her stay it remained there and she fed and cared for it. When it came time for her return, she decided to take it back to New York with her but feared the authorities would not let her, so she hid it in her ample bag and was able to smuggle it through customs. In her Sutton Place home she fed it, cared for it, even spoiled it by letting it sleep in her bed—but it never seemed to get any healthier or stronger.
>
> One morning she awoke and noticed that there was an

oozing mucus around the dog's eyes and a slight foaming of the mouth. Fearful for her dog's health, she rushed it to a nearby veterinarian and returned home to await word on her pet's condition.

The call soon came. "I have just one question," said the vet. "*Where* did you get this dog?"

After pausing, the woman nervously admitted having brought it across the border from Mexico. "But tell me, doctor," she said, "What's wrong with my dog?"

His reply was brief. "I'm afraid it's dying—but it's not a dog; it's a Mexican sewer rat!"

The first observation the folklorist can make is that this story is authentic (reported by independent observers); was told by people in urban settings who believed the story to be true ("it happened to a friend of my wife's aunt," or "it was told to my friend Wendy, who got it from her friend Dennis, who knew the people who knew the woman," etc.); had several variants; and is similar in style and content to other urban legends.

The student of Mexican society is struck by the reference to the dog as a Mexican Chihuahua (especially when "Chihuahua" is not the easiest word for Anglo informants to spell). The Chihuahua originally descended from the small hairless Asian dog, and its ancestors include the short-coated techichi of the Toltec and Aztec Indians. Until recently the Chihuahua and its mute, hairless ancestor suffered from a negative public image. The Spaniards, who introduced fierce war dogs to America, were disgusted by this small hairless dog that was so obviously a part of pagan ceremonies. Even the Aztecs, who fattened the dogs for eating, preferred to disguise their meals by burying the dog meat under a layer of turkey and maize.

As for "Chihuahua," it is a Spanish (i.e., Mexican) place name as well as the name for a species of dog unique because it is indigenous to Mexico. It is appropriate that a legend that expresses a typical North American national and racial bias against Mexico as an unsanitary place would adopt the symbol of the hairless Mexican Chihuahua for its central stereotype.

Like urban legends, urban tales— especially jokes—reflect popular values, attitudes, and practices, and once again testify to the differences and conflicts between Anglo and Hispanic America. Mexicans are often the target of North American ethnic jokes.

In western New York the following riddle joke was circulating during the early 1980s:

"Why do Mexicans always have big noses?"
Answer: "So they'll have something to pick in the off-season."

Like most folklore, this joke is formularized. Usually the New York City version would be:

"Why do Jews have big noses?"
Answer: "Because the air is free."

In both instances, the set phrases and stereotypes are used to ridicule a minority people.

Some jokes are binational, bicultural, and bilingual. The following joke, very likely having its origins in Houston or some other space technology center, is told in the cantinas of Mexico and reveals a common Mexican perception of American attitudes toward Mexicans. As reported by Paredes, it goes like this: A Mexican named Manuel rode on a spaceship with an American astronaut. After having answered a call of nature, the astronaut was heard to say, "I am now going to put it on Manuel (manual)."

The preceding joke is an example of the self-directed anecdote — one that helps the teller to deal with a status of inferiority in some sphere. Another example of the self-directed joke is the *compadre* story retold by Paredes: Two friends in Mexico are discussing the United States and the sensitive issue of Mexican territory lost to the United States during the U.S.-Mexican War of 1845–1848.

"These Gringos are terrible people," says one— "cheaters, liars, and robbers."

"Sure, *compadre*, says the other, "Look what they did in '46. They took half our national territory."

"Yes, *compadre*," says the first, "and the half with all the paved roads."

As historians of the United States and Mexico are quick to point out, the phrase "half our national territory" has been used frequently by Mexican orators denouncing American imperialism from the "manifest destiny" days of 1846, through the Cananea strike of 1906, to the election and monetary devaluation of 1976.

Another type of Mexican joke is the Stupid American jest, a humorous anecdote in which the gringo (often depicted as a tourist) loses face, money, or his wife or girlfriend to the cunning Mexican. For example, the gullible American tourist pays ten thousand dollars for a burro that is supposed to tell the time whenever you heft his testicles. Another, more traditional version has the tourist paying the Mexican for a burro that supposedly "shits money instead of dung."

Another kind of Stupid American jest plays on the gringo's ignorance of Mexican customs, such as a convention of saying "It is yours" for thank you, or replying "My house is your house" when thanking someone for admiring your house. In this vein the joke was told about the late John F. Kennedy, who accepted a wristwatch from Mexican president López Mateos during the Kennedys' visit to Mexico. Kennedy returned the watch when López Mateos expressed his great admiration for Mrs. Kennedy. Whatever the version, the Mexican in the Stupid American jest acquires American dollars and American women, two obvious symbols of power and status. In the process the teller and his audience are able to release aggressive feelings in a socially approved way.

A third type of Mexican urban tale is political humor. In the following example the story is, on one level, another kind of self-directed anecdote. On this national level it contains insights into inter-American relations. On another level, that of class, the story is a populist comment on the Mexican bureaucracy. This story circulated throughout Mexico during the presidency of Luis Echeverría (1970– 76) when Henry Kissinger was Richard Nixon's foreign affairs adviser and secretary of state.

> Once Henry Kissinger visited Luis Echeverría. President Echeverría wanted to know how Kissinger developed such a flair with women. He claimed that he wanted to rekindle the fires of passion at home. Kissinger explained that he used an aggressive macho approach—that he would speed into the driveway, slam on the brakes, screech to a halt, rush to the door, throw it open, burst into the house, grab the woman, and throw her onto the floor. Echeverría decided to try Kissinger's approach. He sped into the driveway at Los Pinos, slammed on the brakes, screeched to a halt, rushed to the door, threw it open, and burst into the hall, where his wife's voice greeted him, "Henry, is that you?"

One immediately notices that here it is the Mexican, not the American, who loses the woman (and face and power). In addition, the story contains a hint of the feeling of powerlessness that many Mexicans experience when dealing with the "Colossus of the North." Taken literally, it is also a statement of the inadequacy and imitative behavior of the Mexican government. (The Mexican president seeks advice from a foreigner from the United States. Then, having resorted to requesting aid, he rushes home to discover that he has suffered the macho's greatest shame, cuckoldry.) The cuckold and other sexual motifs occur often in contemporary Mexican political humor. Their use testifies to the safety-valve theory of humor, in that this kind of joke allows Mexicans to laugh at the politician without risking the more serious crime of attacking the government.

As the preceding examples illustrate, oral traditions do not cease when a people cease to be rural and illiterate. In fact, many of the nonliterary and oral traditions of Mexico are currently to be found in the making and telling in major urban centers of Mexico and the United States, where they continue to be important ethnohistorical documents.

BIBLIOGRAPHICAL NOTE

An excellent source for the beginning student of folklore is Jan Harold Brunvand's *The Study of American Folklore: An Introduction* (New York: W. W. Norton, 1978). The Kennedy ballads are examined by Dan William Dickey in *The Kennedy Corridos: A Study of the Ballads of a Mexican American Hero* (Austin: University of Texas Center for Mexican American Studies, Monograph No. 4, 1978). For an informative account of folk foods, see Peter Farb and George Armelatos, *Consuming Passions: The Anthropology of Eating* (Boston: Houghton Mifflin, 1980). The most complete work on *corridos* remains Merle E. Simmons, *The Mexican Corrido as a Source for Interpretive Study of Modern Mexico, 1870–1950* (Bloomington: Indiana University Press, 1957).

For a thematic issue on Mexican folklore and folk art in the United States see *Aztlán* 13 (Spring and Fall 1982), especially the articles by Américo Paredes on proverbs, Manuel H. Peña on *corridos*, Rafaela Castro on Mexican women's sexual jokes, and José Reyna's review of *The Kennedy Corridos* by William Dickey. The master scholar of Mexican and Mexican American folklore is Américo Paredes. See both his *Folktales of Mexico* (Chicago: University of Chicago Press, 1970) and "The Anglo-American in

Mexican Folklore," in *New Voices in American Studies,* edited by Ray B. Browne, et al. (Mid-American Conference on Literature, History, Popular Culture and Folklore, Purdue University, 1966).

An inclusive if somewhat dated collection of folklore is *A Treasury of Mexican Folkways* by Frances Toor (New York: Crow Publishers, 1947). The Toor study, although lacking in analysis, does contain complete copies of folk songs, tales, myths, legends, names, phrases, and slang usages. For one of the few works on historical methodology and folklore, see Richard M. Dorson, *American Folkore & the Historian* (Chicago: University of Chicago Press, 1971). Dorson argues for natural links between local history and folklore.

University of Utah folklorist Jan Harold Brunvand graciously provided me with three texts of "The Mexican Pet" story. His own pioneering works on urban legends are *The Vanishing Hitchhiker* (New York: W. W. Norton & Co., 1981) and *The Choking Doberman* (New York: W. W. Norton & Co., 1984). Many of the ideas contained in this essay came from conversations with Professor Brunvand. His only request was that I not rename "The Mexican Pet" "The Choking Chihuahua." Finally, Professor William Beezley of North Carolina State University at Raleigh shared the Kissinger-Echeverría story with me. See his paper "Mexican Political Humor," *Latin American Lore* (1985).

5

UNITED STATES–MEXICAN RELATIONS SINCE 1910: A SURVEY

Mark T. R. Gilderhus

With the publication of Diplomacy and Revolution: U.S.-Mexican Relations *under Wilson and Carranza, Mark Gilderhus, chairman of the history department at Colorado State University, first indicated his interest in Woodrow Wilson's diplomacy in the western hemisphere. Wilson's response to the Mexican Revolution was to attempt to protect North Americans and their property and to shape the emerging regime — that is, as Gilderhus says, to reaffirm Mexico's dependence on its northern neighbor. This policy, modified by other international events such as world war and anti-Soviet programs, continues today. Beginning with Wilson, the author succinctly describes the repeated collisions and adjustments between Mexican nationalism and United States interests. Oil, land, and investments had turns as the major issue; bank loans often baited the dependency trap; and presidential policies at times took a back seat to the personalities of the United States ambassadors. After World War II old problems, such as migrant seasonal labor, intensified and new ones, such as drug trafficking, appeared. By 1980, Gilderhus argues, neither nation had much to gain in the continuing controversy over dependency. The tremendous problems that derive from a shared two-thousand-mile border display an interdependency between the United States and Mexico that must be recognized in order to reach mutual solutions.*

No place quite like it exists anywhere else on earth. The border between the United States and Mexico extends some two thousand miles, often through wild and exotic country. It is largely unguarded, and huge numbers of people cross it each day, some with proper papers and some without. The region has unique and hybrid cultural forms and is vivid and stark in contrasts. Any traveler moving south departs from a land of plenty and enters into a land of want, literally in the space of a few hundred yards.

Important conditions, such as geographic proximity and large disparities of wealth and power, have figured prominently in shaping relations between the United States and Mexico in the twentieth century.

In the years since independence, the United States, more dynamic and aggressive, has usually taken the active role. It has made things happen. In contrast, Mexico, the more passive, has had things happen to it. In the nineteenth century, North American expansionists lusted after Mexican territory and in 1848 managed to take possession of half the country. Later, the northern neighbors became content to wield influence less directly and annexed only Mexico's wealth. During the presidency of Porfirio Díaz, from 1876 until 1910, United States trade and investment so pervaded the nation that historian David Pletcher has characterized Mexico as "truly an economic satellite of the United States." Mexicans lacked control of important sectors within their own economy: significantly, transportation, public utilities, and the extractive industries of mining and petroleum.

The great Mexican Revolution beginning in 1910 challenged the existing relationship in many ways. First, the terrible magnitude of the violence, in the course of which some two million Mexicans died, also imperiled North Americans and their possessions in Mexico and elicited countless expressions of horror and outrage. Indeed, the inability of successive Mexican governments to ensure safety and order provoked a chronic diplomatic wrangle. North Americans demanded peace and stability, yet worried about the direction that reconstruction might take, especially when Mexican reformers and revolutionists called into question the prevailing definition of property rights. The United States wanted no deviations from the accepted international norms.

The decade of disorder after 1910 established a pattern in United States—Mexican relations and defined the great issues for many years in the future. They revolved around the question of dependency. Mexicans saw themselves as the subjects of outside domination. According to this perception, foreign interests, principally British and North American, had acquired powerful positions of influence in Mexico and had aided the entrenched ruling oligarchy in oppressing the masses of people and stealing their riches. Mexicans insisted upon the full attributes of sovereignty. For them, the principle of self-determination required that they exercise authority over their country, particularly over the crucial economic sectors, the land, and the natural resources. Henceforth, the principal object of statecraft became liberation from dependency, but the effort aroused tough resistance.

For a decade after the 1910 Madero uprising, policymakers in Washington grappled with a two-sided problem: How could they safeguard Americans in Mexico against the violence and at the same time exert some direction over the course of the Revolution, especially over the process of reconstruction? Ideally, the leaders of the United States wanted a more or less democratic government in Mexico City that would respect the rules of capitalist enterprise and the wishes of the American government. President Woodrow Wilson said on one occasion that he intended to teach the Latin Americans "to elect good men." But he lacked the means and never concluded the events in Mexico to his satisfaction.

Initially, Wilson relied upon the threat of intervention. When General Victoriano Huerta, the interim president, gave offense in the spring of 1914, Wilson ordered a force of navy and marines to take the port city of Veracruz; they held it for nearly a year. Later, when Francisco Villa sacked the border town of Columbus, New Mexico, a column of the United States Army under Brigadier General John J. Pershing gave chase. But such blatant practices entailed certain dangers. They might provoke retaliation against other Americans in Mexico or, even worse, trigger a war along the southern flank at a time of difficulty with Germany.

Wilson, meanwhile, learned about subtlety. When Venustiano Carranza, the first chief of the Constitutionalist armies, achieved some measure of mastery in Mexico, the American president tried to court him, calculating that he might restore order and conform to Washington's wishes. Carranza proved a disappointment. As a patriotic nationalist, he unnerved United States leaders by cultivating an ambiguous policy toward Germany and by staying out of the First World War on grounds of neutrality. He moderated Mexican dependency on "the Northern Colossus" in other ways, too. Most notably, on February 5, 1917, he promulgated a new constitution that altered the rules according to which Mexico conducted its dealings. Henceforth, foreign entrepreneurs would enjoy no special favors. More specifically, under the terms of Article 27, they must renounce special protection from their governments and become "as Mexicans" under the law. Moreover, Article 27 advanced a new conception of property, describing ownership as a privilege rather than a right. Henceforth, private property could exist as long as it served the collective welfare of the Mexican people. When it ceased to do so, it became subject to expropriation, a legal procedure intended to break up the concentration of landholding in immense *haciendas* and to make redistribution possible. Similarly, natural resources, such as oil and minerals, became the property of the Mexican nation, no longer the object of private ownership. In the future, prospective developers could acquire concessions by petitioning the authorities in Mexico City. At the same time, the status of exploitative privileges acquired before 1917 became unclear. Would the Mexican government regard them as still in force?

As an immediate consequence, Article 27 of the Constitution of 1917 ignited a diplomatic dispute lasting more than twenty years. It centered on American property in Mexico but took on additional ramifications, particularly American claims against Mexico for losses during the violence. Much disturbed by the alleged "confiscatory" aims and "Bolshevik" tendencies of Mexico's new rulers, American property owners, mine operators, and oilmen insisted that their government had an obligation to defend their interests. For a time late in 1919, some of them tried to force an intervention, but President Wilson resisted, exploring instead the likelihood of persuading the Mexicans to relax their stand by intimating the possibility of a loan. This ploy, a classic, sought leverage by taking advantage of Mexico's lack of investment capital. It promised rewards for good behavior and penalties for bad. The dilemma always constricted Mexico's ability to maneuver.

An insurrection overthrew Carranza's government in May 1920 and ended with his assassination. It also brought into power the so-called Sonora dynasty. During the next decade, the Mexican Revolution entered a more constructive phase. Under Presidents Alvaro Obregón and Plutarco Elías Calles, literacy campaigns established schools in the countryside, the ideology of *indigenismo* exalted Mexico's Indian past, and labor unions brought organization to urban workers. Moreover, Article 27 provided authority for the breakup of large, landed estates and kept relations with the

United States in constant turmoil. The United States wanted clarification of the intentions and the effects.

Pending some understanding, preferably a treaty in defense of property rights acquired before 1917, the Harding administration withheld diplomatic recognition from Obregón's government. Although Obregón would not nullify constitutional provisions as the price, he hoped for some kind of accommodation by which to put relations on a more regular basis. A decision by the Mexican Supreme Court in 1921 facilitated such an endeavor by articulating the doctrine of "positive acts." If oil companies actually had done something to begin removing oil from their properties before May 1, 1917, the date on which the Constitution took effect, Article 27 could not justify a revocation of ownership. "Positive acts" meant that a company could keep its property. When four subsequent judgments in the lower courts confirmed the precedent in Mexican law, a modus vivendi became possible. In the summer of 1923, commissioners from both countries met at a place on Bucareli Street in Mexico City. In the ensuing "Bucareli agreements," Mexico accepted the doctrine of positive acts as the basis for future dealings with foreign-owned oil companies, and the United States in turn consented to diplomatic recognition. In addition, the two countries concurred in a plan to establish a mixed commission to hear claims by United States citizens against Mexico.

The relationship soured soon after Plutarco Elías Calles took office in 1924. The new United States ambassador, James R. Sheffield, contributed impressively to the deterioration. Characterized by historian Robert Freeman Smith as a "closed-minded" and "self-righteous" corporation lawyer, Sheffield espoused racist views and thought of the Mexicans as barbarians who needed "to be taken over and civilized by sons of 'Mother Yale.' " Such reasoning, an odd attribute of the elitism of the times, regarded the athletic virtues of the playing field as especially useful in coping with savages. Learning the rules of baseball presumably would assist the Mexicans in acting like gentlemen.

When Calles refused to provide additional guarantees beyond the Bucareli agreements, Sheffield, also an alarmist, persuaded his superior, secretary of state Frank B. Kellogg, that a Bolshevik plot now threatened American property in Mexico. In the summer of 1925, Kellogg made a statement to the press in which he said, "The

Government of Mexico is now on trial before the world." Calles, in response, had legislation enacted to put Article 27 into effect. A petroleum law in December 1925 required foreign oil companies to petition the Mexican government for confirmations of their concessions. In bestowing them, Mexico City would adhere to the doctrine of positive acts but imposed a limitation of fifty years.

Relations abruptly became critical. Fortunately, President Calvin Coolidge, no warrior, replaced Sheffield with an old college friend from Amherst. Dwight Morrow, an experienced Mexico hand and a partner in the banking firm of J. P. Morgan, addressed the matter intelligently and assured the Mexicans of his goodwill. He also won Calles over. When Morrow stated his view that the Mexican courts should decide, Calles in all likelihood used his influence to assure an acceptable compromise. The Mexican Supreme Court upheld the doctrine of positive acts but struck down the fifty-year limitation. In this instance, both sides gave a little and avoided a showdown.

The onset of the Great Depression in 1929 diverted attention from the oil controversy for a time. Meanwhile, Mexico suffered additional troubles. The Cristero Rebellion produced chaos in the rural areas and led to the assassination of the president-elect, Alvaro Obregón. Subsequently Calles, *"el jefe máximo,"* ruled by proxy through three short-term, interim presidents. The 1934 election brought about an important change. Lázaro Cárdenas, the former governor of Michoacán, broke Calles's power and displayed new energy. Determined to advance the cause of constructive reform, Cárdenas speeded up the rate of land redistribution and tried to fulfill the promise of the Constitution of 1917. He also brought to a conclusion the oil dispute with the United States.

In the United States, the administration of Franklin D. Roosevelt had proclaimed the policy of "the good neighbor." Fundamentally a response to the Great Depression, the policy proposed to exchange blatant forms of political control for economic advantages. Seeking to obtain markets and cheap resources in Latin America, Roosevelt gave up the practice of intervention. Indeed, he liquidated the remnants of past interventions, abolished the protectorates in Cuba and Panama, and committed the United States to the principle of nonintervention.

Mexico put the Good Neighbor Policy to the test in 1938 when

Cárdenas expropriated the holdings of foreign-owned oil companies. The decision grew out of a labor dispute. Workers in the petroleum industry went on strike for higher wages and better conditions. When an arbitration board upheld the demands but the companies resisted, the Mexican president nationalized their holdings on grounds that they had defied the sovereignty of the Mexican nation. The act produced another crisis. Oil company executives charged Mexico with thievery and attributed it to the influence of communists south of the border. Some extremists wanted to send in the United States Army to throw the rascals out, but Roosevelt took a more prudent course. While putting on the diplomatic pressure, he relied on the tact and skill of Ambassador Josephus Daniels. A negotiated settlement ultimately granted compensation to the companies in the amount of $24 million, substantially less than the $200 million they initially asked for. Nevertheless, the precedent had shattering effects. Henceforth, Roosevelt and his successors tried to find ways to head off similar seizures of foreign-owned property in the rest of Latin America.

One reason why the Americans acquiesced in the expropriation was the intricacy of world politics. Roosevelt had no wish to force Mexico into an association with the Axis powers—Germany, Italy, and Japan. An unduly hard line might have resulted in such an outcome. As it turned out, Roosevelt's flexibility made it possible for Mexico to side with the Allies in the Second World War. When Mexican oil tankers came under attack from German submarines, President Manuel Avila Camacho broke relations and declared war. During the conflict, Mexico aided the cause by sending aviators to fight in the Philippines and supplying vital raw materials.

Another major issue in United States—Mexican relations concerned the movement of masses of people across the border out of Mexico into the United States. Throughout this century, Mexico's inability to control emigration has undercut its claim to the practice of self-determination. The allure of the United States has been irresistible. Peasant people, especially, have fled rural poverty, hoping to find employment among the gringos, working in agriculture or some menial capacity. A great exodus took place during the violent decade 1910–20, driven largely by the bloodletting and carnage. Possibly a million persons left Mexico, followed by similarly large numbers in the 1920s. Very few restrictions regulated the flow during these years. Because of labor shortages in the American Southwest, the residents by and large welcomed the migrants as a seasonal necessity. With the onset of the Great Depression in the 1930s, circumstances changed quickly. Mexicans became competitors for scarce jobs, and the movement of people actually reversed as many chose to return to Mexico.

The issue had several aspects. For the Mexican government, it amounted to an embarrassing confession that the country could not care for all of its people. Another negative feature was the discrimination and abuse that Mexican citizens often experienced in the United States. On the other hand, the migration functioned as a safety valve for Mexico, relieving unemployment and returning needed dollars. During the Second World War, labor shortages again created a hospitable environment for migrants, and the two presidents, Roosevelt and Avila Camacho, struck a formal agreement in 1942 to ensure proper controls, safeguarding Mexican *braceros* (laborers). It provided free transportation, a minimum wage, and a guarantee against unwarranted competition with United States workers, and it remained in effect until 1964 when terminated by joint consent. But the movement of people has remained an issue, taking on large proportions in the 1970s and 1980s.

After the Second World War, United States relations with Mexico became less obtrusive. Sporadic crises no longer gave rise to periodic threats of intervention. Instead, the primary concerns became more routine, centering on such matters as trade, investment, immigration, and energy. Even so, they remained significant. The two countries still acted upon and reacted to one another in important ways.

The anti-Communist impulse in American foreign policy during the Cold War initially directed the United States away from Latin America. When policymakers in Washington became engaged with momentous questions of war and peace in Europe and Asia, they wanted to keep affairs as quiet as possible in the western hemisphere. Accordingly, they undertook a sequence of maneuvers to promote close collaboration with Latin American governments in defense of the status quo. The negotiation of the Rio Pact in 1947 and the creation of the Organization of American States in 1948 provided formal means of military and political cooperation; nevertheless, differences over priorities prevented real intimacy. The United States disregarded Latin American appeals for aid in economic development. Instead, it concentrated resources in Western Europe. No Marshall Plan took shape for Latin America.

In the postwar era, Mexico enjoyed more than thirty years of economic growth and political stability without suffering gross violations of civil rights. Although poverty and the uneven distribution of wealth still had disturbing effects, by the 1970s Mexico had become one of the more industrialized and economically diverse nations in Latin America and the Third World. The country's change of direction came in 1940. During the Avila Camacho presidency and under his successors, Mexican leaders chose to promote industrialization and to obtain some of the necessary capital by admitting foreign investors, this time under strict regulations. Mexican law required that Mexican capital must own the controlling stock in any mixed corporation. Ultimately, Mexican leaders hoped to attain some measure of self-sufficiency in manufactured goods and also the capacity to engage in exports.

Development and diversification made impressive gains in the 1950s and 1960s, and outside money poured in. United States corporations such as Proctor and Gamble, General Motors, and Sears and Roebuck became familiar presences, prompting Mexican nationalists to wonder whether the program of the Revolution had become reversed. Some joked sardonically about the process of becoming Americanized, described after a soft drink as *Cola-Colasado*. The issue of dependency lived on.

A related concern involved trade. Although the volume grew significantly and Mexico and the United States became leading partners, Mexicans worried about too much reliance upon the United States as a market for raw products and as a supplier for finished goods. Marxists and other leftists thought the exchange of low-cost items smacked of neoimperialism.

To counter such claims, Mexican officials tried to keep their distance from the United States on Cold War issues. A consistent champion of nonintervention, Mexico remained aloof from the anti-Communist crusade, fearing the arbitrary exercise of United States power at least as much as the Soviet threat. Mexican leaders showed little enthusiasm in 1954 when the Central Intelligence Agency engineered a *golpe del estado* (coup d'état) to oust a reformist government in Guatemala. The triumph of revolution in Cuba in 1959 also posed a problem. When the United States tried to contain it by means of the Alliance for Progress and also moved directly against Fidel Castro, seeking to overthrow him, the Mexican president, Adolfo López Mateos, upheld absolutely the doctrine of nonintervention. Insisting upon the juridical equality of all states, he refused to condemn the Castro regime, dissented in the vote to expel Cuba from the Organization of American States, and rejected economic sanctions. Only Mexico among the countries of the western hemisphere maintained diplomatic relations and regular air service with Cuba. The war in Vietnam never generated much support, either. At the same time, López Mateos kept clear of the Soviet Union and, indeed, denounced the placing of Russian missiles in Cuba during the crisis in 1962. Independence in foreign policy became a hallmark of Mexican behavior.

Mexico embarked upon a time of troubles late in the 1960s. Dissent created deep divisions. When faced with large-scale student protests just before the 1968 Olympics, the government of Gustavo Díaz Ordaz employed brutal repression. On the night of October 2 at the Plaza de Tres Culturas (Tlatelolco) in Mexico City, several hundred deaths may have taken place in the gunfire, although official statistics put the number at many fewer. Critics, in response, insisted that something terrible had gone wrong. Mexican leaders employed the rhetoric of revolution but behaved like oppressive elites—a very dangerous game, possibly a sign of political schizophrenia, some pundits suggested. Subsequently, President Luis Echeverría, elected in 1970, presided over a demoralized country, filled with self-doubt and buffeted further by the effects of inflation and sporadic terrorism. Disenchanted observers believed that Mexico had come full circle. The present rulers seemed indistinguishable from the *científicos* under Porfirio Díaz. Surely the Mexican Revolution was dead. Critics wondered whether a new round of violence would issue from the failure.

As it turned out, the extremity never took place. Mexicans resiliently retained some faith in the capacities of the government and the Partido Revolucionario Institucional (PRI). For a time in the middle and late 1970s, oil and natural gas discoveries along the east coast spurred a heady optimism. Mexico, the estimates suggested, possessed immense energy reserves, equaled only by Saudi Arabia. President José López Portillo undertook large-scale programs in support of ambitious developmental projects and financed them through international loans, secured by petroleum revenues that were anticipated for the future. The ensuing disaster unexpectedly came close to putting Mexico on its knees early in the 1980s. Oil wealth kicked inflation increasingly higher and produced successive devaluations of the peso. In addition, a downturn in world oil prices destroyed Mexico's capacity to service the debt and introduced a possibility of bankruptcy.

Meanwhile, persistent poverty in the rural areas set large numbers of people in motion. Some headed for Mexico City, making it one of the hugest cities in the world, with more than fifteen million inhabitants. Others went to the United States. The number of "undocumented aliens" without proper papers caused much concern. Estimates ranged from two million up to ten or twelve million. The ensuing debate in the United States took on a degree of desperation and bitterness. Some Americans appreciated the migrants as a source of cheap labor but worried about the inability of the United States to secure its border. A related dimension of that problem entailed drug traffic. Other Americans lamented the abuses suffered by Mexicans at the hands of unscrupulous or prejudiced people and also the tendency to undercut wages.

No easy solutions existed. Mexicans admitted frankly that any attempt to seal off the border would result in a catastrophe. Without the United States functioning as a safety valve, the Mexican government would have difficulty containing rising discontent and might have no choice but to resort to "South Americanization" — that is, the use of unrelenting force to suppress dissent. The United States, for its part, was unsure how to police the border effectively and at the same time maintain traditional safeguards for civil liberties. Meanwhile, Mexico's financial troubles sent tremors of panic through the community of international bankers. If Mexico went broke, along with perhaps Argentina and Brazil, the banks would pay and so would the people of the United States.

The emergent crisis of the 1980s has altered the stakes in important ways. The interconnectedness of issues has taken on a maddening complexity, virtually in defiance of solution. Arguably, neither country by itself has the capacity to act creatively and to bring about settlements. If that is the case, traditional concerns require new definitions in changed circumstances. The tinderbox in Central America makes adaptability all the more imperative. Conceivably, Mexico and the United States have moved from a time when questions of dependency predominated into a new era demanding recognition of interdependency. Whether either country can develop workable courses of action within such a context and remain sensitive to the needs of the other is open to question. Certainly a review of the historic relationship in this century suggests some clues about how not to behave.

BIBLIOGRAPHICAL NOTE

Primary sources are located in the records of the Department of State at the National Archives in Washington, D.C., and the Archivo de la Secretaría de Relaciones Exteriores in Mexico City. Mark T. Gilderhus, *Diplomacy and Revolution, U.S.-Mexican Relations under Wilson and Carranza* (Tucson: University of Arizona Press, 1977) and Robert Freeman Smith, *The United States and Revolutionary Nationalism in Mexico, 1916–1932* (Chicago: University of Chicago Press, 1972) cover the revolutionary period. E. David Cronon, *Josephus Daniels in Mexico* (Madison: University of Wisconsin Press, 1960) examines the 1930s. The contemporary era is considered by Lyle C. Brown and James Wilkie, "Recent United States–Mexican Relations: Problems Old and New" in *Twentieth-Century American Foreign Policy* (Columbus: Ohio State University Press, 1971), edited by John Braeman, Robert H. Bremmer, and David Brody. The recent period is also examined in Tommie Sue Montgomery, ed., *Mexico Today* (Philadelphia: Institute for the Study of Human Issues, 1982), and The American Assembly, Columbia University, eds., *Mexico and the United States* (Englewood Cliffs, N.J.: Prentice-Hall, 1981). The material on immigration is derived from Lawrence A. Cardoso, *Mexican Emigration to the United States, 1897–1931: Socio-Economic Patterns* (Tucson: University of Arizona Press, 1980).

Art. 27. The ownership of lands and waters comprised within the limits of the national territory is vested originally in the Nation, which has had, and has, the right to transmit title thereof to private persons, thereby constituting private property.

Mexican Constitution of 1917

PART II
THE GREAT REBELLION, 1900–1923

During the final decades of the nineteenth century and the first years of the twentieth, Mexico was undergoing a transformation that was integrating it into the world of expanding, global capitalism. This change, sometimes called modernization, westernization, or Europeanization, would eventually increase Mexico's dependency on the United States and intensify the characteristics of underdevelopment. Probably the most important development was the emergence of a Mexican middle class, which sought incorporation into the political process.

Under the dictatorship of Porfirio Díaz (1876– 1911), modernization took several forms. Capitalist production became dominant during the 1890s. Foreign capital, primarily American, British, and German, was invested in extractive industries (mining, petroleum), utilities, and railways. The Mexican state acquired sufficient revenues to develop and maintain a federal army, a rural police force, and an efficient bureaucracy. State authority expanded throughout the nation, undermining the traditional powers of regional oligarchs and municipal councils. The northern frontier, for example, was transformed into a "border" in which communities in Chihuahua and Sonora that had been isolated for years now felt the political influence of Mexico City and the economic influence of the United States.

Modernization was also displacing traditional groups and creating new social classes. In some areas, like Morelos in south central Mexico, railway building and state authority led to the expropriation of free village lands; subsistence farming on communal lands gave way to commercial farming on corporate and *hacendado* lands. In the process, peasant landowners were reduced to peons, sharecroppers, tenant farmers, and day laborers. Many of these individuals were later to join the ranks of the *zapatistas*. Meanwhile, manufacturing centers in the cities and the extractive and processing centers of mining towns housed a new industrial working class that was excluded from the profits of industry and the rewards of political office.

The Pax Porfiriano was being maintained by an aging dictator who was unwilling to rotate offices and incorporate into the bureaucracy a younger, restless, and developing middle class of aspiring *hacendados*, businessmen, bankers, physicians, engineers, lawyers (see Reading 12), and, of course, the ambitious members of the so-called petite bourgeoisie — journalists, schoolteachers, artisans, printers, photographers, small farmers, *rancheros*, and other members of the peasant bourgeoisie. If and when these disparate groups could find a leader, a social volcano would erupt.

Testifying to the events of these years was the lower middle class illustrator and graphics artist, José Guadalupe Posada. Posada (1852—1913) lived and worked during the technological revolution of the late Porfiriato, living long enough to witness the Madero revolt and the first stages of the Great Rebellion.

His prints and etchings provide the historian with a visual record of the modernization of Mexico City (e.g., electric trains, automobiles, street lights, and department stores) and the people of all classes who worked, played, loved, and died there. He depicted the urban, human world of Mexico City, and his images include the rich as well as the poor, bandits and rebels from all levels of society. His prints are an important source for the social historian of the Mexican Revolution. (See Reading 7 and pictorial, "Posada's Mexico.")

Francisco Madero, the man who overthrew Díaz in 1911, was for Posada the man of the hour. Posada interpreted the popular ballads or *corridos* (see Reading 8) in graphic form to illustrate Madero's triumphal entry into Mexico City and his later rule. Posada illustrated other revolutionary themes as well, including strikes by city workers, popular demonstrations, official executions, *zapatista* activities, and the tragic ten days in February 1913 when Victoriano Huerta and Félix Díaz overthrew Madero, supported his assassination, and came to power. (See Reading 9.)

Earlier, again during Posada's later life, one of the first rebels to emerge and confront the dictator was the Oaxacan journalist Ricardo Flores Magón. Forced to flee from Mexico in 1904, he and his followers established a Junta Central of the PLM (Partido Liberal Mexicano) first in St. Louis and later in Los Angeles. As militant revolutionaries who espoused a radical anarchocommunist ideology, the *magonistas* hoped to use the United States as a sanctuary from which arms, finances, and recruits could be sent to launch a revolutionary movement in Mexico. Harassed and hounded by private detectives and United States immigration and justice department officials, the *magonistas* failed to ignite a worker's revolution in Mexico.

At age forty-nine, Flores Magón died in Leavenworth Penitentiary in the fall of 1922. His imprisonment nine separate times by the governments of Mexico and the United States in Mexico City, St. Louis, Los Angeles, Yuma and Florence in Arizona, and at McNeil Island and Fort Leavenworth not only made of him an incarnation of international class warfare, but was also testimony to the fact that the United States was intimately involved in directing Mexico's revolution, not only in Mexico but also in the United States.

The *magonista* revolution was also weakened when many of the less than faithful went over to Madero after 1910. With Madero's death in 1913, a social explosion occurred. In addition to the *zapatista* revolt in the south, three separate rebellions began in the northern states of Sonora, Chihuahua, and Coahuila. Alvaro Obregón, the garbanzo bean king of Sonora, led a middle-class revolt against Huerta. In Chihuahua, the bandit and cattle rustler Francisco Villa attracted a mass of workers, sharecroppers, muleteers, and peddlers to the ranks of his armies. Meanwhile, the *maderista* governor, *hacendado,* and ex-*porfirista* senator from Coahuila, Venustiano Carranza, forged an alliance between revolutionary *hacendados* and middle and lower-class elements.

United at first against Huerta, these men and their followers started to fight each other after the overthrow of Huerta. From late 1914 to January 1915 the armies of Villa and Zapata patrolled the nation. In the spring of 1915 Villa was defeated at Celaya by Obregón, paving the way for Carranza's triumph.

By 1917 the nucleus of a new political and military bureaucracy had formed in Mexico. Middle-class and lower-middle-class elements had risen through the revolutionary armies to positions of power in the new government. With more than two million dead and the uncertain heritage of a four-year civil war, the citizenry and politicians needed peace. The people needed peace in order to survive; the politicians needed peace in order to consolidate their power. The solution was found in a constitutional convention at Querétaro, which resulted in the Constitution of 1917.

The provisions of the Constitution were authored by a new middle class then emerging into the *carrancista* bureaucracy. Through Articles 27 and 123, promises were made to peasants, workers, and businessmen. During Carranza's rule, promises to peasants and workers were broken. Carranza did not hesitate to ignore many of the provisions and selectively interpret others. Primarily, Article 27 guaranteed private property and gave more power to the state (especially the president and the emergency bureaucracy). Carranza could not be deterred from his basic purpose of returning confiscated estates to their former owners. One of those who had his economic power (though not his political authority) restored was the former minister of finance under Díaz, José Ives Limantour.

The military phase of the rebellion came to an end in 1920 when Obregón and the army rebelled against Carranza. Carranza fled Mexico City, was betrayed, and was killed in the mountains outside Veracruz. (See Reading 11.) Obregón had survived them all — Flores Magón, Madero, Villa, Zapata, and Carranza. Now he controlled Mexico.

By 1923 the Great Rebellion was over. The Bucareli agreements of that year, dealing specifically with the petroleum issue, limited the nationalistic goals of Mexicans (as exemplified in the Constitution of 1917) and promoted the interests of American oil companies. It was also that year that the rebel movement in the United States came to an end with the death of Flores Magón and the deportation to Mexico of the remaining *magonistas*. More important, in spite of the violence there was no large-scale expropriation of native or foreign property, and American investments in 1923 were more significant than they had been in 1910. (See Reading 6.) By displacing European interests, American capital assumed a new supremacy in Mexican affairs.

What had happened between 1900 and 1923 was not a social revolution. But historians are still uncertain about how to interpret these events. A populist government had emerged, and the new revolutionary elite was younger, less metropolitan, and more middle class than the government of old. Perhaps this was a Bonapartist-type regime, composed of petit-bourgeois elements who promoted cooperation between the bourgeoisie and the workers. The new state bureaucracy had the necessary authority and power to promote capital development and curtail radical labor movements. Perhaps the fighting had resulted in a bureaucratic political revolution, or maybe it was nothing other than a Great Rebellion.

Many of the participants did not seem to know or care. To quote from the novel by Mariano Azula, *The Under-Dogs:* "Villa? Obregón? Carranza? What's the difference? I love the revolution like a volcano in eruption; I love the volcano, because it's a volcano, the revolution, because it's the revolution." (See Reading 10.) The social volcano was through erupting.

6

THE MEXICAN ECONOMY DURING THE REVOLUTION, 1910–20

John Womack, Jr.

Harvard University historian John Womack, Jr., is a student of Mexican social and labor history and the author of the definitive work, Zapata and the Mexican Revolution. *This essay is an in-depth historiographical analysis of the Mexican economy during the period from 1910 until 1920. Womack rejects traditional accounts by historians and economists who describe this violent decade as nothing more than destruction, disruption, and devastation. He argues that even during the worst violence, aggregate "growth" continued. Womack goes further to state that contemporary Mexican history is largely a function of United States economic history. Because of this the Revolution, instead of being a victory for socialism and the workers, was a defeat of the first massive popular struggle against capitalism in Mexico. In short, the "Revolution" is the history of a foundering bourgeoisie that resorted to a tyrannical state to institute capitalist reforms and curtail the gains of radical labor. Compare this account with that of Ruíz (Reading 12).*

On November 20, 1910, a revolt in the name of the Mexican people began against the Mexican government. Many battles and several governments later, on November 20, 1920, the first official commemoration of the revolt finally proclaimed the triumph of the Mexican Revolution. But commemoration was not an explanation. Despite national agreement on the Revolution's triumph, few agreed on its meaning.

Nearly sixty years later the meaning of the Revolution remains

Reprinted by permission from "The Mexican Economy during the Revolution, 1910– 1920: Historiography and Analysis," *Marxist Perspectives* I (Winter 1978: 80, 83–85, 92, 94, 96–102, 104.

in dispute. Should it rank as one of the first great twentieth-century movements against capitalism, toward socialism? Should it figure as one of the last nineteenth-century campaigns to free capital and labor? For all its violence, should it even count as a revolution, which "brings a new class to power and allows it to remodel society in its own image"? Why not just a civil war? Warlordism? Merely a new political turn? . . .

Examined critically, the historical and economic literature does contain enough to suggest several interesting theses: 1. Whatever the disorder and violence, a Mexican economy functioned from 1910 to 1920. It was predominantly, although not solidly, capitalist, its regions very unevenly developed: the northwest, the northeast, the Federal District, and the Gulf the most; the far south the least. Production of oil and henequen boomed throughout the decade.

2. The circumstances of production during the Revolution varied widely from region to region and year to year. Usually, they were most violent in the north central and the south central districts, especially along the railroads, and in mining, ranching, cotton, and sugar country; not so violent on the west coast and in the far south; still less so along the Gulf and in Yucatán; and least so in Mexico City. Almost everywhere, violence peaked in 1915. Early in the decade many small mines closed for the duration. But the World War so increased foreign demand that the biggest mining companies could meet the higher costs and keep operations going through the most furious fighting.

3. The population, at most, failed to grow during the decade. Its distribution shifted slightly, through migrations to the northwest and Gulf districts and to the cities, above all Mexico City. Emigration to the United States became sizable, mainly out of the north central districts, especially after the United States entered the War in Europe.

4. Death, emigration, conscription, and the retreat into subsistence reduced the total labor supply. But in the large manufacturing centers, the supply and demand increased.

5. In most regions some urban and rural property changed hands, but this redistribution scarcely changed the pattern of concentration, except for a while in a few south central districts. There, preeminently in Morelos, the pattern broadened. In 1917 the new Constitution transferred "original" ownership of the country's

natural resources to the "nation." But private control remained
intact.

6. Changes in land use were most extensive in the north central
districts, where range went back to the lizards and hawks, and farms
grew up in weeks; in the northwest, which turned seriously to
commercial crops like cotton and chickpeas; and in south central
districts, where commercial crops gave way in part to weeds and in
part to corn, beans, and chile for the household. Nationally, food
harvests were lowest in 1915, when they declined to about half their
normal volume. The worst export losses were in sugar and rice.
Herds of cattle, sheep, and goats were depleted.

7. Physical destruction and deterioration of the railroads
became serious after 1913. More costly was use of the railroads by
military and political factions, which encouraged black markets and
extortion. The number of mules and donkeys doubled during the
decade. Trucks and airplanes first came into use.

8. In some places, because of the war, many artisan shops
closed, but many others opened elsewhere. The war caused little
physical damage to manufacturing plants, sometimes cutting off
their distant customers but expanding their immediate markets.
Difficulties in transportation caused severe slumps in most northern and central provincial manufacturing centers by 1913, and in
Mexico City in 1914–15. But the major centers steadily increased
their output from 1916 through the end of the decade, by which time
most had at least regained their 1910 levels. In these centers
mechanical power came increasingly from oil and hydroelectricity.
Because of the Revolution, however, Mexican industrial entrepreneurs lost some of the opportunities that the World War gave for
import substitution, which their counterparts were undertaking in
Argentina, Brazil, and Chile.

9. In some places relations of production changed. In the north
central districts and in Yucatán, peonage waned; in south central
districts, peonage disappeared, and small traditional communes
reappeared. In industry, mainly transportation, mining, printing,
electricity, and textiles, as well as among commercial employees,
unions organized and tried to confederate nationally. Weak everywhere, they were strongest in the Federal District, Hidalgo, Puebla,
and Veracruz. In all sectors both capitalists and workers came under
strong although disjointed political pressures, constitutionally so

after 1917. The government itself administered expropriated *haciendas* in the north and south, major railroads throughout the country, and henequen sales in Yucatán.

10. Despite difficulties in internal transportation, the oil companies not only supplied a growing domestic market, which in 1920 consumed almost twice as much oil as in 1910, but also supplied the intensely demanding foreign markets, which took next to nothing in 1910, 50 percent of a much greater production in 1912, and 95 percent of an enormously increased production in 1920.

11. The collapse of the banking system by 1914 dispersed financial authority in 1915 – 16, compelled improvisations for credit, and allowed the Constitutionalists, who controlled the largest commercial centers, to fight their hardest military campaigns on the cheap.

12. After the promulgation of the new Constitution, concurrent with United States belligerence in the World War, the Mexican economy began a recovery more heavily dependent than ever before on developments in the United States.

In short, costs of production rose everywhere in the country, but for different reasons in different regions, and not so much or for so long in some regions as in others. Generally, in an economy already unevenly developed, the Revolution redistributed productive forces across regions and sectors still more unevenly. Theoretically, this should have encouraged enterprise and negotiation. . . .

The standard interpretation is clear. Logically, it moves through a series of three discrete stages. First, between 1880 and 1910, the economy became externally dependent upon Great Britain and the United States and internally cramped by the *hacienda*, which wasted land, capital, and labor.

Second, between 1910 and 1920 the Revolution destroyed the old economic organization. Although it wrecked much capital and killed many people, it broke the country's international dependence, demolished the *hacienda*, and released domestic capital and labor for more efficient operations. It also emancipated the Mexican soul, freeing Mexican entrepreneurial and cooperative spirits of production. Hence the importance of Revolutionary policy and legislation and above all the 1917 Constitution, for curbing foreigners, prohibiting monopoly, and penalizing proprietors or usufructuaries who did not produce.

Third, there then ensued the constructive stage. Repudiating the earlier abdication to institutionalism, Marxists and neoclassicists resumed their respective lines and language. After 1920, because of the Revolutionary destruction, the country supposedly enjoyed more independent, easier, and more deliberate shifts of productive forces through new means, relations, and structures of production. Mexicans had more fat years than lean and piled up a substantial gain in product, especially in manufactured product, increasingly for their own use. In Marxist jargon, they enlarged the "actual economic surplus" invested in productive facilities. In neoclassical jargon, "economic development" issued in "growth." . . .

On the big difference the Revolution made, the great majority of historians and economists sing in harmony. Over the long run the meaning of the Mexican Revolution lies in its repudiation of foreign checks on the country and its destruction of an internally blocked system, which allowed the subsequent reorganization of land, capital, and labor into a dynamic system. On this interpretation the Revolution amounted to the historic overthrow of an internationally dependent, semifeudal, semicomprador oligarchy, its replacement by an authentic bourgeoisie, and the shift from a neocolonial dictatorship to the rule of a nationalist party that evoked broad popular consent. So the lesson appears, for example, in the influential writings of Arnaldo Córdova and Juan Leal.

The dissent from this view has long lacked coherence and professional respectability. Far from a minority interpretation, it seems to have consisted only of objections, some indirect, some contradictory, some moral, some self-serving. But lately, especially during the last ten years, these protests have pulled more closely together. And unlike the standard argument, they have historical bases. Their implications are highly significant.

The first objection flatly challenges the supposition of changes in Mexico's international role. Instead of waxing independent because of the Revolution, the country's productive processes in fact involved more foreign operations than before. During the Revolution and the decade following, American and British ownership of wealth in Mexico increased, absolutely and relatively. In the 1930s, during the depression, aggregate foreign ownership of assets in Mexico declined absolutely, but American ownership of them increased proportionally.

Fig. 1. **Comparative Growth of Mexican and U.S. Economies, 1900–1965.**

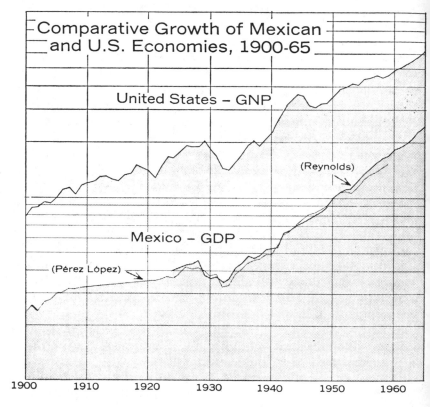

Source: Clark W. Reynolds, *The Mexican Economy* (New Haven: Yale University Press, 1970), Chart 6.1.

Note: The two Mexico series are based on indices in millions of 1950 pesos, the U.S. series on one in billions of 1958 dollars.

Buying and selling abroad led deeper into the same nexus. After the Revolution, while the ratio of Mexico's foreign trade to its domestic product remained about the same as before (about 20 percent of GDP), the pattern of trade fastened the country more tightly to the United States economy. In the 1900s Mexico typically bought 50 percent to 60 percent of its imports from the United States; in the 1920s and 1930s it typically bought 60 percent to 70 percent. Its dependence on the U.S. market for its exports remained about the same in the 1920s as before — 70 percent to 80 percent. In the 1930s U.S. demand slackened, and Mexico sent only 50 to 60 percent of its exports to the United States. But by 1940 the proportion going to "the Colossus of the North" climbed back to more than 80 percent.

In principle, the place to look for basic explanations of these changes is not in Mexico but in the world economy — in the tremendous competition among U.S., British, and German monopoly capitalism to concentrate and centralize capital internationally. For an immediate explanation, at least since the turn of the century, Mexican economic history has been largely and increasingly a function of United States economic history. (See Fig. 1.)

A second objection concerns the standard concept of "growth." As historians in other fields have observed and as economists themselves have insisted, "growth" registers change in money-measured product only. From a historical perspective, it therefore overstates changes in total product during the monetization of archaic and feudal economies and during periods of primitive accumulation. Over the long run the historian should not just count the value of commodities in the capitalist market, but also assess that of goods outside it. These estimates could not be nearly so precise as those now relied upon to calculate GNP, but they would more truly reflect the big changes in a country's real wealth. In Mexico between 1880 and 1940 they would indicate that the big change occurred during the 1890s. It was then, not after the Revolution, that capitalist production became dominant and began the modern expansion of total product.

A third objection concerns the difference the Revolution made to the country's mode of production. If capitalism had already become dominant in Mexico before the Revolution, and if it remained dominant afterwards, eventually to flourish, what in the long run did the Revolution accomplish?

Here [Adolfo] Gilly's thesis is suggestive. Since the *campesinos* and the working class remained strong in 1920, he concludes that they retained the potential under the right leadership to resume the Revolution — openly for socialism. But a more historical conclusion would give greater respect than he does to the class that actually won the 1910–20 round and has kept control to date. After all, the specific contest that the victors have taught the world to call the Mexican Revolution amounted to the defeat of the first massive popular struggle against capitalism in Mexico. The difference the so-called Revolution made to the country's modern history was therefore not a radical transformation but simply a reform, accomplished by violent methods but within already established limits. If a model from European history is necessary, it would not be the French or Russian Revolution, but the Italian Risorgimento or the Spanish Revolution of 1868–74.

Fourth, there are objections to institutionalism, in fact and in theory. In fact, as regards the *hacienda:* 1. Already before the Revolution many estates functioned as capitalist firms. 2. The Revolution did not do away with them, except in a very few districts. 3. Even by 1940 more than three-fifths of the country's farm and ranch land remained in large private holdings (1,000 hectares or more), two-fifths of it in very large estates (10,000 hectares or more). (See Table 1.)

As regards capitalists: 1. Already before the Revolution *sociedades anónimas* (corporations) were numerous in the Mexican economy, and afterwards they proliferated. 2. The changes the new Constitution mandated for many firms—provision of housing, schools, etc. for their workers—reimposed a moribund paternalism. 3. The regional and national business associations formed during the Revolution promoted policies to guard business from competition, not to raise productivity.

As regards morale: It may be that spirits were freer. From the early bets on nationalism to the latest speculation on the Revolutionary Ethos, the claims are manifold that the Revolution made Mexican proprietors more enterprising and Mexican farmers and workers more cooperative than before. But so far no scholarship proves either differences or similarities between pre- and post-Revolutionary psyches. Until it does, claims that "the psychological factor" explains "development" will continue to serve as propaganda for the newcomers.

If changes nevertheless occurred in regional, sectoral, and industrial movements of capital, uses of land, and relations of production during the Revolutionary decade, as well as industrialization and "growth" afterwards, theoretically how did they happen?

In this dissenting view, the explanation should come first from the study of markets. If the modern Mexican economy had already

Table 1. Estimates of Distribution of Farm and Ranch Land in Mexico, 1910–1970 (in hectares).

Year	Land in Ejidos	Solares (0.1-10)	Granjas, and Ranchos (10.1-200)	(200.1-1,000)	Haciendas (1,000.1-10,000)	(10,000.1-more)	Total
1910	2,373,877	1,800,000[a]	38,200,000[b]		27,101,764 18.0%	80,898,236 53.8%	150,373,877
	1.6%	40,000,000 26.6%			108,000,000 71.8%		100%
1923	3,098,571	1,693,069 1.4%	8,988,937 7.6%	12,579,351 10.6%	26,073,186 21.9%	66,573,234 55.9%	119,006,348
	2.6%	23,261,357 19.6%			92,646,420 77.9%		100%
1930	8,344,651	1,421,225 1.1%	7,545,645 5.7%	11,401,400 8.7%	34,137,600 25.9%	68,744,000 52.2%	131,594,521
	6.3%	20,368,270 15.5%			102,881,600 78.2%		100%
1940	28,922,808	1,564,158 1.2%	8,733,214 6.8%	10,167,028 7.9%	24,947,000 19.4%	54,415,000 42.3%	128,749,225
	22.5%	20,464,400 15.9%			79,362,000 61.6%		100%
1950	38,893,899	2,065,600 1.4%	11,314,300 7.8%	12,269,000 8.4%	28,209,500 19.4%	52,764,600 36.3%	145,516,943
	26.7%	25,648,900 17.6%			80,974,100 55.6%		100%
1960	44,497,075	2,006,900 1.2%	14,404,400 8.5%	15,526,400 9.2%	32,276,892 19.1%	60,372,508 35.7%	169,084,208
	26.3%	31,937,700 18.9%			92,649,400 54.8%		100%
1970	69,724,102	1,658,643 1.2%	12,422,949 8.9%	14,222,359 10.2%	22,368,958 16.0%	19,471,179 13.9%	139,868,191
	49.9%	28,303,951 20.2%			41,840,137 29.9%		100%

a. Land in holdings of 0.1 to 100 hectares.
b. Land in holdings of 101 to 1,000 hectares.

Sources: Aguilera Gómez, La reforma agraria en el desarrollo económico de México (Mexico, 1969), Table 13; Manuel Bonilla, Apuntes para el estudio del problema agrario (Hermosillo, 1914), in Silva Herzog, ed., La cuestión, III, 224–248, 254–256, El Colegio de México, Estadísticas sociales del Porfiriato, 1877–1910 (Mexico, 1956), 1–61; Eyler N. Simpson, The Ejido: Mexico's Way Out (Chapel Hill, 1937), Appendix A, Tables 17, 30, and 39; Frank Tannenbaum, The Mexican Agrarian Revolution (Hamdon, Conn., Archon Books, 1968; reprint).

formed before the Revolution, then the basic reason for its productivity afterward was not new habits, new policies, and new laws, but the new material circumstances in which capitalists sought profits and workers sought wages. Schematically, as the violence during the Revolutionary decade deepened already severe regional disparities, the economy increased its rate of accumulation, which it at least maintained during the 1920s and 1930s, building the capacity for enormous expansion later. . . .

Only in these terms do institutions enter the explanation. As the country's productive forces shifted rapidly during the Revolution, they translated socially and politically into the new arrangements framed constitutionally in 1917. These represented not a liberation, but only a new order of capitalist control. And afterwards the new capitalist organization remained the basic condition and code for the elaboration of the new state.

A fifth objection to the prevailing consensus, already announced by advocates of free enterprise in Mexico during the 1920s and 1930s, denies the Revolution credit for post-Revolutionary "development" or "growth." That the Revolution was succeeded by "development" and "growth" does not prove that the Revolution caused them. Rather, the country simply recovered from the Revolution, to resume the cycles that the violence had stopped. . . .

Although such a variety of objections could not readily coalesce into a definite dissenting position, Jean Meyer's recent review offers a probable preview of the coming revisionist argument. In this interpretation, history moves not through a positivist series of stages but dialectically, the contradictions working all the time. The Revolution means the fortification of United States against British imperialism; the many new advantages that foreign and native capitalists gained in the country's most developed regions—so many that even during the worst violence, aggregate "growth" continued; and the despair of working people, urged by the Revolutionaries to demand justice, but crushed by them when they struggled for it themselves.

Thus, the Revolution would represent not a historic replacement of an *ancien régime* by a new republic, but the historic failure of the Mexican bourgeoisie ever to take shape as a ruling class— before, during, or after the uproars from 1910 to 1920. Hence, a bourgeoisie always floundering in conflicts between broadly ambitious and locally entrenched factions, critically losing popular confidence during the Revolution, relying on a regional faction to end the violence, eventually resorting to the state to conduct social and political reform, incapable of evoking popular consent, and constantly though tactfully supporting tyranny.

7

POSADA AND THE POPULAR TRADITIONS

Jas Reuter

Translated by Marigold Best

Jas Reuter, a former dean of the Faculty of Social Sciences and the Humanities at the Universidad de las Américas, Puebla, Mexico, is now on the staff of the Dirección General de Culturas Populares, Mexico City. He is a student of folk music and art.

This essay describes the work of Mexico's foremost graphics artist, José Guadalupe Posada. Posada lived and worked during the late Porfiriato (after 1900) and the early Revolution. He died in 1913. Reuter indicates how Posada the journalist and illustrator, "a common man with uncommon talent," reflected the popular culture and social history of early twentieth-century Mexico when its technological revolution was undoing the traditions of the past. As Reuter notes, Posada's illustrations and lithographs affected and created, as well as reflected, Mexico's folklorist traditions, from the descriptions of a baptism ritual for a newborn peasant baby to the calaveras *or death images of the Day of the Dead celebration.*

The very fact that the work of Posada is known throughout Mexico and in other countries — there were exhibitions in Chile in 1971, in Germany in 1975, and in China and the United States in 1979, to mention only a few — is a sign that this Mexican artist enjoys a certain international popularity, a popularity that is ever increasing. Since the mid-twenties — when Jean Charlot published in Mexico City the first article acclaiming Posada as the "precursor of the Mexican art movement" and thus, together with Orozco, Rivera, and other artists and intellectuals of postrevolutionary Mexico, drew attention to the popular genius of our engraver—there have

Reproduced from *Posada's Mexico,* edited by Ron Tyler (Washington, D.C.: Library of Congress, 1979), pp. 59–61, 63–64, 72–77, 81, 83.

been a growing number of essays and studies, mentions in histories of art, monographs, and collective and individual exhibitions devoted to José Guadalupe Posada. In the intellectual circles of Mexico — still centered in the country's capital — the work of the modest engraver from Aguascalientes is highly esteemed and, in that sense, popular.

This popularity has grown year by year in part thanks to the references that are made to Posada in connection with the Day of the Dead, when newspapers, magazines, and broadsheets publish so many *calaveras*. The importance that Mexican artists accord to Posada can also be inferred from the fact that many of them wish to recognize him as in some way their "artistic father." This claim is sometimes legitimate but very often put forward merely in an attempt to bask in that great creator's reflected glory — which many artists would like to think has descended upon them.

Posada, the Journalist

José Guadalupe Posada gave an account, almost every day, of some noteworthy occurrence in Mexico or in other areas from which news was received. He was, therefore, a graphic reporter, guided by an infallible journalistic "nose" — probably in fraternal collaboration with the no less keen noses of his principal colleagues in the workshop — for news items likely to interest his public. Many modern professionals with university degrees in communication techniques could learn more than one lesson from Posada.

In fact, Posada knew, partly by intuition and partly by experience, what most interests the ordinary man. First of all he is interested in himself, his family, his work, his livelihood, and his loves and amusements; second, in his neighborhood and his city; third, in those government measures that affect him directly (taxes, high prices, or shortages) and the repressions to which he is subjected by the public authorities, together with the gossip and anecdotes concerning the people responsible for those measures and repressions; next, in the uprisings, gory accidents, earthquake, fire, and flood; then, in religion and the beliefs and superstitions connected with it in the mind of the people, scabrous or morbid fantasies, and the alarming world of the supernatural, with its miracles, its monsters and its magic; and finally, in extraordinary happenings in other parts of the world. . . .

The journalistic weapon of Posada is not the word; he does not write articles, reports, news stories, or gossip columns. If anyone has demonstrated the truth of the saying, "one picture is worth a thousand words," it is precisely our artist. His journalism is graphic, it is the direct image, which strikes the eye with an immediate, overwhelming impact. Nevertheless, Posada nearly always linked his pictures to some text, and the content of the text served him as a guide in the execution of his work. In this sense Posada is an illustrator.

We are using two meanings of the term *illustrate* here. On the one hand Posada illustrates in the sense that he enlightens; he teaches his semiliterate readers and brings to their notice a series of facts — and fancies — about both the nearby and the far-off worlds. His lessons are sometimes objective, but at other times they are weighted so as to become graphic comments, reflecting the critical position of their author. Thus, in the series of engravings dealing with bullfighting, he shows us the most characteristic passes made by the matador in a style that is clear, dynamic, and supremely realistic. The engravings of the El Buen Tono cigar factory enlighten us about the conditions of work in that enterprise. The portraits of politicians, actors, singers, and kings enlighten the buyers of the news sheets about how such personages dressed, about their appearance and aspects of their lives that the said buyers rarely had the opportunity to discover in person. The covers of history books illustrated by Posada for schoolchildren and adults shows Spanish and Creole fashions in dress from the sixteenth to the nineteenth century — as well as the dress of Indians and friars, conquistadors and viceroys, lawyers and soldiers. His engravings of events abroad — showing such things as balloon ascents, Russian and Japanese styles of dress, and polar bear hunts — were the only source available to thousands of readers among the populace for forming an idea of these realities. In this sense, part of Posada's work was didactic. His educational technique was what today, in other media, we call audiovisual.

In fact, the second meaning of *illustrate* is linked to the second part of the term *audiovisual*. The *audio* element was the text to which most of Don Lupe's works were attached. Several dozen of his works have such expressive force that words are superfluous; engravings like the *Segunda aparición de la Virgen de Guadalupe, El ahorcado (The Hanged Man)*, and a number of the *calaveras* need no explanation at all. In fact, any text only particularizes and restricts the universal message of the picture. On the other hand, hundreds of Posada's other admittedly excellent engravings—apart from those that are merely ornamental and commercial—take on their full significance thanks to the text that accompanies them. Likewise, hundreds of the texts and verses that describe extraordinary events in journalistic, ironic, or humorous form, in prose, in allusive posters, or in vulgar verses take on *their* full significance thanks to the engravings that illustrate them. . . .

Among the popular types drawn by Posada we may mention the following, stressing that their costumes and settings are always very exact: The shoemaker and the carpenter, wearing their workman's aprons but, as befitted their social class, dressed in white shirts and ties, are portrayed in their workshops, adorned with an image of the Virgin. The restaurant chef appears with his apron and cap, and the cook in a popular inn, with her braids, her full skirt, and her belted blouse. The water-seller, with his thick cotton trousers, barefoot and wearing a straw hat, pulls a cart with a barrel from which he supplies water to those homes that lack it. In Posada's engravings appear the house painter, the musician, and the *peladitos*, urchins who vociferously sell newspapers and play in the streets. The housewife goes to market with her basket on her arm, dressed in a wide skirt and wrapped in her *rebozo*, or shawl, the garment most characteristic of working-class women in Mexico. The peasant who has migrated to the city retains his white cotton clothing, sandals, poncho (or else serape), and big straw hat. The half-breed farmer or the horseman, with his tight trousers elegantly decorated with buttons, his tie, vest, and short jacket, boots and wide felt hat, and the boastful expression of the *muy macho Mexicano* are included among the types depicted. The blacksmith hammers the red-hot iron on his anvil, the boatman travels in his flat-bottomed boat; the market women sell vegetables, fruit, tortillas, and cheeses; and street vendors offer flowers, candies, and toys in baskets carried on their heads or in wooden trays slung around their necks. In Posada's drawings we find the building laborer plastering a wall, the fireman hurling streams of water onto the blaze that is destroying a building, and all those engaged in the daily activities of the people, right down to the police, likewise of the people, but the antagonist of all the others mentioned when they come into conflict with law or morality. And who does not occasionally come into at least some degree of conflict with a law, a morality, and a public order imposed for the benefit of a ruling minority?

Calaveras

All the human and social types mentioned so far, from the most elegant, affected ladies to the *tamal* seller in the Indian market, from generals and bishops to the Indian in his sandals and cotton pants, appear in Posada's famous *calaveras*. What is most popular in our engraver, and has become most popular in his work, is precisely the multitude of uninhibited illustrations that he engraved year after year, with evident pleasure, during the last days of October and first days of November when all in Mexico celebrate in their own very special way what is called All Saints' Day, All Souls' Day, or, most commonly in Mexico, the Day of the Dead.

Death has a unique persona in Mexico, which is not found anywhere else in the world. In the pre-Hispanic cultures, death was just a further step in life itself, a step that offered a security and serenity markedly contrasting with the sufferings and worries that afflict mankind in this world of hardships. Life and death complement each other. With their dualistic and dialectic system of thought, the ancient Mexicans believed that life issued in death just as death issued in life, the two engendering each other in unending cycles.

When a person died, he was buried with clothing, food, and his most personal possessions — in the case of a rich man, with jewels and weapons and sometimes even with his servants. In this way his survivors hoped to ensure to the departed certain comforts on his long journey to the Beyond. Death was not something negative; even the man who was sacrificed to the sun, as a guarantee that it would continue to come out every day, felt himself deified when he became a messenger between the living and the gods.

In the pre-Hispanic world there was no fear of Death, perceived as a country that under the name of Mictlan was imagined as a backwater toward which our troubled and agitated life flowed. In the world of the living, the important thing was to sustain the collective life of men, animals, plants, valleys, and seas; the life of the individual was not important. Hence the constant reference to death as linked in unbroken continuity with life. Hence also the fact that death is represented plastically in so many forms, starting with its Lord, Mictlantecuhtli, and ending with the Lady of the Serpent Skirt, Goddess of the Earth and of Resurrection— and of Death— Coatlicue. The skull and the complete human skeleton appear in an infinite range of shapes and materials. Made of stone or clay, painted on walls or pots, cast in gold or carved on seals or cake molds, thousands and thousands of skulls and skeletons decorate temples and palaces, clothing and personal ornaments, ritual and domestic utensils, and weapons. In ancient Mexico, death goes hand in hand with life.

In the sixteenth century, the European concept of death reached the New Continent. It was a terrible, frightening Death, doubly inflicted by the conquistadors: once as a physical death in the form of slaughter, torture, and alien illnesses that decimated the indigenous population; a second time as death in the abstract but no less threatening form that was depicted as fearful torment by the Christian Catholic clergy, inheritors of the medieval anguish about the end of the world and of the stories about epidemics and plagues that wiped out cities and villages. This second death was hell, to which sinners would be consigned after the Final Judgment. And those missionaries and priests gradually brought in the countless images of European Death: worm-eaten corpses, Death with a sickle cutting short our lives, and Death carrying off lovers and prancing out its universal triumph in a danse macabre.

Over and above all these Deaths is the sacrificial death of Jesus Christ, so akin to the pre-Hispanic sacrifices that immediately after their evangelization the indigenous converts began to carve, sculpt, model, and paint crucified Christs in a tradition that continues up to this day.

The present-day indigenous Mexican, the Indian, after centuries of being exploited and despised in a collective martyrdom, does not fear death. He feels anguish at the thought of dying and sorrow at the disappearance of a loved one, but he still essentially preserves the attitude of his distant ancestors. Apart from the symbiosis with Catholicism in the matter of ritual and Christian names, the great change that the indigenous people have undergone is that they have largely abandoned the religious and cosmological dualism that governed pre-Hispanic thought in order to focus their attention no longer on Death itself but rather on the dead, on the spirits. And so the Mexican—and not only the indigenous Mexican! — celebrates every November 2 the return for one day of his "dear departed," who, as ethereal souls, come back to their burial place and the home where they lived, to keep their loved ones company. The living lovingly and painstakingly prepare the funeral altars with candles, fruit, bread, and toys for a child or bottles of brandy for an adult; they go to the cemeteries to sweep the graves and decorate them with flowers. And at night they take food and drink to the tombs to share with the visiting spirits. One frequently hears a harmonium or a band of musicians playing anything from funeral marches to sensual tropical dances in order to gladden the departed. The air is full of the heavy, oversweet scent of copal, the pre-Hispanic incense. Prayers, tears, and lamentations are saved for the official ceremony celebrated by the priest in church.

It was probably in the eighteenth century that pictures and models of Death as a comic skeleton were first made. Through this genuinely popular genre, the drama, and for many the tragedy, of everyday life was momentarily forgotten in order to concentrate for two or three days upon a friendly, amusing, caustic-tongued and mischievous Death. Puppets and masks, figures made of clay, paper, and cardboard, toys, and candies (from little sugar skulls to the bread of the dead) began to fill Mexico's popular markets with the image of the skull and the shape of the skeleton, and all received the same name — calavera, which means, literally, skull. In our own time, the variety of calaveras (or calacas, as they are often colloquially called) is enormous; every November 2, Mexico adorns herself with Death. In homes, schools, offices, and museums, markets and bakeries, theaters, and even on television one lives with Death, a satirical and humorous Death that has very little in common with the memento mori of the engravings of Holbein and Dürer.

To a large extent, the boom in representations of the human skeleton in the twentieth century is due to José Guadalupe Posada. He took the popular traditions and gave them a material form of such expressive vigor that the macabre surrendered to the dynamic and jovial vitality of his images. More than any other artist known to us, Posada breathed life into Death, a human life reminiscent of the fables of Aesop and La Fontaine, in which men with their characteristic traits, their passions, and their ideas were ironically portrayed in the shape of animals.

Following a tradition established for some decades in the

Mexican press, Vanegas Arroyo published in his gazettes and broadsides humorous verses in which he spoke a few homely truths about his contemporaries, either politicians or other well-known figures or his own neighbors, always referring to them as if they were already dead. The verses thus appeared as ironical epitaphs, secular requiems, or parodies of the usual lapidary inscriptions. And Posada illustrated them. The term *calavera* could be used to describe the verses alone, or the illustration by itself, or the whole sheet. This tradition of composing *calaveras* about public figures or fellow office workers continues up to the present. The irony is mischievous but rarely intended to wound or insult the presumed "departed."

The majority of Posada's depictions of human types of the Mexico of his time are *calaveras* intended to amuse the public. There are even literary *calaveras,* like that of Don Quixote, who, with his lance poised, will not let any of his contemporary *calaveras* escape criticism, or that of Don Juan Tenorio, a classical figure of the Spanish theater, whose story, in the version by José Zorrilla, is staged every year at this same season of early November.

Perhaps the most calaveresque of Posada's *calaveras* are from the scene in which several skeletons are selling skeleton pictures and skeleton candies and the scene in the cemetery where a number of skeletons are lamenting the death of one of their companions.

The Popular Traditions

José Guadalupe Posada was not a folklorist, either as a person or as an artist. As a person, according to the little that is known about him, he was serious, hardworking, responsible, and punctilious. He was ordinary and undistinguished in appearance, with a kindly expression and a calm temperament. As an artist he belongs too much to the lower middle class — neither a pitiable peasant nor a mean-minded bourgeois — to detach himself from the customs and traditions of his people sufficiently to display those customs and traditions as the curious and exotic habits of backward, ignorant human beings. For all his caricatures, his humor, and his critical sarcasm, Posada portrays his people in the setting of their customs, taking these for granted rather than stressing that they are in fact popular traditions. He depicts the people as they are, and that's that.

So much so that most of the time the elements of traditional popular culture are not themselves the theme of the engraving in which they appear; rather they create the atmosphere that brings out the full significance of the theme Posada is presenting. For example, in the illustration for the children's story "The Toyseller" he shows a typical, late nineteenth-century Mexican domestic scene: a fashionably dressed lady and gentleman, country-style furniture—a table, two chairs, a stool— a chest full of dolls and other toys, a sewing-basket, a few ornaments hanging on the walls, and various photographs around a large image of Our Lady of Sorrows, beneath which is fixed a candleholder. These objects serve as the setting for the little girl holding a doll, but at the same time they reflect a whole way of life. To give another example; in the pre-Christmas season, to denounce the constant harassment inflicted on the people by the *caciques*—those minidictators who have done so much harm in the Mexican provinces—Posada used the old tradition of breaking the piñata to deliver his allegorical message. During the nine days before Christmas Eve the whole of Mexico celebrates the *posadas,* gatherings of family and friends to reenact the pilgrimage of Joseph and Mary to Bethlehem and their search for lodging. In the most strongly traditional towns, which are numerous, the whole neighborhood still joins in singing the verses and the pilgrims, with their dozens or hundreds of companions— many dressed up as shepherds and nomads— end up in the parish church to hear a sermon specially intended for the children, who are the principal participants. The high point of the nonreligious activities occurs amid tumultuous excitement, when in a courtyard or in the street the children hang up a huge clay pot decorated with colored paper and filled with fruit and candy. One child after another is blindfolded and tries to break the piñata with a stick. When it breaks, and the oranges, candy sticks, *jícamas* (a tasty kind of potato), and other good things rain down on the children, they all rush to grab as much booty as possible.

Posada sometimes represents the carol-singers' search for lodgings with appropriate seriousness, to illustrate religious booklets of Christmas verses. But in the case of the piñata he uses the tradition simply because it is so widely known and practiced that all his readers will understand the allegory when Mrs. Arbitrariness, aided by Mrs. Authority, wields a stick called "Cacicazgo" (a local dictatorship) to hit the piñata, labeled "People." The satire is more immediately effective than if he had used European-style allegorical figures which, on other occasions, he does not in fact disdain. In his engravings, for instance, we find Justice blindfolded, cherubs fluttering in the clouds, Liberty in a Phrygian cap, and Freedom of Thought with her wings clipped.

The *calavera* itself is a Mexican tradition that Don Lupe uses as a means of expression. For any Mexican, a *calavera* by Posada immediately calls to mind the celebrations of the Day of the Dead. In this connection, it is true that Posada's engravings played a significant role in bringing the *calavera* to its present height of popularity.

The principal popular traditions that appear in Posada's work, apart from costume and the Day of the Dead, revolve around other celebrations and holidays, food and drink, music, games and toys, and, finally, love.

In Mexico one of the distinctive things about celebrating holidays — especially the religious ones, which are in the majority — is the way the whole population takes part, amid the noisy excitement produced by music, dances, traditional foods, a fair, games, and often a market or even a rodeo and cockfights. Devotion is combined with the enjoyment of all kinds of activities that are out of the ordinary. And Posada reflects this when he shows processions, pious multitudes crowded into the courtyards of sanctuaries, apparitions of the Virgin, images of the diversity of saints venerated in Mexico, and men and women kneeling in a church. On the other hand, there is the humor of the *calaveras*, the satire of the caricatures, and the drunken sprees and music that form part of every good holiday. Besides Christmas and the Day of the Dead, there is the New Year — a secular holiday — and Holy Week, in particular what was called until recently the Saturday of Glory (now Holy Saturday), the day on which by tradition the people take revenge for the betrayal of Jesus by Judas Iscariot by burning large painted cardboard effigies of the devil, Death, a policeman, and the most detested politicians, all considered villains and traitors. In Posada's time this "Judas-burning" was frequently banned precisely because of its mockery of high personages. The tradition, very much alive at the beginning of the century, has been dying out during the last twenty years as a result of the changes that

Mexican culture is undergoing, partly because of its internal development and partly from being overrun by the cultural products imposed through the mass media.

The diet of the Mexican people, as is well known, is based on maize, a plant that originated in the Americas. With it all kinds of goods and even drinks are prepared. Among the typical dishes that appear in Posada's engravings are tortillas (cooked on the equally traditional flat clay or iron *comal* after the dough has been prepared on the *metate*, which is of pre-Hispanic origin), tamales, and enchiladas. Posada illustrated a whole recipe book entitled *La Cocina en el Bolsillo* (*Cookery in Your Pocket*).

And if nowadays the most popular cool drink in Mexico is probably beer, the drink that in the old days held first place and still holds first or second in the rural areas is *pulque,* prepared by fermenting the juice of certain species of maguey or agave. There are several engravings in which Posada shows a *pulquería,* where the clients are quaffing the delicious beverage in the traditional *catrinas,* glass jars that have now practically vanished. Together with the *pulque* goes the whole background of women fighting, drunkards, children, stray dogs, and guitar players.

One must also mention Posada's illustrations of the typical Mexican candies, with their endless variety of ingredients, shapes, textures, and flavors, when describing the foods important in his work.

Mexicans have always been a people of great musical sensitivity. The variety of popular musical instruments still played in the country today is enormous: The range includes purely pre-Hispanic instruments, such as various drums and tambourines and flutes; others, like the guitar and the violin, that are purely European; and still others that are local adaptations of European instruments and even one African instrument — brought to perfection in the south of Mexico — the marimba.

Whether it is a question of festivities, of love, or of sadness, there is always a guitar, a harp, or a violin to convert transient human emotions into art. José Guadalupe Posada shows these instruments in dozens of his engravings. His illustrations for songbooks may feature a young man or a girl strumming a guitar. When he engraves a popular dance — whether of the *vivitos* ("dear living") or the *muertitos* ("dear departed") — musicians are playing the dance tune on the harp or the violin, the clarinet, and the guitar.

During Holy Week the rattle of the traditional *matraca* is heard. In the streets the barrel-organ player turns the handle of his aged mechanical instrument, actually made in Germany, whose nostalgic strains still today . . . float through some districts of Mexico City. Even when engraving illustrations for horoscopes, Posada uses two mandolins to represent the sign Gemini.

Posada illustrated in a more subtle vein, but perfectly recognizable for the people of 1900 and even today for devotees of Mexican traditional music, the verses and songs that, although they refer to contemporary events and personalities, are based on old ballads and even on children's singing games. This is the case with the verses of the Fandanguito of Veracruz in the *Semanario destinado exclusivamente a la defensa de la clase obrera* and also in the parody of the children's game Doña Blanca.

This brings us to another traditional field that Posada cultivated with evident affection: children's traditions. He illustrated several of the covers for a series of children's booklets, which included plays, riddles, and stories. He also designed various board games in which dice are used to move a counter along a series of little squares to reach a goal. Among these games, once very popular but now replaced by television, are snakes-and-ladders and smugglers-on-horseback. Many of the miniature drawings identifying the little squares along which the player has to move his counter also represent popular traditions, as do decorations that surround the actual game. Thus we find on these boards depictions of leapfrog, marbles, skipping, bowling a wood hoop with a little stick, or a little girl hugging a doll. And in other engravings we find more dolls; a top, which a little boy spins on the ground by means of a string; a cup-and-ball; a rocking horse, for the smaller children; and even one of the puppet shows, which then, as now, enjoyed great popularity in Mexico. Most of the games depicted are things of the past, at least in the big cities, but adults remember them nostalgically. They belong to a time before a surfeit of mass-produced toys, which encourage passivity instead of stimulating the development of their physical and mental powers, brought on the indolence of so many modern children.

Several games for adults are documented in the work of Posada. Among them are billiards, which attracts many young people on weekends, particularly in the small towns, and pitching pennies, in which the players throw a coin at a line and the one whose coin is the nearest to the line is the winner. These are games still much played in Mexico today.

Speaking of adults, we include here some spectacles that were very popular in Mexico at the beginning of the century: horsemanship and bullfighting, both derived from the activities of the great cattle ranches. In several engravings Posada depicts demonstrations of skill with the lasso and confrontations between bull and matador. Another spectacle, now confined to the towns, is boxing, which reflects one side of life in the poor quarters of many cities: the sublimation of the violent instincts, the actual helplessness of the spectators, and the pugilists' desire literally to fight their way up in the world.

Finally, a spectacle that for centuries has exerted a strong fascination over children and many adults is the circus, with all its aura of exoticism. Posada ranges from the most elementary form of circus — the trainer making his performing bear dance in the streets — to the grand circus with acrobats, clowns, lions, bareback riders, and performing elephants. The strangeness of distant Africa, the agility of the gymnasts, and the frequently risqué jokes of the clowns used to delight the popular audience. At the present time there are still circuses in Mexico, but they are clearly in decline through having been replaced in the popular taste by television, the cinema, and professional soccer.

The reader may be astonished to find the theme of love included among Mexican traditions. It is obviously a universal tradition and could perhaps have been discussed between games and spectacles. The reason for mentioning love here is to be found in Posada himself, since he illustrated many covers for books of love songs and collections of love letters to serve as models for lovers writing to their sweethearts. Posada's illustrations, suitable as always to their theme, reflect the kitsch that has surrounded flirtation and courtship among young people since at least the rococo period. Bashful damsels and dashing, moustachioed youths appear surrounded by cupids, bleeding hearts, fluttering butterflies and doves, fans, and luxuriant creepers and bunches of flowers. There is no lack of languishing glances, proposals by kneeling suitors, and theatrical indignation from future parents-in-law. Posada is here an artist of the belle époque, the fin de siècle.

Alongside these products for the consumption of young people of the lower class, he has a whole series of caricatures on the same themes that allow one to suppose that Posada himself was inclined to consider tasteless the illustrations in those newspapers and cheap magazines specifically destined for "the ladies." Among these half-serious, half-humorous engravings we will mention only one, a very typical one. It is a broadside containing one four-line and four ten-line verses (lyric forms very popular in Mexico) in which the "young ladies of forty" beseech "the miracle-working St. Anthony of Padua" to grant them a husband, no matter if he is an old man, a thief, or even a demon. The engraving shows half a dozen spinsters begging the saint for this miracle. Their attitudes and expressions are as pathetic as the initial quartet accompanying the engraving:

> St. Anthony of miracles
> With bitter tears I beseech you
> Find me a good husband
> For I am getting along in years.

There is one work of Posada on the subject of love that neither contains the affectations we have just mentioned nor caricatures the theme ironically. On the contrary, it reflects with great human understanding and tenderness the affection between two human beings who will not see each other for some time. I am referring to one of Posada's masterpieces, *La despedida del revolucionario* (*The Revolutionary's Farewell*).

What a good psychologist Don Lupe was!

Posada. Calaveras. Dancers. Courtesy Amon Carter Museum, Fort Worth, Texas.

Posada. Calavera. Streetcleaners. Courtesy Amon Carter Museum, Fort Worth, Texas.

Posada. Calavera. Women workers. Courtesy Amon Carter Museum, Fort Worth, Texas.

Posada in his shop. Prints and Photographs Division, Library of Congress, Washington, D.C.

8

MADERO AND THE COMET:
CORRIDO

In June 1910, Francisco I. Madero was sent to prison in San Luis Potosí for opposing the election of Porfirio Díaz. Escaping on October 6, he fled to San Antonio, Texas, where he issued his manifesto "To the American People" and his plan for a new government. This was the beginning of Madero's revolt, a rebellion that led to the overthrow of Díaz by May 1911. These events were seemingly foretold by the omens of 1910, especially Halley's Comet. The corridos, *Mexico's popular folk ballads, retold the story from the* campesino *point of view. The* corrido *"De Madero" can be used by the social historian to get a "people's" view of events. This* corrido *was taken from Vicente T. Mendoza's* El corrido *mexicano; the commentary is by W. Dirk Raat.*

> Cometa, si hubieras sabido
> lo que venías anunciando,
> nunca hubieras salido
> por el cielo relumbrando;
> no tienes la culpa tú,
> mi Dios, que te lo ha mandado.
>
> ¡Ay qué Madero tan hombre,
> bonitas son sus *aiciones!*
> Mandó a los cabecillas
> echar fuera las prisiones.
> ¡Madre mía de Guadalupe,
> llénalo de bendiciones!

"De Madero" was reproduced from Vicente T. Mendoza, comp., *El corrido mexicano* (Mexico: Fondo de Cultura Económica, 1974), p. 25. The translation of the *corrido* was done by W. Dirk Raat, and it and the commentary were taken from *Revoltosos! Mexico's Rebels in the United States, 1903–1923* (College Station: Texas A&M University Press, 1981), pp. 203–204. Reproduced by permission of Texas A&M University Press.

On the evening of May 18, 1910, Halley's Comet brushed the earth with its long, spreading tail. At various points, intermittent flashes were seen "resembling an arch of glowing white surmounted by a crest of crimson." It took less than fifteen seconds for the comet to travel from Veracruz to Mexico City, only sixty-six seconds to cross the North American continent. American tourists traveled to fancy Alpine resorts to view it; "comet picnics" were organized in Berlin and Potsdam. Thousands of immigrant workers in Pennsylvania refused to enter the coal mines, fearing that the earth would be destroyed. Indiana's poor squandered their savings on a Last Judgment party. In Colorado, Mexican and Italian workers at the Leadville and Cripple Creek mines remained underground to avoid possible contact with the tail of the comet.

Near El Paso, hundreds of Mexicans from villages along the border gathered about crucifixes erected on the hills, awaiting the appearance of the comet they feared would destroy the world. For ten days they sought to avert the impending disaster with music, incantations, and prayers. They searched for refuge in caves and canyons in the mountains. When the comet passed without catastrophe, dancing and feasting replaced the religious ceremonies. Yet all knew that this glare, which had destroyed the quiet of night and had made the cattle uneasy, was an announcement. Elders told the young that the coming of the comet meant famine and plague.

The village shamans understood the signs of nature. Had not the eruption of Mt. Colima the year before been correctly seen as a promise that the powerful Old Ones were to come and sweep the wicked away? Even in the city the scribes and historians knew that significant events always accompanied the coming of Halley's Comet. In 44 B.C. Halley's Comet blazed for seven days after the assassination of Julius Caesar—the time it took for the soul of Caesar to be received into heaven. In A.D. 30 the comet signaled the crucifixion of Christ; in 1066 the comet blazed a trail followed by the Norman conquerors of England. For Mexico the meaning of the portent was clear—civil war, death, and a new life were at hand.

Later the *corridos*, Mexico's popular folk ballads, would retell the story. In "De Madero" the villagers sang:

Oh comet, if you had but known
What it was you prophesied,
You never would have come out that way,

Lighting up the sky;
It is not your fault, God knows
That you were ordered to do it.

Oh, what a man this Madero,
How good are his deeds!
He commands all the wrong-headed ones
To free and release their prisoners.
O Lady of Guadalupe
Bestow blessings upon him!

The world of Don Porfirio and Doña Carmelita was coming to an end. The Day of Judgment was at hand, and the Lord had sent an Apostle of Democracy called Madero to act as judge and deliverer.

9

DECENA TRÁGICA

Henry Lane Wilson
and William F. Buckley

An army coup began on the morning of Sunday, February 9, 1913. It had been in the planning stages for months. Fighting erupted and continued for several days throughout the city. General Victoriano Huerta, who had initially refused to join into an alliance with the rebels, subsequently changed his mind. Shortly before midnight on the evening of February 22, the "Tragic Ten Days" came to an end when President Francisco Madero and Vice-President José María Pino Suárez were taken from the national palace and shot. The officer in charge, Francisco Cárdenas, who personally killed Madero, was later promoted by Huerta. In spite of this, Huerta's guilt is believed by recent scholars to be circumstantial at best.

What follows are two previously unpublished and unknown accounts of these events. The first is from Henry Lane Wilson's "History of Mexico, to the death of Obregón." The second is a memo to Wilson from William F. Buckley dated June 29, 1928. Wilson (no relation to Woodrow Wilson) was United States ambassador to Mexico from 1910 to 1913. He later wrote **Diplomatic Episodes in Mexico, Belgium, and Chile** *(1927). Buckley was an entrepreneur interested in Mexican oil affairs. (His son, William F. Buckley, Jr., is the well-known conservative writer and editor.)*

Both men were eyewitnesses to the general events surrounding the fall of Madero, and both were less than disinterested observers. An interesting project would be to compare the views of Wilson with those of the State Department, or his views with those of the German ambassador, Paul von Hintze. Von Hintze, unlike Wilson, favored keeping Madero alive as a counterweight to United States influence in Mexico. The reader should be alert to the international intrigue associated with the events of the Decena Trágica.

Reprinted by permission of Kenneth E. Parrish.

On the night of February 8, 1913, the inhabitants of Mexico City went undisturbed to their slumbers, and away in the castle of Chapultepec Madero rested, if not in tranquillity, at least without apprehension of impending dangers. If there was not a positive feeling of security, there was nevertheless nothing sinister in the air. Outbreaks were occurring from time to time, sometimes formidable, sometimes insignificant, but the government had met them promptly and disposed of them largely without publicity.

But the conspiracy was afoot. Its movements were secret and rapid. In the early hours of the night the Tlalpam cadets, stationed at the suburban town of Tlalpam, marched to the military prison and released General Reyes and General Felix Diaz. The revolt spread to other contingents of the army, and before dawn a small but respectable force stood ready to obey the commands of Generals Diaz, Reyes, and Mondragon, a distinguished Mexican general not in favor with the Madero government. These forces were divided — one detachment under the leadership of Reyes marching on to the government palace, and the other, under General Felix Diaz and General Mondragon attacking the Citadel, the depository of arms and ammunition of the Mexican government. The Citadel was so situated as to command with its guns the entire city. It yielded immediately, probably in compliance with a previous arrangement, and Diaz and Mondragon established themselves there, maintaining a direct line of communication with the environs of Mexico City which was not to be broken at any stage of the engagements which followed.

The attack made by General Reyes and his followers on the national palace was not so successful. The night alarums had spread, and the inmates of Chapultepec Castle, rudely awakened, were faced with a revolutionary movement that had already obtained a substantial foothold in the city. Madero did not lack courage or energy in this crisis, and rapidly betook himself to the national palace, summoning to his side officers of the government and loyal troops.

When, therefore, Reyes appeared before the palace to take possession, he was met by a vigorous defense, and in the attempt to force an entry, was mortally wounded. In those hours, too, other fierce and bloody reprisals took place. General Ruiz, commander of the Rurales, who was present in the palace, being under suspicion, was stabbed to death, and four Tlalpam cadets were summarily dispatched. By morning the situation had taken on a different character. Felix Diaz and Mondragon were in possession of the Citadel, or arsenal, and their position was apparently invulnerable against anything but an attack en masse.

With some misgivings Madero had summoned General Huerta and placed him in command of the government forces. The city immediately reflected the dangerous condition which existed. Banks, newspaper offices, business houses, and private residences closed and barred their doors. The streets were deserted and there was an ominous silence broken at intervals by the firing of engaging forces or the booming of cannon from the Citadel or palace.

The diplomatic corps resident in Mexico City, in so far as they were able, gathered at the American Embassy, which remained the center of refuge and assistance in the bombardment which followed. The attitude of the diplomatic corps during the bombardment has been frequently in question. It is enough for the historian to say that through the efforts of these diplomats they secured an armistice from the contending forces, and that while it was in force, the non-combatant population was permitted to escape to the suburbs and out of danger; that they furnished a temporary refuge to all classes of the foreign population of Mexico City; that they supplied thousands of people with food and drink; that they unofficially conveyed a warning to Madero, which, if he had heeded it, would have saved the lives of the President and hundreds — perhaps thousands — of unfortunate Mexicans.

Fighting in Mexico City, accompanied by a vigorous bombardment, lasted for ten days, during which time some eight thousand soldiers were killed, and an enormous destruction of property made. In the last days of the bombardment, Madero brought up forces under General Angeles from the south, and announced that forces under General Blanquet would arrive soon in his support from the north. General Blanquet did arrive from the north with five thousand men, but he encamped on the outskirts of the city and turned his guns toward the castle of Chapultepec. This was accepted by the public generally as an evidence that Blanquet was acting not for the government but against it, and was intending to cooperate with the forces in the Citadel. A startling confirmation of this opinion was soon given. The guards in the national palace were replaced by soldiers from Blanquet's army, and the President and his Cabinet by this change became prisoners in the national palace.

Events followed rapidly. The only force that remained loyal to

Madero was that of General Angeles, who stood in the suburbs awaiting the command to advance. The government of Madero was finished. The Mexican Senate marched in a body to the palace to advise Madero to resign; the Supreme Court went there on an identic[al] mission, and the diplomatic corps sent an unofficial representative to advise Madero of the dangerous situation and of the necessity of acting promptly to prevent further violence.

The conspirators, with whom undoubtedly was leagued General Huerta, acted swiftly. They seized Gustavo Madero while he was dining in a restaurant near the palace and conveyed him to the Citadel, from whence he was not to emerge alive. A small deputation of soldiers led by Colonels Riverol and Isquierda entered the room where the President and his Cabinet were assembled and formally asked him to resign, and th[u]s prevent further bloodshed. The President's reply to this petition, which he probably regarded as the first signal for his seizure, was to open fire with a revolver on the representatives of the army, killing these two colonels, and two, or perhaps four, private soldiers. The President then escaped from the room, and was about to take the elevator to escape from the palace when he was arrested by General Blanquet and placed in the palace prison.

The revolution against Madero had triumphed, but two rival armies contesting for supremacy still occupied the city. Unless these two contending forces could be brought into sympathy and understanding the bombardment would go on, and chaos would ensue. On this same day Huerta addressed the American Ambassador, as dean of the diplomatic corps, advising him of the overthrow of Madero and his de facto control. The Ambassador replied, asking for the release of the members of the Madero Cabinet and the protection of the life of Madero. Huerta immediately freed all of the Cabinet, and gave positive assurances of protection to Madero. Late in the day the American Ambassador asked General Huerta and General Diaz to come to the American Embassy under the protection of the American flag, the purpose being to induce them to submit themselves to the Mexican Congress and dissolve their forces. The meeting took place at the hour fixed, and resulted in a complete understanding between Diaz and Huerta, the substance of which was that Huerta should remain as provisional president with a Cabinet entirely composed of Diaz adherents, and that Diaz should be free to prosecute his candidacy for the presidency. This arrangement, though ultimately not loyally carried out by Huerta, was temporarily the cause of great rejoicing in Mexico City and throughout the republic.

The formal performance of the first stipulations of the contract was quickly carried out. Lascurain, Madero's Minister of Foreign Affairs, and next in succession to the presidency, was formally declared President by the Mexican Congress. He assumed office and appointed Huerta Minister of Interior (Gobernacion) [sic] and then resigned. Huerta therefore became Provisional President in comformity [sic] with the Mexican Constitution. He immediately named his Cabinet of Diaz adherents, established de facto relations with the resident diplomatic corps, and the government began to function normally and with authority.

There remained, it is true, a very active fly in the ointment. The deposed Madero and Pino Suarez, the vice-president and legitimate heir of the succession, though both had formally resigned, lay in the palace prison, and there was much speculation in regard to them. Huerta, who had some elements of kindness in his character, was not disposed to deal harshly with these two men. He was, however, anxious to be rid of them, and in carrying out promises made to the American Ambassador and the German Minister, he arranged for their exit from the country. A special train was prepared and lighted in the station ready for the reception of Madero and all of his family. Everything was ready at Vera Cruz, and had prudence governed the councils of the Madero family, probably all would have been well.

But the inevitable conspiracy frustrated the plans of Huerta. Telegrams were intercepted between the military commander and certain members of the Madero family or following, which revealed the intentions of the military commander at Orizaba to stop the Madero train and free Madero. The discovery of this plot led to immediate changes in the plans of the Huerta government. Huerta then summoned the American Ambassador and the German Minister, showed them the intercepted telegrams, and announced his intention of either confining Madero in a lunatic asylum, or of trying him before Congress for violation of the Mexican Constitution. To neither of these courses was it possible for a diplomatic officer to object, and evidently no comment was made.

Returning from this visit to the Provisional President, the American Ambassador and the German Minister found Mrs. Madero in the Embassy awaiting them. She had come there to secure the intervention of the Ambassador in the matter of Madero's imprisonment, and carried with her a letter of appeal from the Maderos to President Taft. Though relying confidently on the promises made by Huerta, the American Ambassador and the German Minister returned to the national palace seeking a reaffirmation of Huerta's promise to protect the lives of Madero and [Pino] Suarez, and also to ask—a suggestion of Mrs. Madero—that these prisoners might be moved to a more comfortable place of confinement. Huerta renewed the promise he had made to these gentlemen, and acceded to their request for the transferance [sic] of Madero to other quarters. He did say, however, that there "are those about us who are eager for the lives of these men. They are not safe here."

On the same night a solitary automobile drew up in front of the palace and but a few steps from the palace prison. Madero and [Pino] Suarez [sic] were immediately brought out and placed in the automobile, within which were Major Cardenis [sic] and two private soldiers, carrying instructions to take Madero to the military prison and hand him over to the officials there. Whether there were secret instructions or a conspiracy in the official circle unknown to Huerta are details of history which will perhaps never be known. The automobile containing these state prisoners passed silently through the heart of the city, attracting no attention, but arriving at a point near the military prison—as subsequently reported—fire was opened from an adjoining house. The account which is now generally accepted is that Madero was shot by Major Cardenis [sic] who sat beside him; but whether Cardenis [sic] fired the fatal shot in a moment of panic, or in accord with a previously arranged plan will remain a mystery. Madero and [Pino] Suarez were done to death, but whether their sudden taking off was due to the indiscretion of friends or to the hatred of enemies remained, and probably will remain undetermined.

The American Ambassador immediately asked for a suspension of the reception of the diplomatic corps which was to be given on the day following these events, and asked Mr. de la Barra, the Mexican Minister of Foreign Affairs, to come to the Embassy. Mr. de la Barra came without delay, but seemed to have no information that would clarify the situation. He promised, however, to institute an immediate and independent investigation of the facts and report to the Ambassador, stating at the same time that if the government were guilty he would immediately surrender his portfolio.

Later in the day he returned to the Embassy announcing complete faith in the innocence of the government and General Huerta, and corroborating in full the details which had already reached the public. The Ambassador had known Mr. de la Barra for many years, had served with him in Belgium, and had been in active touch with him while de la Barra was stationed in Washington as Mexican Ambassador, and ad interim President of Mexico. He had, and subsequently retained deep faith in de la Barra, and accepted the version given, not only because of his faith in him, but because the needs for complete pacification of the country were very great.

The taking off of Madero and [Pino] Suarez, if the government were guilty, was a savage and barbarous act. If the death of these men were brought about by members of Huerta's Cabinet, who became cognizant of the proposed transfer of Madero, it may be accounted as simply an act of vengeance. If it was the result of an unwise attack by the friends of Madero to free him, the act was foolish, as those who intervened must have known that the lives of these men would be placed in immediate jeopardy.

In passing it might be well to note as indicative of the curious reactions in Mexican psychology that the violent death of Madero apparently made little if any impression o[n] the Mexican people. Whether this circumstance was because of the universal desire of the people for a firmer type of government, or whether it was born of a satiety of heroic words and unheroic performances, the indifference of the public was marked and curious. Later on, when it was found that the name of Madero was something to conjure with, in the political game, and useful as an appeal to the sympathies of the American people[,] he was enshrined as a political saint, his virtues recited and his misdeeds forgotten.

But now that this tragedy had gone its way, shocking the world and placing an indelible stain on the new government, the work of reducing Mexico to order went on vigorously and successfully[.] Huerta's methods and enterprise were well known, and Mexico recognized her master. Chieftain after chieftain made terms and surrendered to the government, and before many days had elapsed, peace and order were restored throughout the republic.

One man only hesitated to recognize the new government and submit to it—Venustiano Carranza, governor of the state of Coahuila. Carranza had been at odds with the government of Madero over the distribution of certain funds placed in his hands for the treasury of the state of Coahuila, and was apprehensive of being called upon to account for these moneys to the Huerta government. He was disposed to surrender upon the receipt of certain guarantees that he would not be required to make an accounting. He conveyed his views to the Huerta government through the medium of the American consul, who communicated them to the American Embassy at Mexico City. The Ambassador then brought the proposition unofficially to the attention of the Provisional President, who seemed not averse to the arrangement, but with Napoleonic foresight, began an immediate military offensive against Carranza. Thereupon Carranza took alarm, and with a small contingent of troops[,] fled to the state of Sonora, being there hospitably received, although not officially, by those who were afterwards to give him military support. Carranza remained a mere speck on the horizon from this time, and undoubtedly would have eventually paid the penalty of his rebellion or passed into obscurity.

But this speck on the horizon was sufficiently large to excite the imagination of those in power in the great republic in the north. President Wilson and Secretary Bryan evidently believed Carranza represented the toiling and sweating population of Mexico, and by withholding recognition of the defacto government of Huerta, gave an importance to Carranza and those who were supporting him to which they were entitled neither by their formidable numbers nor honesty of purpose. So those who had laid down arms took them up again, and the revolution in the north slowly gained impetus and respectability.

Editor's note. Buckley to Wilson, June 29, 1928, pp. 2–4 of an eleven-page memorandum. Buckley's page numbers refer to Wilson's unpublished manuscript reproduced here.

New York City, June 29, 1928.

Memorandum for Mr. Henry Lane Wilson:

. . .

Page 22. My recollection of the conspiracy of February 9, 1913, is as follows:

General Felix Diaz was in the penitentiary as the result of his Vera Cruz fiasco. General Bernardo Reyes was in the military prison of Santiago as the result of his revolutionary sortie in northern Mexico. General Mandragon [sic] was the man who instigated and planned the revolution. As an ex-army officer he was in touch with disloyal officers in Madero's army. This propaganda was done in behalf of and in the name of Felix Diaz. Reyes was not taken into consideration but at the last moment, because of the request of his son, Rodolfo Reyes, or of other partisans, it was decided to liberate Reyes also.

Arrangements had been made that the commander of the garrison at the National Palace would surrender. The revolting army was delayed so long in reaching the Palace (partly because Felix Diaz took 50 minutes to shave) that Madero found out about the conspiracy and rushed General Lauro del Villar down to take charge of the Palace. Diaz and Mandragon [sic] were not aware of this change and marched up to the Palace door. General Reyes, who had had no part in the conspiracy but wanted to be in the lime light, rushed ahead of them and was killed by the machine gun turned on them at the order of General del Villar.

True to Mexican character, no plan had been made as an alternative to the surrender of the Palace and Felix Diaz and Mandragon [sic] did not know what to do. It was the general belief in Mexico City that at this juncture our old friend Harry Berliner rushed up and advised Felix Diaz to take the "ciudadela."

Page 28. The general impression is that Madero was shot by Cárdenas who sat immediately behind him in the car. My only point here is that it would probably not be necessary to say that "fire was opened on it from one or perhaps two houses," as this might raise an unnecessary controversy.

Page 29. A point might be made in connection with the assassination of Madero that I do not think has been made in any book on this revolutionary period. The assassination of Madero did not shock Mexicans of any class or political affiliation. The enemies of Madero were elated and Madero's friends and partisans all admitted it was good politics, and that it was what they would have done to Huerta if conditions had been reversed. It was only when the Madero partisans found out to their surprise that the American people were shocked and that President Wilson was disposed to take a hand, that they decided to make political capital out of this normal Mexican political expedient.

Page 30. It seems to me that a little more detailed statement might be made of Carranza's offer of loyalty to Huerta for a consideration. . . .

10

I LOVE THE REVOLUTION THE WAY I LOVE AN ERUPTING VOLCANO!

Mariano Azuela

The following short selection comes from Mariano Azuela's novel of the Mexican Revolution, Los de Abajo *(The Underdogs). Azuela (1873–1952) was one of the first Mexican writers to grasp the reality of the Revolution. Like that other great novel of the Revolution,* The Eagle *and the* Serpent *by Martín Luis Guzmán, this work reveals fiction and reality as almost indistinguishable. There is a naturalistic fatalism in Azuela's works. The protagonist, Demetrio Macías, is propelled into the Revolution as a means of defending himself. He ends his life story where it started, ambushed at the scene of his first victory. Earlier, when his wife asks him why he keeps fighting, he answers, tossing a pebble into an* arroyo: *"Look at that stone, how it keeps on going." In this passage Demetrio has just learned of the defeat of Francisco Villa at the battle of Celaya. Note the somewhat fatalistic response of Valderrama to this bit of bad news. The reader should ponder the uses of fiction for history, and the relationship of fiction to history.*

"Why are you hiding?" Demetrio asked the prisoners.

"We're not hiding; we're just following our trail."

"Where?"

"To our country — Nombre de Dios, Durango."

"Is this the road to Durango?"

"Peaceful people can't go by main roads now. You know that, chief."

From Mariano Azuela, *Two Novels of the Mexican Revolution: "The Trials of a Respectable Family" and "The Underdogs,"* translated by Frances Kellam Hendricks and Beatrice Berler, pp. 251–53. Copyright 1963 by Principia Press of Trinity University Press. Reprinted by permission of Trinity University Press.

"You're not really ones who aren't fighting; you're deserters. Where do you come from?" persisted Demetrio watching them sharply.

The prisoners became disturbed; they looked at each other in perplexity without finding a ready reply.

"They're *carrancistas!*" one of the soldiers observed.

The prisoners instantly recovered their fortitude. The terrible enigma posed for them from the first by the unknown troops no longer existed.

"Us *carrancistas!*" replied one of them haughtily. "We'd rather be pigs!"

"It's the truth, we're deserters," said another. "We got cut off from General Villa this side of Celaya, after the skinning they gave us."

"General Villa defeated? Ha! Ha! Ha!"

The soldiers laughed uproariously. Demetrio, however, frowned as though a black cloud had passed before his eyes.

"The son of a — isn't born yet who can defeat General Villa!" proudly exclaimed a coppery faced veteran with a scar from his forehead to his chin.

Without altering his expression, one of the deserters stared fixedly, saying,

"I know who you are. When we took Torreón, you were with General Urbina. In Zacatecas you came with Natera and there you joined the troops from Jalisco. So?"

The effect was abrupt and conclusive. The prisoners were able to give a detailed account of the tremendous defeat of Villa in Celaya.

They listened, silent and stupefied.

Before resuming their march, they built fires to roast some meat. Anastasio Montañés, who looked for firewood among the huisache trees, saw some distance away among the rocks the cropped mane of Valderrama's little horse.

"Come here, you loon, we haven't massacred anybody yet," he began to call out.

Valderrama, that romantic poet, always disappeared for the whole day when there was any talk of shooting. He heard Anastasio's voice and must have been convinced that the prisoners had been set free, for in a few minutes he appeared near Venancio and Demetrio.

"You heard the news?" Venancio said to him very seriously.

"I don't know a thing."

"Very bad! A disaster! Villa defeated in Celaya by Obregón. Carranza's winning everywhere. We're all washed up!"

Valderrama's gesture was as disdainful and as solemn as an emperor's.

"Villa? Obregón? Carranza? X, Y, Z! What difference does it make to me? I love the Revolution the way I love an erupting volcano! The volcano because it is a volcano; the Revolution because it is the Revolution! But the stones left above or below after the cataclysm, what do they matter to me?"

There shone on his forehead the reflection from a white bottle of tequila as bright as the noonday sun. With rejoicing in his heart, he turned his horse around abruptly toward the bearer of such marvelous news.

"I sort of like that loon," said Demetrio smiling, "because he sometimes says things that make you stop and think."

As they resumed their march their uneasiness was translated into a gloomy silence. The other catastrophe was silently but inevitably dawning on them: a defeated Villa was a fallen god. Fallen gods are no longer gods; they are nothing.

Cordoniz expressed the feelings of all of them,

"Well, that's it boys—each spider to its own web."

11

LUCIFER FALLS AGAIN

Carleton Beals

Carleton Beals (1893–1979) was for many years the dean of correspondents in Latin America. He was a colorful, crusading journalist and adventurer. An independent columnist, he wrote more than fifty books, made numerous contributions to several more, and wrote articles for an almost unending list of encyclopedias, magazines, and newspapers in the United States, Latin America, and Europe. He did most of his writing in Mexico, Spain, Italy, and Peru, and in the United States. During his long career he visited forty-two countries and covered many revolutions and guerrilla uprisings, including four Mexican rebellions, a guerrilla war by Augusto Sandino against United States Marines in Nicaragua, the overthrow of Cuban president Gerado Machado, and the rise of Mussolini in Italy. Among his Mexican works are Mexico: An Interpretation; Porfirio Díaz: Dictator of Mexico; Mexican Maze; *and the book from which the following excerpt was taken,* Brimstone and Chili: A Book of Personal Experiences in the Southwest and in Mexico.

This selection gives a firsthand account of Venustiano Carranza, the military men around him, and the circumstances of his fall from power and subsequent death. In typical Bealsian fashion the account includes a digression in which Beals rants against ignorant gringos he has met in Mexico. The reader is cautioned not to confuse his antimilitarism with anti-Mexicanism and his dislike of Yankee excesses for inverted racism. Beals was a passionate man whose candid and outspoken support for the underdog alienated many people. Yet he was one of the most important observers of the Mexican scene, and his views were shared by his intellectual friends in Mexico City, including painter Diego Rivera, photographer Edmund Weston, and folklorist Frances Toor.

Reprinted by permission from Carleton Beals, *Brimstone and Chili: A Book of Personal Experiences in the Southwest and in Mexico* (New York: Alfred A. Knopf, 1927), pp. 324–28, 330–33.

My acquaintanceship was steadily widening. One day in summer one of the members of the board of trustees of the American School suggested that I make application for a position in the high school. I presented my credentials and was appointed at once. In a few months I was raised from teacher to principal.

The work occupied only the mornings, so that by taking afternoon and evening classes I could keep on with the Institute.

To do my writing, to which I had now dedicated myself in good earnest (I had started my book on Mexico), I rose at five or six in the morning and wrote until nearly eight; many times I also spent the fag-end of the evening at the typewriter.

About this time some of the prominent club women of the American colony asked me to give lectures on English literature once a week, and to this end a Shakespeare club was formed, which met in the homes of the various members and lasted as long as I stayed in Mexico.

In addition I was frequently called upon to do special tutoring in mathematics for children expecting to enter universities in the States. So that all in all I was busy sixteen to eighteen hours a day, and enjoying it.

As though I were not sufficiently occupied, another opportunity presented itself at this time. I had made the acquaintance of one of the officers of President Carranza's personal staff, and one day when we were in one of the cafés drinking cocktails, he suggested that I give the staff special lessons in military English. Hardly had I accepted when George Poltiol suddenly decided to go back to the States. He willed the Institute to me for a hundred pesos, the remainder of his original investment. I could find no satisfactory person to tend to things properly during the hours when I was obliged to be absent; so I sold it out, furniture, pupils and goodwill, for about six hundred pesos.

My new work with President Carranza's staff afforded me an opportunity to meet many interesting military types. The classes were held in the offices of the Secretary of War, General Barragán (General Urquizo was acting minister in Barragán's absence), which were located above the north entrance of the Palacio Nacional opposite the street leading down to the national university. My class-room was the reception *salon* between the offices of General Urquizo and General Mariel. About twenty young officers attended—a jolly barrack-room crowd.

Here I met most of the leading military lights of the Carranza régime, Generals Murguía (shot years later in Telehuanes, the Durango city where I had been treated so hospitably), Mariel, Diéguez, Mújica, Sánchez, Aguilar, and many others, most of whom have since been shot in various uprisings.

The most amusing to me, I think, was General Mariel, a big-bodied, black-bearded brute with a feline treacherousness. Some months later he was killed with Carranza in the mountains of Vera Cruz but in the days when I knew him he was the very essence and excrescence of militarism, more important than a puffed toad. Frequently he strode from his office to that of Urquizo, who was himself a nasty little vulgarian, with a heavy yet hurried tread, causing my class to rise precipitately to stand at attention. This happened time after time. Though I always kept on talking or writing on the black-board, this interruption was very annoying to me, and one day I requested him to excuse the class from standing at attention every time he passed through. He drew himself up with the air of a vaudeville comedian — braid and chest and insignia — to inform me with a sneer that I was very ignorant of military discipline. But thereafter he treated me with more punctilious courtesy than before — he was, in short, a typical silly, strutting Uniform, vanity-fed by mob adulation and the hysteria of over-sexed females.

I also met President Carranza several times. He was a white-haired patriarch, without much warmth, chilly and inscrutable behind his flowing whiskers and blue spectacles. He always received me in such wise that his face remained in the shadow, mine in the light. His office had statues of Napoleon and Diaz, giving me a subtle clue to understanding his inflexible obstinacy. He saw the explanation of the failure of Madero, the first leader of the Revolution, in Madero's clemency. Carranza, himself, had determined to rule with an iron hand, at a time when force should have expressed itself in cunning rather than overt power. As a result he merely drove the ablest men, including Alvaro Obregón, from his side and became surrounded with the cheap military clique I have described, men without principles or patriotism, whose one desire was loot and more loot.

Life was vivid, yet some of my contacts were rather insipid, above all many of those in the American colony. The American who comes to Mexico is too frequently a colourless nobody whom race

prejudices have filled with strutting pretensions; or he is a bar-
barian or an adventurer trying to forget his origin. In Mexico the
American who at home would be a mere train conductor learns to
despise the Mexican, becomes a superintendent, a school trustee,
puts on a dress suit, swells at the country club, learns to play golf,
but never quite conceals the lack of education and culture underneath. The best and most companionable are those who do not try
to put on ludicrous trained-monkey airs, but retain their true
vagrant spirit and can be taken for what they are. But by and large
the Americans I have met in Mexico (with some remarkable exceptions) when speaking Spanish will ask you to sit down in the past
subjunctive tense or commit some worse *faux pas;* will call the
Mexicans from whom they should be learning something "yellow-
bellies," and do their travelling in Hotel Regis in Mexico City, and
are quite unfamiliar with the country and its ways, with Spanish-
Mexican history, literature, and traditions. These people, who
believe in race superiority, who are decades behind in politics, fully
convinced that everything in the United States and elsewhere in the
world should be run as it was back in Podunk, Arkansas, twenty
years before — these people will never learn the heart, the spirit,
the soul of the Mexican people.

My polite contacts with the good women of the Shakespeare
Club to whom I gave lectures, the gossip of the teacups, did,
however, have the good effect of driving me to drink. Association
with them was quite too prophylactic, and my fondness for good,
honest, low-brow association would violently reassert itself. Perhaps I am just using the good ladies as an excuse for youthful
exuberance and curiosity; but, at any rate, after my talk to them I
would go down to a cheap, dingy Chinese café on my beloved
Dolores Street to drink coffee and "chew the rag" with a bunch of
American rough-necks and Mexicans till late at night. Perhaps my
giving these ladies talks was the self-same affectation in me for
which I condemned them, but after hearing myself called gush-
ingly: "My dear Doctor, what an excellent talk you gave on *Romeo
and Juliet!*" reaction promptly set in, though I well knew that such
varied and, in some cases, disreputable contacts would jeopardize
my position in the American school. . . .

Just a few weeks before the success of the Obregón revindicat-
ing revolution, after Obregón had escaped from a faked-up treason
charge to Balsas, one by one the officers of Carranza's staff began

disappearing from the class, without any explanation. By the time Obregón's troops were closing in on the capital only three of my pupils remained. The others had all gone out to join the revolution. Later I was to see some of my ex-pupils in the victorious parade of Obregón troops that swept down the Paseo de la Reforma. Of the three pupils who remained in my class, two remained loyal, fleeing with Carranza when he deserted the capital, and remaining by his side until he was assassinated in the wild mountains of Vera Cruz. Later these returned to Mexico City and, through back-door connections, were reinstated in better positions than they had lost. The third became the personal aide of Treviño, one of the rebel officers, who became Minister of Commerce and Labour. Another young fellow was named head of the aviation school, and still another was placed in charge of the Mexico City headquarters of General Pablo González, one of the most important participants in the Obregón turnover.

Those last days before the arrival of the rebel army were hectic. Little authentic news came through the press, but wild rumour was rampant. Dramatic defeats of the Carranza forces sifted through: the annihilation of the crack army of General Diéguez; the fall of Zacatecas, Guanajuato, Guadalajara, Querétaro; tawdry yellow journals appeared with flaring scareheads; the cafés buzzed with talk; long files of cavalry rattled down the avenues to take the field. One morning a lurid poster appeared on the walls of Mexico City, signed by General Murguía, Commandant of the Forces of the Valley of Mexico, that the Government would never falter but would maintain itself to the bitter end.

But up in the Secretaría, where I gave my class, I found everything in wildest confusion. The government was attempting to pack up its effects and skip out to Vera Cruz, still held by General Cándido Aguilar, the loyal son-in-law of the President. Men were tearing in and out of the offices with telegrams, orders, news. Bearded, travel-stained officers, in from the front strode nervously to and fro.

The War offices were being stripped; soldiers and officers were bawling about like so many calves; everything was being hauled out: old bugles and broken drums, hoary with dust; pins, furniture, type-writers, files — a long stream of heaped-up objects was being passed from hand to hand, down to the lower floor and loaded on motor trucks. This saturnalia of mad last-minute packing was going on in every public building. The Government had completely lost its head.

Down in the train-yards fourteen trains were waiting to transport the departing Government and its effects to Vera Cruz. There, too, everything was in the wildest disorder. Great ragged heaps of records, files, furniture, stood along the tracks waiting to be loaded — even the treasury of the nation: great open coffers full of gold coins had been flung down haphazardly, spilling their valuable contents over the runway under the very heels of the frantic train-hands and pacing officials.

The train bearing President Carranza did not leave until the next morning. I hired an auto and dashed out to Guadalupe Hidalgo, the first stop after Mexico City, where I saw Carranza's patriarchal figure on the rear of the presidential car, leaning over the gilded grill-work, grandiloquently flinging coins to scrambling Indians.

A week later he was assassinated in the mountains of Vera Cruz, and I recalled then those two statuettes of Napoleon and Diaz that I had seen in his office, and pictured him galloping over the wild mountains, his white beard blown in the wind, driven by some strange freak of destiny down to an ignominious grave. He died in that traditional elegant fashion that Mexicans love to die in.

There too, in Guadalupe, I saw the last Government train wrecked by a mad engine sent hurtling after it down the tracks by the rebels, a box car of soldiers smashed to smithereens, a wild dash of cavalry up the hills; Red Cross autos whizzing to the capital with the wounded.

Rebel troops streamed into Mexico City. Fifteen minutes after the last Government trains pulled out, horsemen began arriving, straight from the hills, galloping wildly, bent low over their lean, wiry ponies. They circled with thundering hoofs, guns at the hip, into the Plaza Constitucional — Zapatistas, Yaquis, Tarascas, Huachinangos, all hoary with dust, weary from long hours in the saddle — bearded faces streaked with sweat. Long whirling columns of cavalry — handsome devils in wide sombreros and red kerchiefs — rattled down the paved avenues. The revolution was over.

A great mass of people swarmed into the Plaza Constitucional, fifty thousand of them massed in the great central plaza. The bronze bells of the cathedral rang out over the assembled multitude, a ceaseless, wind-tossed tolling that continued all that day and far into the night.

I wedged my way into this enormous throng that had trampled over grass and shrub and fence and was jammed solid into the enormous quadrangle. Bit by bit, shoving my way, hauled about, at times almost swept off my feet, deafened by the roar of bells above me and the cries of the crowd, I managed, somehow, to get close to the balcony of the National Palace. General Treviño stepped out and in a few brief words read the announcement of the deposition of Carranza and the substitution of the new revolutionary government.

No sooner had he finished speaking than the crowd began fighting to leave the plaza. At that moment, about three yards away, I caught sight of a familiar face. A girl in a modish blue hat and spring dress. Evangelina! My companion of the train trip!

I fought to get over to her. But the vast heaving crowd had become as irresistible as an ocean. Arms pinned to my sides, I was swept along, a helpless chip on the powerful human tide. Evangelina was lost to sight! I never saw her again.

Some weeks later I said good-bye to my former landlady who had been so kind to me — Doña Concha, and the two children — dropped in at Avellaneda's for dinner, joked with Guadalupe and Consuelo, flattered Doña Teresa, and after a long, tearful parting from Rosa (to whom I had given the American flat), I bought a steerage ticket to Spain, the land of the Hidalgos.

12

A PROFILE OF REBELS

Ramón Eduardo Ruíz

Ramón Eduardo Ruíz is professor of history at the University of California, San Diego. He is the author of several articles and books on Cuba and Mexico, including Cuba: The Making of a Revolution *and* Labor and the Ambivalent Revolutionaries, 1911–1923. *The following excerpt was taken from his award-winning* The Great Rebellion: Mexico, 1905–1924. *In this account Ruíz describes the rebel bourgeoisie, a group of middle-class leaders who emerged as victors during the years of the great rebellion. Note that the profile does not include skilled and unskilled industrial workers,* campesino *spokesmen, or peasant leaders. As Ruíz notes, "peasant leaders were conspicuously missing from cabinet posts captured by the victors." Instead one finds lawyers, journalists, schoolteachers, engineers, physicians, bankers, entrepreneurs, and* hacendados. *As suggested elsewhere, petit-bourgeois and proletarian elements followed the* magonistas, *the great losers of the great rebellion. As for the peasantry, their voices died with Zapata.*

Don Porfirio, addressing Congress for the last time in 1910, had spoken of an uprising of peasants, humble dirt farmers, in the western mountains of Chihuahua. History proved him only partially correct. Not peasants but small-time entrepreneurs and others eager to improve their station in life, mature heads of families, *rancheros,* the owners of lands often left behind in the care of their sons, swelled the ranks of the Maderistas. They were men "with the good fortune of knowing, although perhaps poorly, how

Reprinted from *The Great Rebellion: Mexico, 1905–1924* by Ramón Eduardo Ruíz, by permission of W. W. Norton & Company, Inc. Copyright © 1980 by W. W. Norton & Company, Inc., pp. 213–24, 226–35, 237–38.

to read and write, able to think for themselves." All the same, their chieftains and political bosses were almost always a notch or two above them in social class and learning. With few exceptions, moreover, the Great Rebellion turned into a young man's crusade. An astonished Vicente Blasco Ibáñez, the Spanish writer, described don Venustiano, then sixty years of age, as the "principal of a school" who surrounded himself with "generals of 26 years of age and cabinet ministers who took on airs of importance at the ages of 29 and 30." When dealing with General Francisco Múgica, a distinguished architect of the Constitution of 1917 and a man he esteemed, Carranza called him "son."

Despite the anarchy of the early years, the thinking of rebel leaders, whether young or not, early or latecomers, began to reflect certain basic tenets, particularly moderate social and economic goals. A pattern of continuity with the past slowly emerged, notwithstanding the rhetoric of revolution. To cite an interpretation popular among the rebel bourgeoisie of the day, the Constitutionalist's crusade, like an oak born of an acorn, had risen as an offshoot of the nineteenth-century Revolution of Ayutla, the door to political power for Benito Juárez and his Liberals. The goal, said one partisan, was to transform into reality the Charter of 1857 and the laws of the Reforma. To the president of the Club Liberal of Acula, a small hamlet in Veracruz, Carranza had picked up the baton dropped by Madero. For disciples of this view of private property, no less so than in the United States and Western Europe, were worshipped, along with the other sacred symbols of capitalism. As one loyal colonel confided to Carranza, the solution for the country's ills was to "boldly protect private enterprise while offering guarantees to commerce and banking." With that sagacious opinion, particularly during the days of Madero, went a fear, at times bordering on panic, of widening the conflict to include the peasantry. To recall the observation of one gentleman from Jalisco to Madero, if the guerrillas operating in the vicinity of Cocula were to receive help from the Indians, it would be difficult to put down the rebellion.

From the start, these views testify that moderates, the timid prophets of reform, discovered a home in the rebel camp. Equally to the point, the opportunistic Luis Cervantes in Mariano Azuela's *Los de Abajo*, a stinging indictment of the corrupted rebellion, had countless counterparts among the rebels. "It is public knowledge,"

Rivas Iruz told Carranza, "that many persons . . . although claiming to be revolutionaries and sympathizers . . . have never fully supported the Great Redemptionist Movement . . . but, instead, exploit it for personal profit." In the opinion of another friend of the First Chief: the men who have taken up arms in Chiapas "do so solely for selfish gain." Or, according to Salvador Alvarado, a successful general from Sonora turned enemy of Carranza, the First Chief had about him a flock of "servile sycophants hoping to line their pockets with money."

Alvarado exaggerated, but he did not entirely distort the truth, for the upheaval set off by Madero unlocked channels for opportunistic men. Not a few equated the new order with the possibility of making a "fast buck." Emiliano P. Navarrete, one of an army of Constitutionalist's generals, in asking his First Chief for a special concession to build a railroad between Matamoros and Tampico, put the matter well: "revolutionaries stuffed with energy and with blueprints for new enterprises" felt "a moral duty to help develop the country." That he would undoubtedly profit from his venture he left unsaid. In a Sonora mining company with 10,000 shares of stock, one alert colonel had cornered all but one share. "If you want to increase the number of your followers," a sympathizer candidly advised Carranza, "you must stop the outrageous chicanery of your underlings," for even their subordinates, he explained, "censured them, men who took for themselves the homes and automobiles of friends and foes alike and, on occasion, even the furniture."

The grab for the almighty peso, so went the national lament, too often coexisted with the willingness to shed old loyalties and convictions. With startling dexterity, as Zapata remarked, erstwhile stalwarts of dignity and honor climbed on and off political bandwagons to emerge eventually with a distinct set of principles or, at least, of allegiances. A mere minority in the higher echelons of the rebel phalanx probably kept their political honor unblemished. More typical were the ideological adventures of General Francisco Coss, a native of Ramos Arizpe, who began his rebel career with Ricardo Flores Magón, switched to Madero, served the Constitutionalists, and ended up siding with the abortive *cuartelazo* of 1923, discarding, in the course of a decade and a half, one set of commitments for others at the opposite extreme.

Of the rebels who climbed the ladder of high public office nearly all were at least of middle class status. Not illogically, in a tug-of-war pitting Mexico City, the seat of power of the Old Regime, against the malcontents, the left-outs, most of the new *politicos* and bureaucrats had come from the small towns of the provinces. Yet of the rebel luminaries, the bosses of ministries and their coterie of subordinates, only a handful had come from rural villages. Peasant leaders were conspicuously missing from the cabinet posts captured by the victors.

Instead, lawyers were the most dominant among the high public officials. Typical of the early dissidents was Emilio Vásquez Gómez, whose brother, Francisco, hunted game with don Porfirio. A liberal reformer, he helped smuggle arms to the Zapatistas while serving briefly in the cabinet of Francisco León de la Barra. However, judged by the convictions of radical agrarian reformers, he was at best a tepid rebel. José María Pino Suárez, Madero's vice-president and also a lawyer, had rallied together malcontents in Yucatán. The son of a wealthy family from Tabasco, Pino Suárez, nonetheless, had worked for Simón Bastar, the owner of rubber and cacao plantations in Tabasco. The cautious Madero placed him on the national ticket because he felt comfortable with his ideas. Pedro Lascuráin, who replaced Manuel Calero as minister of foreign affairs in Madero's cabinet, was a noted jurist, a rich urban landlord, and an active Catholic layman. A few months later, wittingly or not, he delivered Madero into the hands of Victoriano Huerta. Antonio Díaz Soto y Gama, a rebel of a different stripe from Vásquez Gómez and Pino Suárez and offspring of a middle-class family in San Luis Posotí, had fared poorly under Díaz, having to work as a law clerk for an American firm. He catapulted to fame as part of Emiliano Zapata's kitchen cabinet after a short sojourn in the Casa del Obrero Mundial, becoming a congressman, head of the National Agrarian party and oracle for Obregón. In 1911, however, he labeled the old military the "guardians of democracy" and increasingly became disenchanted with reform. Another politician from the bar was Rafael Zubarán Capmany, an astute wheeler-dealer who, during his life, championed Díaz, Bernardo Reyes, Madero, Carranza, the government of the Aguascalientes Convention, Carranza again, Obregón, and then De la Huerta in 1923. Along the way, he held choice appointments as minister of *gobernación,* head of the Department of Industry, Commerce, and Labor, and mayor of the Federal District. Often in the shadows of political intrigue, he helped widen the rift between Pancho Villa and Carranza. A partisan of the De la

Huerta uprising, he later offered to sell its records and papers to Obregón who had earlier dismissed him from the cabinet, accused, along with his brother, Juan, a Campeche congressman, of peddling their influence.

One flamboyant lawyer, José Vasconcelos, appointed minister of education by both Eulalio Gutiérrez, chief of the government of the Convention of Aguascalientes, and Obregón—itself a feat not to belittle, had been a member of the Ateneo de la Juventud, a small circle of young intellectuals who took it upon themselves to bring down the philosophical edifice built by the positivists. By conviction and temperament miles apart from radicals, and a worshipper at the altar of classical beliefs, he looked across the seas for his inspiration, to the ancient history of the Mediterranean world. He thought himself the Ulises Criollo of Mexico, a facsimile of the legendary hero of Greek mythology he knew and loved so well. To educate Mexico, including its dirt farmers, he had printed and distributed the writings of Dante, Homer, Cervantes, Pérez Galdós, Rolland, and Tolstoy, although those masters had not written for illiterate Mexican peasants. A disciple of José Ortega y Gasset, he believed in the superiority of an educated aristocracy. His idol was Faustino Domingo Sarmiento, the headstrong, conservative Argentine thinker and politician of the nineteenth century. He believed Argentina's success was due to Sarmiento's racist attack on the rustic *gaucho*. For Vasconcelos education was a moral crusade, upholding platonic ideas, stressing the three R's, and scorning the thrust of modern pedagogy, finding his inspiration in the ancient Greeks and the Spanish friars of the conquest. Education was primarily a defense of culture, rather than a matter of economics. He envisaged a school to develop Mexico's peculiar brand of culture, primarily along Hispanic lines, Spanish and Latin-European. His values excluded the Indian contribution. Mexico was Hispanic; where not, its civilization must be made so.

Andrés Molina Enríquez, lawyer and polemicist of the middle road, trusted advisor of Luis Cabrera, distinguished scholar and bumbling *politico*, served Reyes, Huerta, the Constitutionalists, and Obregón. His *Grandes Problemas Nacionales*, published with funds provided by Reyes and written with a positivist slant, hardly concealed his racist views of Indian Mexico. With his Plan de Texoco, he was among the first to raise the standard of revolt against Madero. Huerta's chief of the Department of Labor, Molina

Enríquez, survived this mistake to become a key advisor to the committee that drew up Article 27 of the Constitution of 1917. Afterwards, as a member of the National Agrarian Commission, he labored mightily on behalf of small, private property and to halt the spread of the collectivist *ejido.*

No one, however, better exemplifies the cautious lawyer turned politician and reformer than Luis Cabrera, a brilliant thinker, journalist, and confidant to Carranza. Son of the owner of a small bakery in Zacatlán de las Manzanas, Cabrera, after a short stint as a school-teacher, obtained a law degree in 1901. He practiced law first with Rodolfo Reyes, son of the *caudillo* of Nuevo León, and from 1909 to 1912 with the law firm of William A. McLaren and Rafael L. Hernández, the latter being the wealthy and conservative uncle of Madero. He joined Madero because Reyes, whom he supported, refused to take on Díaz. Cabrera, baptized "the voice of the ideological Revolution" by Antonio Manero, fell out with Obregón during the days of the Aguascalientes Convention and lobbied against his presidential designs in 1919. For his part, Obregón distrusted Cabrera, once telling him in a letter that "no one believes what you say because you never say what you think." Carranza, however, relied on Cabrera for advice on financial affairs, naming him minister of the treasury in 1914, a post he filled for two years, and again in April 1919. Cabrera had long thought highly of Carranza, having suggested him for the vice presidency in 1911. . . .

School-teachers, too, supplied a large share of the political nabobs and rebel officials. One Mexican historian has noted the similarity in the role of the insurgent schoolmaster with that of the lower clergy during the wars for independence a century before. Yet, while the list of school-teachers turned rebels was long and impressive, only a handful were actual radicals. The straight and narrow, moderate reform, appealed to most of them.

Teachers entered the fray early. Esteban Baca Calderón, one of their precursors, helped instigate the strike at Cananea in 1906; before that, he had taught school in Tepic. According to rumor, Braulio Hernández, teacher and personal secretary to Abraham González, inspired his cautious boss to rebel in Chihuahua. The son of a wealthy family from Guanajuato, Praxedis Guerrero, the first to unfurl the flag of rebellion in Chihuahua, was also a school-teacher. David G. Berlanga, a rebel dignitary, had been superintendent of public education in San Luis Potosí. Luis G. Monzón, unlike his companions a radical and a delegate to the Constitutionalist Convention at Querétaro, was a native of Sonora and the former director of the Escuela de Varones in Moctezuma. Born in San Luis Potosí in 1872, Monzón had come to Sonora during Ramón Corral's efforts to expand and upgrade public schooling. One of the handful of left-wing ideologues, he had collaborated with Ricardo Flores Magón on *Regeneración*. For siding with Flores Magón, he was exiled from Mexico and jailed in Douglas, Arizona, as a syndicalist agitator. In 1923, he joined the Communist party, and eventually died honest but poor. Manual Chao, governor of Chihuahua in the time of Villa, less radical and more successful than Monzón, had spent his youth in Tuxpan, a port of Veracruz. A graduate of the teachers college in Japala, Chao answered Madero's call as a teacher in Chihuahua, served Villa and Carranza, and lost his life for supporting De la Huerta in 1923. Chao, whose thinking ran with the mainstream of rebel thought, had taken the field against Huerta to defend "democracy" and "the rights of man." Born and educated in Saltillo, capital of Coahuila, Gertrudis G. Sánchez, a teacher in Agua Nueva, became a commandant of *rurales* in return for his support of Madero. Sent to Guerrero, he initially sympathized with Zapata. But when Madero faltered, he fell in step with Huerta, and then with the Constitutionalists because, as he said, Carranza "upheld his principles." He stayed out of the quarrel between Carranza and Villa; when he regained his loyalty to the Constitutionalists, the Villistas killed him. Meanwhile, during the course of his vacillations, he had abandoned Zapata. In like manner, Antonio I. Villarreal, another schoolmaster from the north, became a stalwart of the Constitutionalists after finding the climate of the Partido Liberal Mexicano, an allegiance of his early political days, overly invigorating. Once a backer of land reform, he ultimately shed this conviction, rejecting even Obregón's cautious stance.

Of the schoolmasters of moderate bent, Plutarco Elías Calles undoubtedly stood at the head of his class. Unlike most of his companions, however, Calles had forsaken the schoolroom even before don Porfirio went into exile. A man of ups and downs during his early life, Calles was the illegitimate son of Plutarco Elías Lucero, an influential *hacendado* in Sonora, and doña Jesús Campuzano. His step-father, from whom he took his last name, was Juan B. Calles, while his half brother, Arturo M. Elías, as a diplomat served Díaz and Huerta and later the Constitutionalists. Calles launched his teaching career in the Colegio de Sonora, one of the many schools built by Corral, and then moved to Guaymas as its school superintendent. When he lost his job in Guaymas, because of his heavy drinking, he moved to Fronteras where he unsuccessfully tried farming. Fortunately for him, at the urging of Governor Rafael Izábal, the city council of Fronteras appointed him its secretary, while his natural father made him the *mayordomo* of one of his *haciendas*. To add to his income, Calles also managed the local flour mill. By 1909, given his multiple activities, he was earning 300 pesos a month, a goodly sum for that time. Yet again, circumstances, probably of his own making, compelled Calles to leave Fronteras for a job as manager of the Hotel California in Guaymas.

Calles' political life dated from 1911, when he ran unsuccessfully for Congress. Like Obregón, with whom he was closely linked, Calles did not support Madero, preferring to watch events from the sidelines. But, he and José María Maytorena, appointed governor of Sonora by Madero, shared mutual friends, who prevailed upon Maytorena to appoint Calles chief of the police of Agua Prieta and Cananea. Maytorena wanted someone he could count on to curb the activities of disciples of the Flores Magón, for whom he had no sympathy. True to his orders, Calles kept Agua Prieta from falling into the hands of the Magonistas. With the death of Madero, Calles pledged his allegiance to the Constitutionalists, siding with Carranza in his quarrel with Villa and Maytorena. Between 1915 and 1918, he was Carranza's minister of industry, commerce, and labor, governor of Sonora, and its military boss. In 1919, he abandoned Carranza for Obregón, served briefly as minister of war under De la Huerta, later as Obregón's minister of *gobernación,* and then as president of Mexico.

Until 1927, the year of his conversion to conservative principles (some say with the encouragement of Dwight Morrow, the Yankee ambassador), Calles had occasionally toyed with unorthodox doctrines. To his enemies, he symbolized the radical fringe of the Sonora dynasty. W. A. Julian, the American consul in Nogales, described with horror Calles' ideas during his term as governor. Calles, he said, had started a "back to the farm" movement, while harboring "hatred" for the Cananea Consolidated Copper Company and the Cananea Cattle Company. Still, whatever the validity of this opinion, Calles had another side. As military boss of Sonora, alleged Villarreal, Calles had not only become the scourge of urban and rural workers but had two precursors of Mexican socialism, Lázaro Gutiérrez de Lara and Manuel H. Hughes, shot. He ruled with a brutal hand, as one Mexican physician who clashed with Calles, then military chief of Nogales, testified. Only the timely intervention of Obregón had saved the doctor from death by a firing squad for having, against the wishes of Calles, gone to the United States in search of medical help for a stomach ailment.

The former schoolmaster quickly left behind the austerity of the classroom. He built not only a "political clan," but a "financial dynasty reminiscent of the *cientificos*." The "radical" who had sent shivers of fear down the spine of the American consul in Nogales became the proud owner of the Hacienda Santa Barbara on the outskirts of Mexico City—lands originally designated for sub-division into small farms. By 1921 he could speculate, at a loss of 50,000 pesos, on the purchase of El Tramado, a lead and silver mine. He owned the controlling stocks of the Compañía Mercantil y Agrícola de Sonora, and shared the others with members of the Elías family. In 1925, Rodolfo, one of his sons, on the advice of Obregón, purchased 390 hectares of land in the Río Yaqui Valley by writing a check for 50,000 pesos on his father's account. In the meantime, another son, Plutarco Elías, Jr., had acquired the Hacienda Soledad de la Mota in General Terán, Nuevo León, where he cultivated cotton, alfalfa, corn, and citrus fruits. . . .

Engineers furnished an additional contingent of the public officials and planners. Like the men they obeyed, they wanted reform and not revolution, and easily mastered the art of adapta-bility, the need to adjust to political realities. Adalberto Tejeda, for one, the son of a distinguished family from Veracruz, chief of staff of General Cándido Aguilar, Carranza's son-in-law, and Constitu-tionalist senator from 1916 to 1920, became governor of his native state under Obregón. To his credit, he worked hard for reform. Pastor Rouaix, an engineer from Durango, helped write Articles 27 and 123 of the national charter. Wealthy and successful, he had been governor of Durango, which under his leadership was the first state to adopt a land reform program. While loyal to Carranza and no kin of radicals, Rouaix nevertheless boldly broke with his chief's timid recommendations at Querétaro in order to sponsor meaningful labor and agrarian measures. At the time, Rouaix was Carranza's minister of agriculture and *fomento*. Yet, for all his contributions,

Rouaix, a believer in private property, merely hoped to update Mexican capitalism and to add a measure of social justice. . . .

Barring scattered exceptions, neither did the physicians who jumped into the political fray fit the picture of the social revolutionary. From middle-class background, and not uncommonly from wealthy families, the physician who heeded the siren call of politics cherished moderation and distrusted unorthodox schemes. Occasionally, one of them, Jenaro Amezcua, for instance, a physician with the Zapatistas, battled vigorously for social change. Still, Amezcua never sided with the die-hards in Zapata's camp, advocating from the start ties with the Constitutionalists. He ended his political career as the agent of Obregón's Ministry of Agriculture in Morelos, scarcely a place to shape national policy.

More typical was Francisco Vásquez Gómez, brother of Emilio and a physician who entered politics by linking his fate to Bernardo Reyes. A man who went hunting with don Porfirio, Vásquez Gómez, while to the left of Madero, bid farewell to his orthodox views when he lost his political prestige. When Reyes left his admirers high and dry, Vásquez Gómez, like others in the identical plight, turned to Madero. Although he belatedly tried, with the help of his brother to keep the rebel militias alive, Vásquez Gómez never felt at home with the radicals. Yet, to his credit, after Madero cut him off, he ultimately accepted the necessity for some kind of land reform. José Manuel Puig Casauranc, another physician and officeholder in the 1920s, rode to fame on the shoulders of Calles. Before that, he had cared for the sick of El Aguila, a foreign oil company. According to Jorge Prieto Laurens, Calles had once judged Puig a "reactionary" and a *burgués*. But Puig had the good sense to side with Calles in his battle with De la Huerta, and as a reward, became minister of education where, happily for public education, a coterie of dedicated pedagogues did his work for him. Puig died a millionaire with a palatial home in the Lomas de Chapultepec in Mexico City. . . .

Middle-class journalists were also among the *politicos* of the coming order. A muckraking newspaperman, Silvestre Terrazas, publisher of *El Correo de Chihuahua* and a stubborn critic of the local bosses, supported Madero and served briefly as governor of Chihuahua. By choosing Villa over Carranza, Terrazas cut short his political career. Yet despite his angry denunciations of the ruling clan in Chihuahua, he hardly fitted the picture of the wild-eyed radical; instead, he displayed a sharp eye for profitable invest-ments, having acquired a small fortune of 200,000 pesos by 1912. Besides his newspaper, he owned real estate in the city of Chihuahua and rural property. With the approval of Villa, who also was savvy in business matters, Terrazas, in 1915, had signed an agreement with Generals Manuel S. Avila, the military commander of Chihuahua, and Fidel Avila, giving him one-fourth of the profits from two coal mines on public lands. At the time, Terrazas was the *secretario de gobierno* of Chihuahua. . . .

Even bankers scaled the heights of exalted public offices. One of them, Adolfo de la Huerta, son of "one of the most beloved and most powerful merchants of Guaymas," and a graduate of the Preparatoria in Mexico City, had majored in the unlikely combina-tion of accounting and voice. When not performing on the stage, he kept records for the Banco de México. From that job he went on to be manager of the Negociación Industrial, and by 1909 ran one of the largest companies in Guaymas, the tannery-*hacienda* of San Germán. In the waning of Díaz' regime, De la Huerta flirted briefly with the Partido Liberal Mexicano, but its intoxicating idealism proved too strong for don Adolfo who, while a reformer of sorts, stopped short of embracing militants. Occasionally a friend of labor, kind and generous, De la Huerta, perhaps one of the most liberal in the Sonora dynasty, also advocated streamlining Mexican capital-ism, not its elimination. When governor of Sonora, he sanctioned the small, private farm over the *ejido*. To the delight of the American consul in Nogales, he displayed a "conservatism that has proven a surprise to most persons"; an American mining mogul, according to the consul, after a conversation with De la Huerta, had returned "agreeably surprised by the governor's reasonable attitude." He was a diplomat for Carranza in Europe and Obregón's minister of the treasury. Had Obregón picked him as his successor, the two would have lived happily ever after. When he marched off in a huff over the political rebuff, quixotically along with a large body of workers, he also drew the applause of the rich, greedy generals and die-hards.

Abraham González, banker, cattle buyer, and governor of Chihuahua for Madero, like De la Huerta, toyed momentarily with the Flores Magón but quickly discovered that he had no heart for their socialist doctrines. Well meaning, he envisaged reform within a political framework, giving his attention to municipal autonomy and state's rights, both, he believed, trampled by the old oligarchy in Mexico City. As governor of Chihuahua, and as a cabinet minister for Madero, he never swore to destroy the huge *latifundia*. Had he outlived Madero, in all likelihood he would have loyally served Carranza as well as Obregón. . . .

"Unquestionably, men of business and property sympathize with your administration," a merchant told Madero. We want to help you, he added, "not just with our hearts but with guns in our hands." Shopkeepers and merchants, almost always from towns in the provinces, from the start participated in the rebellion; eventually, large numbers of them filled government jobs, and some in key positions.

The list of salesmen, clerks, and merchants on the make who swore allegiance to the Constitutionalists is particularly long. General Celedonio de Villarreal, for example, a native of Nuevo León and the son of wealthy parents, had run a produce and dairy business in Monterrey. Another Constitutionalist general, Ildefonso V. Vásquez, had been a student in a commercial college in Fort Worth, Texas. Captain Ernesto Martínez had sold Singer sewing machines in the coal towns of Coahuila. Former store clerks, Crispín Treviño and David R. Neave became respectively a colonel and a general for Obregón. Everardo G. Arenas, a traveling salesman, distributed Maderista propaganda, including *La Sucesion Presidencial*, in the state of Puebla. In 1909, he founded in the city of Puebla, where he made his home, the Club Central Anti-Reeleccionista and worked closely with Aquiles Serdán, the young newspaperman who fired the opening shot of the Madero rebellion. Made a general by Madero, Arenas helped organize Puebla for him, and subsequently became its attorney general, a political bellwether, and an inspector for the army. With Madero's death, he went over to the Constitutionalists. Ramón F. Iturbe, governor of Sinaloa and a man who knew how to benefit monetarily from the influence of public office, owned a small grocery in Alcoyonque. Another storekeeper, Eulalio Gutiérrez, went from mayor of Concepción de Oro, his home in Zacatecas, to general and eventually became president of Mexico. Gutiérrez, who surmounted the misfortunes of his aborted rule, acquired a mine in San Pedro, where he paid his miners poorly, and a *tienda de raya* that sold goods at inflated prices. . . .

Of somewhat different fabric were two other former entrepreneurs. One was Pascual Orozco, the son of a shopkeeper in San Isidro, a village in Chihuahua, who hauled goods between the mining camps on mule-drawn wagons, and with two companions, ran a lumber and feed store. Until quite late in the movement, Orozco paid scant heed to politics. But, when a business competitor received special privileges from the Terrazas clan during the aftermath of the crises of 1907, Orozco joined the foes of re-election and took to the hills with Madero. Denied a post he coveted, the governorship of Chihuahua, Orozco rebelled against Madero, advocating in the Plan de la Empacadora, a concoction of liberal reforms, including land distribution, and conservative panaceas. However, behind his revolt stood the Terrazas and the old oligarchy in Chihuahua. Defeated, he ended up in Huerta's camp. Salvador Alvarado, once a leading Constitutionalist and afterwards one of its critics, had owned a profitable drugstore in Potam, Sonora. Born in Sinaloa, he had come north with his parents, proprietors of a small business. A rival of Obregón, he became military boss of the southeast and eventually governor of Yucatán, where he ran a well-oiled political machine. Sympathetic to labor, he helped found the Socialist party of Yucatán. Yet, despite his scores of worthwhile social measures and his socialist rhetoric, his most acclaimed accomplishment was a committee to regulate the price and sale of henequen to foreign buyers. The henequen planters, nonetheless, outlived his term in office. Not so the priests, most of whom he drove out of Yucatán. Always unhappy with Obregón, he joined De la Huerta's coup in 1923 and paid with his life for his treason.

Not every petty job holder or entrepreneur, however, proved timid or cautious in his politics or ideology of reform. Two, in particular, left their imprint on the history of revolution. One was Lucio Blanco, who came from Nadadores, the town in Coahuila that gave Pablo González his start in politics. The first rebel to subdivide a *hacienda*, Blanco was the offspring of a prominent family and had gone to school in Saltillo and Texas. One of his ancestors was Miguel Blanco, minister of war for Juárez. Blanco's godfather, Atilano Barrera, a backer of Madero, presided over the state legislature. Until he took up arms, Blanco had managed his father's properties. Unfortunately, Carranza punished Blanco for daring to subdivide a *hacienda*, and sent him to serve under Obregón in Sonora. A partisan of the government of the Aguascalientes

Convention, and one of the few northerners to want to patch up the rift with Zapata, Blanco died at the hands of former companions in arms. As the lives of Blanco and Zapata illustrate, social revolutionaries often paid dearly for their convictions. A similar fate befell Felipe Carrillo Puerto, an engineering student and later a train conductor in Yucatán. A supporter of Zapata and a Socialist, Carrillo Puerto became governor of Yucatán in 1922, and spent his short span in office attempting to help the peasants, eradicating illiteracy and combating the clergy. Of impeccable reform credentials, Carrillo Puerto committed the mistake of organizing the peasants against the henequen lords, and lost his life for his efforts. During the De la Huerta uprising, his enemies captured and shot Carrillo Puerto and his brothers. . . .

Hacendados, too, strangely enough, attended the banquet of the victorious rebels, either as sympathizers or as "revolutionaries" who had, in the course of their adventures, made themselves masters of *haciendas.* No one knows how many successful rebels acquired estates, but no one disputes that many did. Not surprisingly, a handful of *hacendados,* whether of Porfirista vintage or of the newly inaugurated, championed reform, but rarely land redistribution. Antenor Sala, *hacendado* and proponent of land reform, walked a lonely path. Madero and Carranza, vintage *hacendados,* died, so to speak, with their boots on; neither lost his lands during his stay in office. Nor did Obregón, a "revolutionary" *hacendado.*

From the start, Madero, Carranza, and Obregón counted *hacendados* among their friends and backers. Carlos Morton, an *hacendado* in Hidalgo, even borrowed money from the Banco de Monterrey to help equip his brother-in-law who had taken up arms on behalf of Madero. Genaro Dávila, a landlord in Coahuila, lent the rebels nearly 10,000 pesos and gave lands for Carranza to distribute among the landless of Zaragoza to insure, as he said, the "pacification" of the country. Manuel Cuesta Gallardo, an *hacendado* and former Díaz *político,* from his haven in New York was telling Carranza in 1915 that he was a "devoted follower of the Constitutionalists, whose victory he awaited so that Mexico might savor an era of peace, prosperity, and progress." Unquestionably, some of the enthusiasm of *hacendados* for Carranza, particularly during the period of factional fighting, reflected a fear of the more radical rebels. Manuel Ruíz Lavín, an *hacendado* in the Laguna, to cite one instance, pledged his allegiance to Carranza while offering to dispatch his own soldiers to combat the "Villista yoke." At that time, Villa had taken to rewarding his *compadres* with lands of *hacendados* he disliked. Roberto Castro, master of the Hacienda San Miguel in Puebla, probably turned Constitutionalist in order to protect his properties.

Still, landlords did go to battle to challenge the rule of Díaz and his puppets. Such a landlord was José María Maytorena, who governed Sonora for Madero and was the son of an *hacendado*. His father, the offspring of a distinguished family, had long waged political warfare against Lorenzo Torres and Corral, the state's *caciques*. The Maytorenas were allies of the Pesqueira family, another landowning clan that broke with Díaz. A moderate politically, Maytorena had studied at Santa Clara College in California and had backed Reyes. He owned eight *haciendas*, mines of silver and copper, and urban real estate in Guaymas. He employed large numbers of Yaquis on his *haciendas*, and at times, before casting his lot with Reyes, had received special permission from Governor Alberto Cubillas, a Corral henchman, to recruit additional Yaquis to harvest his garbanzos. Yet, Maytorena became one of Madero's earliest disciples in Sonora, as he claimed, "to defend its sovereignty." When Obregón asked him to break with Huerta, Maytorena replied that he could not: "It is useless to ask me to do it," he replied. I have family ties with the elements you label *científicos*, and anyway, my stomach is not up to eating raw meat in the mountains." Huerta's soldiers, he abjectly confessed, "would destroy my properties and burn my *haciendas*, and frankly, I am simply not cut out for it." . . .

Additionally, students, similar to others in the *carnaval*, as José Clemente Orozco called events from 1910 to 1920, had their quota of politicians, public officials, and generals. Aarón Sáenz, intimate of Calles, abandoned law school on behalf of rebellion and ended up a cabinet minister, presidential hopeful, and a millionaire. Emilio Portes Gil, president of Mexico between 1928 and 1930 and also a millionaire, rose from the ranks of the law students, along the way serving as a clerk in the law courts of the Huerta regime, and if Prieto Laurens' version is authentic, as an "enthusiastic Huertista." He wrote articles in defense of Huerta, but finally made his peace with Carranza and Obregón, becoming senator and political boss of Tamaulipas. To his credit, as president of the Republic, he pushed ahead with land reform. General and politician Juan Andréu

Almazán, with an "impressive talent for hoax and skulduggery," had been a medical student in Puebla and then, as he proclaimed, a loyal adherent of Madero. However, with the triumph of Huerta, he changed colors, parroting Huerta's condemnation of Zapatismo as "the banner of bandits who kill, rob, and pillage." It was a "flag to be destroyed completely . . . because it was a shameful blot . . . on the motherland." Yet Almazán, an opportunist hostile to social reform, held high public office, won national honors and died a rich man.

"No soy un guajolote para morir en las vísperas."
"I am not a turkey to die at dusk" [for a real man dies at noon].

Primo Tapia, agitator, organizer, *magonista*, revolutionist, and Tarascan Indian, to his mother (1917)

PART III
MEXICO UNDER CALLES AND CÁRDENAS, 1923–40

In 1923 President Obregón designated Plutarco Elías Calles as his successor and, with arms and munitions from arsenals in the United States, suppressed the Adolfo de la Huerta revolt. There was a price for this assistance, for Obregón assured his American backers that the radical provisions of Article 27 of the Constitution would not be enforced retroactively.

Calles began his political campaign with a pilgrimage to the tomb of Zapata. Agrarian revolt and peasant uprisings continued throughout the 1920s and 1930s, first in Michoacán (see Reading 14), then in the *zapatista* province of Morelos, and finally in Zacatecas, Guanajuato, and Veracruz. To deal with the many voices of mass anger, Calles supported the formation of a National Agrarian Party and allowed the restoration of some *ejidos* (semi-communal lands) and the creation of *ejido* banks. Yet the struggle between subsistence and commercial agriculture would continue, in part because the state and Calles were anxious to modernize agriculture and because the state and Calles looked at the *ejido* as a detour on the road to capitalism in the countryside.

One of the peasant struggles of the 1920s involved the larger traditional issue of Church-state relations. Religious leaders and their lay followers were concerned about the anticlerical provisions of the Constitution of 1917. What began as a Church-state struggle in 1925 soon led to the Cristero religious war against the Mexican Revolution, 1916–29. (The Cristeros were dirt farmers who took up arms to protect their religion from the Revolution; see Reading 15.) Although interim president Portes Gil brought an end to the Cristero War in 1929, Church-state conflicts continued into the late Cárdenas era with the nonviolent Sinarquista groups (literally "without anarchy"; a religious "law and order" movement in the countryside) in the anticlerical centers of Veracruz and Tabasco in 1937 and after. By 1939 the National Action Party (PAN), a conservative, procleric party, was founded to oppose Cárdenas's Party of the Mexican Revolution (PRM).

In 1935 President Lázaro Cárdenas emerged to lead Mexico out of chaos. As in Europe and in other parts of Latin America at this time, the two major ideologies circulating throughout Mexico's workingman circles were socialism and nationalism. The Great Depression had revealed to many Mexicans their dependency upon the industrial creditor nations, and a wave of economic nationalism spread from the city to the countryside. There it merged with indigenism, a type of regional pride based on ethnic and tribal loyalties. Intellectuals and artists expressed these themes in the cultural nationalism of the day. Diego Rivera used native themes in his murals to express pride in the Mexican past and anger at the European and North American invaders. (See Pictorial: Art and Indigenism.) Similarly, indigenism informed the mood and content of *El Indio*, the national prizewinning novel by Gregorio López y Fuentes (see Reading 16) and the poem "Tarahumara Herbs" by Alfonso Reyes (see Reading 19).

As for socialism, Cárdenas enlisted the support of Marxist Lombardo Toledano and the Confederation of Mexican Workers (CTM) to usher in his "socialist" state. (See Reading 17.) Socialist education was introduced into the schools. In foreign affairs Cárdenas recognized the Republican and Communist factions of Spain's civil war and supported the enemies of Franco. He readily accepted political refugees from the Spanish civil war and even opened his arms to fugitives from Stalin's Russia, including the world-famous revolutionist and ideologue Leon Trotsky.

In 1938 Cárdenas reorganized labor from the top down. He brought the CTM into an alliance with the government at the same time that the CTM was instrumental in providing Cárdenas with popular backing when his government nationalized the foreign oil industries. (See Reading 18.) Meanwhile, on another front, the government assisted the peasants in their struggle with the landlords. Rural militias were formed to do battle with the private armies of the *hacendados* known as White Guards (see Reading 16), and by the summer of 1938 Cárdenas had formed a National Peasant Confederation (CNC) from regional leagues and unions. These leagues were active in attacking *haciendas* and restoring *ejidos*. Finally, again in 1938, Cárdenas, the great organizer, created a new labor central for bureaucrats known as the Federation of Unions of Workers at the Service of the State (FSTSE).

At the party's national assembly after the oil expropriation of 1938, Cárdenas herded workers into the newly created sectors of the renamed party, the PRM. The peasant sector was the CNC. The labor sector was composed of the giant CTM and some smaller groups like the CROM, the CGT (a syndicalist group), the miners' union, and the electricians' union. In the popular sector stood the bureaucrats' FSTSE, surrounded by associations of professionals, intellectuals, shopkeepers, women, and youth. The industrialists, although not a part of the party proper, influenced the popular sector through organizations like the Chamber of Commerce, the Bankers' Association, and the Chamber of Industry.

Calles and Cárdenas had created a heritage for contemporary Mexico known as the corporate state (see Reading 13), and the party sectors were tools for promoting state and corporate capitalist interests. Whatever the rhetoric of the populist revolution, the kind of socialism that emerged after Cárdenas was closer to national socialism than to Marxian socialism.

13

THE CALLES-CÁRDENAS CONNECTION

Lyle C. Brown

Lyle C. Brown is director of graduate studies and professor of political science at Baylor University. He is coeditor of Religion in Latin American Life and Literature *(1980), coauthor of* Practicing Texas Politics *(five editions, 1971 – 83), and author of various articles on Mexican political history and United States – Mexican relations. In 1978 he received the Walter Prescott Webb prize for "Cárdenas: Creating a Campesino Power Base for Presidential Policy," published in* Essays on the Mexican Revolution: Revisionist Views of the Leaders, *edited by George Wolfskill and Douglas W. Richmond (1979). The following essay on the rise of the corporate state is an original contribution to this volume.*

In reading this article on the Calles-Cárdenas heritage, that is, the rise of a political machine that is dominated by the president of Mexico, the reader should be aware of the following issues and problems: Did this era bring an end to the traditional powers of the soldier, priest, and landlord? If so, was this an era of political or social revolution? What is a corporate state? If Mexico had a corporate state by 1940, how did it develop and how did it function? Was Mexico's corporatism under Cárdenas a form of state capitalism, national socialism, or Marxian socialism? Did the military and political bureaucracy that emerged from the revolutionary armies consolidate or lose power during this era? Was Mexico by 1940 still a Bonapartist state in which political power was separate from economic power? Finally, did reform (or revolution) come from above or below during the 1930s?

For more than half a century, Mexico's politics have been dominated by a national political organization claiming to be *the* party of the Revolution. Established as the Partido Nacional Revolucionario (PNR) in 1929 and transformed into the Partido de la Revolución Mexicana (PRM) in 1938, this party was renamed the Partido Revolucionario Institucional (PRI) in 1946. Since 1929, the Revolutionary party's presidential candidates have triumphed in every national election, and the party has exercised a near monopoly of elective and appointive offices at local, district, and state levels.

The Calles Era, 1924–34

Because the Constitution of 1917 prohibited reelection, General Alvaro Obregón was barred from seeking another presidential term in 1924. When Obregón indicated that the minister of the interior (Gobernación), Plutarco Elías Calles, should be Mexico's next president, few were surprised. After all, Obregón and Calles had been comrades-in-arms since 1913, and both were Sonorans. Although not inclined originally to challenge this imposition, minister of finance and public credit Adolfo de la Huerta (another Sonoran but not a military man) first became embroiled in a personal conflict with Obregón over the handling of state elections in San Luis Potosí. Then de la Huerta resigned his cabinet post in September 1923, and on November 22 the former interim president (June–November 1920) was nominated as the presidential candidate of the Partido Cooperativista Nacional.

Backing de la Huerta were several generals who had followed Obregón's leadership for a decade but who refused to accept Calles as Mexico's next chief executive. These military men decided not to bother with the formalities of an election contest that could result only in a vote count that would favor Calles regardless of how a majority of ballots might be cast. On November 30, word reached Mexico City that General Rómulo Figueroa had revolted in Guerrero. Fearing arrest, de la Huerta slipped out of the capital on December 5 and joined General Guadalupe Sánchez in Veracruz. Two days later, de la Huerta issued a declaration denouncing Obregón's plan to impose Calles as his successor.

Although confronted with an insurrection involving almost half of his army, President Obregón moved swiftly to crush the rebels. Sending General Eugenio Martínez to deal with insurgents in Veracruz and southern Mexico, Obregón took personal command of operations in the west, where a large rebel force under General Enrique Estrada controlled most of Jalisco and Michoacán. As Obregón prepared to move government troops westward along the railroad from Querétaro to Guadalajara, he ordered General Lázaro Cárdenas to lead a column of two thousand soldiers from

Michoacán into Jalisco. Appraised of this movement, rebels under General Rafael Buelna attacked the column. In the fighting that followed, Cárdenas was gravely wounded and then taken prisoner as his men were routed at Huejotitlán on December 23. Less than two months later, however, Obregón's main force scored a smashing victory at Ocotlán, and Estrada's troops were dispersed or compelled to surrender.

Sporadic combat continued in southern Mexico during the remainder of 1924 as rebels were pursued into remote regions, but the conflict did not impede Calles's election campaign. On September 27 the Chamber of Deputies announced that he had defeated his opponent, General Angel Flores, by a count of 1.34 million votes to 250,000 votes. Calles claimed that he had made no commitments to any political party; but the office of minister of industry, commerce, and labor was awarded to Luis N. Morones, a corrupt labor leader who headed the Confederación Regional Obrero Mundial (CROM) and its political arm, the Partido Laborista. Although Morones's party had received important presidential patronage at the beginning of Obregón's administration, toward the end of his term Obregón had given more support to a rival organization, the Partido Nacional Agrarista. Under the Calles regime, however, the CROM expanded its membership at the expense of other labor unions, and the Partido Laborista was virtually the official party of the government.

Like many other revolutionaries, Calles was an outspoken critic of the Catholic clergy; but conflict between the Catholic Church and the revolutionary regime was kept at a relatively low level until 1926. In that year Archbishop José Mora y del Río publicly affirmed the Church's opposition to implementation of anticlerical provisions of the Constitution of 1917. The Calles administration reacted by deporting alien priests and nuns, expelling the apostolic delegate, closing Catholic schools, and ordering priests to register with civil authorities. In an effort to counter this repression, the Catholic hierarchy decided to suspend all religious services as of July 31. Subsequently, with the blessing of exiled bishops, thousands of Mexican Catholics—especially peasants in Jalisco, Colima, Michoacán, and Guanajuato—took up arms against the government. Invoking the name of Cristo Rey (Christ the King), these Cristero rebels waged a guerrilla war against federal troops and their civilian supporters.

While the Cristero rebellion still raged in western Mexico, the national Constitution was amended to provide a six-year presidential term and to allow reelection after an intervening term. Angered by this constitutional change, which would allow Obregón to seek another term in 1928, General Francisco Serrano and General Arnulfo Gómez declared themselves to be opposition candidates and plotted rebellion. The outcome of this development was a brief and unsuccessful uprising. Serrano was arrested and executed on October 3, 1927; Gómez was captured on November 4 and shot the following day.

Enthusiastically supported by the Partido Nacional Agrarista, Obregón was reelected on July 1, 1928—much to the displeasure of Morones. Two weeks later, while attending an electoral victory banquet, Obregón was assassinated by José Torral, a militant Catholic mystic. In the weeks that followed, there was speculation that Calles might continue in office beyond the end of his four-year term; but in his state of the union address on September 1, Calles declared that he would not under any conditions serve after November 30. He also emphasized that the time had come for Mexico to pass from a system of "government by *caudillos*" to a "regime of institutions and laws." Subsequently, on September 25, Mexico's congress named Emilio Portes Gil, a civilian, to serve as provisional president from December 1, 1928, to February 5, 1930. At the same time, the congress fixed November 20, 1929, as the date when Mexico's voters would elect a new president for the remainder of Obregón's six-year term.

On December 1, 1928, the day after Calles ended his presidency, he led other politicians in issuing a manifesto calling for formation of the Partido Nacional Revolucionario (PNR). Only a week later, however, Calles announced that he would retire completely from political life. Although General Manuel Pérez Treviño succeeded Calles as head of the PNR's organizing committee, Calles did not become an ordinary citizen. Instead, he continued to make important political and administrative decisions even after Portes Gil took office. Indicative of Calles's role as the country's most powerful leader were his unofficial title, Jefe Máximo de la Revolución (First Chief of the Revolution), and use of the term *Maximato* to describe Mexico's six years of government and politics between the end of his presidency and the beginning of the Cárdenas administration.

General Aáron Sáenz, a lawyer who had been closely associated with Obregón, emerged early as the likely presidential candidate for the PNR, which was scheduled to begin its first national convention on March 1, 1929. At that time some nine hundred delegates representing many local political organizations, labor groups (not including the CROM), and peasant leagues met at Querétaro to establish the PNR and nominate a presidential candidate. Sáenz had already been named as the candidate of the Partido Nacional Agrarista, and his supporters were certain that Calles wanted him to be the PNR's candidate as well. But they were to be disappointed. Sáenz was not nominated by the PNR—perhaps because he was a Protestant, or perhaps because he was too moderate for radicals, or perhaps because he was distrusted by some of the generals, or perhaps for a combination of these and other reasons. At any rate, General Pascual Ortiz Rubio, an engineer who had been abroad on diplomatic missions, emerged as the PNR candidate—in spite of the fact that Sáenz's sister was Calles's daughter-in-law, the wife of Plutarco, Jr.

Even as the PNR convention was engaged in the nominating task, a revolt was launched by a group of *obregonista* generals led by General José Gonzalo Escobar. With rebel forces operating in Veracruz, Sonora, Sinaloa, Durango, and Chihuahua, Portes Gil named Calles as minister of war. Forthwith, Calles assumed direction of military operations against the rebels. From Michoacán (where he had been serving as governor of the state and commander of federal forces combating Cristero rebels), General Lázaro Cárdenas was summoned to join General Juan Andreu Almazán and General Saturnino Cedillo in leading loyal troops against insurgent forces in the north while General Miguel M. Acosta dealt with rebels in Veracruz. By the end of April 1929, the Escobar revolt had been quelled; at the same time, through the good offices of United States Ambassador Dwight Morrow, progress was being made toward ending the Church-state conflict. Finally, on June 22, 1929, President Portes Gil and Archbishop Leopoldo Ruíz y Flores issued announcements to the effect that an understanding had been reached concerning terms for resumption of public worship and termination of the Cristero rebellion.

Opposing PNR candidate Ortiz Rubio in the election of November 20 were General Pedro Rodríguez Triana, candidate of the small but vocal Partido Comunista de México, and José

Vasconcelos, representing the Partido Nacional Antireeleccionista. Claiming the mantle of Francisco I. Madero, Vasconcelos aroused widespread enthusiasm as he campaigned vigorously throughout the country; however, election returns announced on November 28 showed the following totals: Ortiz Rubio, nearly 2 million votes; Vasconcelos, almost 111,000; Rodríguez Triana, a little more than 23,000.

Ortiz Rubio's administration began under unfortunate and ominous circumstances. On February 5, 1930, the day of his inauguration, the new president was wounded by a pistol bullet fired by a mentally deranged dissident. In the months that followed, Ortiz Rubio's political health also suffered. First, he followed a policy of ratifying all policy decisions made by Calles; then when public ridicule prompted the weak president to attempt independent action, lack of *callista* support made governing impossible. Finally, on September 3, 1932, Ortiz Rubio submitted his resignation and departed for New York on the following day. Among the highest-ranking political figures of the brief and troubled administration of Ortiz Rubio was Lázaro Cárdenas, who served as president of the PNR from November 1930 to May 1931 and as minister of the interior from August to October 1931.

Following Ortiz Rubio's resignation, the national congress filled the presidential vacancy by electing minister of war Abelardo Rodríguez, a long-time Calles supporter and one of the richest revolutionary generals, to serve out the remaining two years of Obregón's term. Although Calles continued to play a dominant role in affairs of party and state, there were signs that the PNR apparatus was growing in strength at the expense of its semiindependent components: labor groups, *campesino* leagues, and local political organizations. In part this was due to a growing party bureaucracy financed by contributions of seven days' pay by each government employee—a requirement originally imposed by interim President Portes Gil. Further strengthening of the party resulted from an extraordinary convention of the PNR called by the party's National Executive Committee. Although the convention was held in Aguascalientes in October 1932 for the announced purpose of proposing a return to the rule of no reelection for the president of México under any circumstances (a proposal that became part of the national Constitution within five months), delegates were directed by Calles to reorganize the PNR along hierarchical lines.

Formerly a loose confederation of regional and local political bodies, the PNR became a highly structured political pyramid consisting of party organs and nominating conventions at *municipio,* state, and national levels.

The Cárdenas Years, 1934–40

At the end of 1932, President Rodríguez brought General Cárdenas (then serving as *jefe de zona* in Puebla) into his cabinet as minister of war, an office that had been used as a springboard by other generals who aspired to the ultimate promotion: the presidency. Even before Cárdenas assumed this cabinet position on January 1, 1933, however, his name was being mentioned by many as a possible PNR presidential nominee for 1934. It is true that Cárdenas was known to be a champion of land reform, whereas Calles had become strongly opposed to such agrarian measures; but the two military men were bound by strong personal ties first formed in 1915. In March of that year, Cárdenas led four hundred *convencionista* troops into the *constitucionalista* camp at Agua Prieta and joined Calles in defending this strategic border town. Operating under Calles's command, Cárdenas helped to turn back Villa's attack and then contributed significantly to the destruction of *villista* forces in Sonora.

General Manuel Pérez Treviño, president of the PNR, was another prominent political figure who appeared to be a strong contender for his party's presidential nomination in 1934; but everyone knew that Calles would make the final decision regarding selection of the candidate for this national office. By June 7, 1933, the Jefe Máximo had decided in favor of Cárdenas, for it was on that date that the more conservative Pérez Treviño announced his withdrawal from the contest. Subsequently, on December 6 of that year, Cárdenas was nominated by acclamation at the PNR convention meeting in Querétaro. Another achievement of the convention was adoption of a party platform known as the Six Year Plan, forced upon the convention by radical *cardenista* elements within the party. Revolutionary provisions of the plan committed the new administration to programs designed to promote growth of labor organizations, speed up distribution of land to small farmers and *ejidos,* carry out extensive public works projects, and implement socialist-oriented public education.

Cárdenas's opposition in the 1934 presidential campaign took the form of three candidates: Adalberto Tejeda, the leftist governor of Veracruz and candidate of the newly organized Partido Socialista de las Izquierdas; Antonio I. Villarreal, a veteran revolutionary who had supported the unsuccessful Escobar revolt and who received the presidential nomination of the loosely confederated Confederación Revolucionaria de Partidos Independientes; and Hernán Laborde, the general secretary of the Partido Comunisto de México, who entered the election campaign under the banner of the Bloque Obrero y Campesino. Despite the weakness of the opposition and the certainty of his election, Cárdenas campaigned vigorously throughout the country during the months between nomination and election. Traveling by plane, train, horse, and foot, he came face to face with millions of Mexicans and emphasized his determination to carry out the promises of social and economic reform that were spelled out in the Six Year Plan and authorized by the Constitution of 1917. Official results of the election conducted on July 1 gave Cárdenas a landslide victory with more than two million votes, while each of his opponents was credited with less than twenty-five thousand votes.

Shortly after Cárdenas took office at the end of November 1934, Mexico was convulsed by a series of strikes resulting from interunion conflict and the president's openly expressed sympathy with labor's demands for higher wages and better working conditions. When Calles criticized the strike activities of Vicente Lombardo Toledano and other labor leaders, Cárdenas interpreted these statements as constituting an unwarranted and intolerable intervention. Most politicians had expected that the thirty-nine-year-old president would defer to his patron, but Cárdenas defended the labor unions and indicated that he would allow no interference by the Jefe Máximo.

After *callista* deputies and cabinet members were quickly removed from office at Cárdenas's direction, Calles left the country; however, he returned to Mexico at the end of 1935 and began organizing an opposition movement. Once more Cárdenas was quick to respond to a challenge to his leadership: generals of dubious loyalty were reassigned to new commands; *callistas* were expelled from the PNR; and pro-Calles governors and senators were purged from office. Finally, on the evening of April 9, 1936, Calles was placed under house arrest. During earlier and more violent periods of the Revolution, Calles's conduct most certainly would have resulted in execution before a firing squad; but Mexico had changed, and Cárdenas's techniques were not those of Villa or Obregón. Thus, on the morning of April 10, the former president and Jefe Máximo was placed aboard a plane and exiled to the United States.

Another challenge to Cárdenas's authority had a more violent ending. Following a lengthy labor-management dispute in the petroleum industry, on March 18, 1938, Cárdenas announced that the government would expropriate the oil companies. Subsequently it was rumored that General Saturnino Cedillo, long-time political boss of the state of San Luis Potosí and former minister of agriculture in Cárdenas's cabinet, was conspiring with agents of the oil companies to bring about the overthrow of the federal government. When ordered to assume command of the 21st Military Zone in Michoacán, General Cedillo requested retirement on grounds of poor health. The request was granted, although Cárdenas insisted that Cedillo's health was not a problem. Any doubts concerning Cedillo's intentions were soon resolved when San Luis Potosí's state legislature issued a manifesto denouncing the Cárdenas regime and calling on other state governments to do likewise. Then on May 15, 1938, the governor of San Luis Potosí, Colonel Mateo Hernández Netro, issued a decree withdrawing recognition of Cárdenas as president of the republic and naming General Cedillo as commander-in-chief of the Mexican Constitutionalist Army. Cárdenas responded to this challenge by rushing to the rebelling state and throwing a strong contingent of federal troops against the insurgents. Without support in other parts of the country, the uprising was short-lived. Within a few weeks Cedillo's forces were dispersed and their leader was forced to take refuge in the mountains. Finally, on January 11, 1939, he was brought to bay and slain in the course of a brief skirmish; subsequently, Cedillo's body was displayed publicly in the plaza of the state capital.

Realizing that education of the masses represented Mexico's most pressing need, and aware of the fact that teachers could be utilized as agents for disseminating propaganda in support of his policies, Cárdenas sought to expand the country's public school system; but anticlerical elements of his socialist education program provoked strong opposition from the Catholic hierarchy and from many parents. Convinced that a prolonged religious conflict would interfere with programs in other areas, Cárdenas appeased the clergy by modifying some of the more radical features of his educational program while at the same time using his influence to ensure the opening of more churches and to lift state restrictions on the number of priests allowed to function. Attempts by rural Catholic militants to renew the Cristero conflict failed, and the most significant Catholic political action took the form of the fascist-style Sinarquista movement, which emphasized nationalism and nonviolent demonstrations.

Cárdenas made good his campaign promises to protect labor; and among Mexico's peasant masses he distributed 49 million acres of land to nearly 800,000 beneficiaries, most of whom were members of *ejidos*. But while promoting the interests of labor and carrying out his land reform program, Cárdenas also insisted that Mexican workers and peasants be organized into separate confederations. Lombardo Toledano, the country's most prominent labor leader at that time, wanted both peasant and labor elements united within a single proletarian organization; but Cárdenas was too shrewd a politician to accept a plan that might have led to the expansion of Lombardo Toledano's power at the president's expense. Thus, Cárdenas supported the Marxist labor leader's efforts to unify labor unions within the Confederación de Trabajadores Mexicanos (CTM); but he designated responsibility for achieving unification of peasant leagues to the federal government and the PNR. Although the CTM came into existence early in 1936 and included a majority of the country's industrial workers, it was not until the summer of 1938 that a single peasant league had been organized in each state and territory, and that these leagues had been brought within the Confederación Nacional Campesina (CNC). While Cárdenas insisted that the CTM and the CNC were created in order to give the proletarian sectors greater influence in public affairs, it was only too evident that they were also designed to broaden the base of the president's political power and make him less dependent upon support from professional politicians, government employees, and military personnel.

Beginning shortly after the meeting of the Seventh Comintern Congress in Moscow in 1935, the Partido Comunista de México (PCM) sought to create a popular front along lines laid down by Stalin's spokesman, George Dimitrov. The highhanded methods employed by PCM officials soon alienated both CTM and PNR leaders, and a Mexican popular front movement under Communist guidance failed to materialize. Late in 1937, without giving any indication that he might have been influenced by PCM efforts, Cárdenas called for a transformation of the PNR so as to create a corporative structure featuring four sectors: labor sector (the CTM, a few smaller federations, and some independent unions), peasant sector (state *campesino* leagues in the process of being unified under the CNC), military sector (army and navy units), and popular sector (a mixed bag including government employee unions, cooperative societies, professional associations, and groups not included within the other three sectors). Consequently, the Partido de la Revolución Mexicana (PRM) came into being in 1938. No longer were all elements of the revolutionary party involved in selecting candidates for each local, district, and state office. Instead, nominations for certain offices were allocated to each sector; then sector nominees were supposed to be supported by all party members in the general election. Majority support by delegates in three of the PRM's four sectors was required to nominate the presidential candidate at a national convention.

In November 1939, under Cárdenas's guiding hand, the PRM's presidential convention passed over General Francisco J. Múgica, author of some of the most radical provisions of the Constitution of 1917 and for many years one of Cárdenas's closest collaborators and advisers. Instead of supporting the candidacy of his fellow *michoacano*, Cárdenas preferred conservative General Manuel Avila Camacho, his long-time comrade-in-arms and minister of war. The principal opponent of the PRM's candidate was General Juan Andréu Almazán, a veteran revolutionary who was nominated by the newly organized Partido Revolucionario de Unificación Nacional (PRUN). Also participating in the campaign was General Rafael Sánchez Tapia, an independent candidate and former minister of national economy in Cárdenas's cabinet.

Despite the president's promise of an orderly election, the voting on July 7, 1940, was marked by numerous riots, especially in Mexico City, where pro-Almazán sentiment was strong. Dozens of people were killed or wounded during the course of various shootouts when *almazanistas* and *avilacamachistas* fought for control of polling places. In many voting precincts, separate polling places were established by the warring political groups, and the canvassing boards that were convened in each district on July 11 were controlled by the PRM. Consequently, it was declared that all congressional contests had been won by PRM candidates; and as for the outcome of the presidential race, the following voting results were announced: Avila Camacho, 2,265,199; Almazán, 128,574; Sánchez Tapia, 14,046. Later, the official tally increased the number of votes for Avila Camacho and Almazán to 2,476,641 and 151,101, respectively, while the number for Sánchez Tapia was reduced to 9,840.

Claiming to be the victim of gross election fraud, the PRUN insisted that its congressional candidates had won a large majority of seats and that Almazán had been elected as Mexico's president. Thus, the big question was whether *almazanistas* would attempt to use violent methods to obtain the offices that they claimed. During the late summer and early fall of 1940, there was a very real possibility that General Almazán would attempt to launch an armed revolt; but after spending several weeks in the United States vainly seeking some assurance that the Roosevelt administration would adopt a policy of neutrality in the event of civil war in Mexico, Almazán became convinced that his presidential bid was a lost cause. Therefore, Cárdenas was able to transfer presidential power to Avila Camacho and leave office at the end of November after having served a full six-year term.

During the four years of Calles's presidency (1924–28), Mexico was the scene of violent Church-state conflict and chronic political instability. The religious problem was largely resolved by suppression of the Cristero rebellion in 1929, when Calles was no longer president but was recognized as the country's Jefe Máximo. As for the political turmoil of the 1920s, it was a characteristic of the *caudillo* system featuring personalist politics and revolts led by ambitious generals. Upon leaving the presidency, Calles established the PNR as a means of centralizing political authority and controlling elections. While directing the development of this political structure, Calles dominated Presidents Portes Gil, Ortiz Rubio, and Rodríguez during the era of the Maximato (1928–34), but he was unable to exercise similar control over the Cárdenas administration (1934–40).

In part, Calles's failure to dominate Cárdenas was due to the latter's strong sense of personal pride and independence, and in part it was because Cárdenas was supported by radical elements that were dissatisfied with the growing conservatism of the Jefe Máximo. Ironically, Cárdenas was able to free himself from Calles's tutelage because the young president knew how to manipulate the party organization that Calles had built. Then Cárdenas reorganized the Revolutionary party, creating the four-sector PRM in which peasant and labor organizations received representation but became subject to greater presidential control.

Both Calles and Cárdenas were pragmatic politicians with distinct styles of leadership that served them well in a political environment where assassination and rebellion were ever-present dangers. To presidents of the post-1940 period (all civilians after 1946), they bequeathed a political machine that is still used to monopolize power, to maintain political stability, and to transfer power without precipitating armed revolt or other types of mass violence. This is the Calles-Cárdenas heritage.

14

AGRARIAN REVOLT IN NARANJA

Paul Friedrich

Paul Friedrich is professor of anthropology and linguistics at the University of Chicago. He is the author of Agrarian Revolt in a Mexican Village, *the first detailed ethnological history of an agrarian revolt in one village, and the source from which this excerpt was taken.*

In his summary discussion, Professor Friedrich describes seven causes of the agrarian revolt that occurred between 1920 and 1926 in the village of Naranja de Tapia, a Tarascan Indian community in the Zacapu valley of Michoacán. Of the causes mentioned, which are primary and which are secondary? Are any of the components of the material conditions of revolt psychological ones? How did the Great Rebellion from 1910 to 1923 serve as a model of arbitrary violence? What was the general role of ideology, and how important was the ideology of magonismo *to Primo Tapia? How did kinship affect Primo Tapia's revolutionary role? Finally, compare this essay with the following one on the Cristeros (Reading 15). After so doing, ask yourself if the insight gained from the Naranja case can be used to improve your understanding of the previous* zapatista *movement in Morelos and the later Cristero revolt in central and western Mexico.*

For agrarian revolt in Naranja, a total of seven causes have been isolated, ranging from material factors, to political ideology, to local organization, to physical violence, to gifted leadership, to preexisting patterns of local social structure (especially kinship), and the encapsulating politico-governmental organization. These will now be discussed in turn.

The primary precondition for an agrarian revolt, which in-

Reprinted by permission from Paul Friedrich, *Agrarian Revolt in a Mexican Village* (Englewood Cliffs, N.J.: Prentice Hall, 1970), pp. 136–42.

volves land by definition, is a condition of the natural environment and man's relation to it—and I find it simpler to think of the matter this way than in terms of the familiar terminological categories of "environment, ecology, material culture, economics," and so forth. One must distinguish, of course, between overt and covert, between explicit ideology and underlying motivation. Many revolts have been superficially political or religious, but latently agrarian; and the opposite type, though rarer, has also been known to occur—where, for example, a nominal "agrarian struggle" is motivated by a prior division based on caste differences and invigorated by vendetta obligations. But barring some hypothetical mass psychosis, there will be objective, soil-related preconditions. Villagers themselves think material causes are primary and necessary, and differentiate sharply and consistently between the "true" or "real" agrarian revolt or struggle as against "pure politics" or "the religious question" or "a question of skirts." They explained the revolt in terms of such ultimate life symbols as corn, a shortage of tortillas, and the expropriation of the land.

The material condition also consists of other components. In the present instance, the village abutted on a huge marsh, the source of [corn] and other basic foods and of raw materials for the mats and hats that the villagers exported; location in a distinct ecological niche impinged on politics. But these villages also were subject to the vast program of national economic development under the Díaz dictatorship, which was perceived by the ethnocentric peasants as an alien and dangerous force. The two preconditions of local ecology and national economic policy were brought together by the expropriation of the fertile marsh by Spanish capitalists. The most direct consequences of the expropriation were physical deprivation, including hunger, and the need to have more traffic with Spanish-speaking peons and foremen, whether on the new [e]states or in the tropical plantations; such interaction often was thought to imply the rape of native women.

The ill-treatment and exploitation of the peasants contrasted in the strongest possible colors with the affluence and physical power of the intrusive landlords, and with the fabulous bumper harvests of the basic food, corn. The contrasts between the haves and the have nots might have motivated agrarian unrest anywhere; by the 1890s, agitation had been initiated in the state capital, and local committees were formed during the first decade of this century. But while such material preconditions were indispensable, they did not generate revolt in isolation as "objective facts," or even when mediated by the attitudes and traditional value systems of the population.

The material conditions had to be not only apprehended and verbalized by the peasantry but critically evaluated and persuasively tied to an ideology. By ideology I do not mean any system of values or an unconscious or subconscious normative system, but an explicit, articulated evaluation of the pros and cons, coupled with ideas about effectuating the desired change; in the present case, the agrarian ideology evaluated the expropriation as "the rape of the pueblo" (in Mexican Spanish terms) and enjoined the peasant to participate in the "just struggle for the land." Ideology, of course, can develop in considerable independence of agrarian conditions, as when soft-palmed urban intellectuals make a revolutionary case of "the plight of the peasant" where agrarian redistribution might actually make conditions worse; in other cases, an ideology of forceful expropriation may develop precisely during the years when agrarian conditions are actually improving. But even in these admittedly exceptional cases, there is a meaningful relation to material reality, usually an objective inequity in land distribution. In the Zacapu valley, and also in the nearby Eleven Pueblos, an agrarian ideology began with legal and agitational work around the turn of the century, in obvious response to the glaring inequities and the seizure of ancient lands by outside entrepreneurs.

Ideology itself appears to have had at least two causes. Several major ingredients like anticlericalism were certainly stimulated by the political theorizing and propaganda of the so-called Liberals during the 1890s and the first decade of this century. Additional components were contributed by the Russian-Spanish anarchosyndicalism of the Flores Magón brothers—notably the total expropriation of the landlords and other propertied classes in favor of the workers and tillers of the soil. But the growth of counterpoised agrarian and conservative ideologies also was motivated by the drastic shift in political power within Naranja: (1) the rise of the two small mestizo families to positions of control through caciques, in close collaboration with the clergy and the landlords, and (2) the fall of the Tarascan leaders, and specifically of the numerous first and second cousins of the large Cruz—de la Cruz name group; thus, ideology was a product of local social change and of theorizing in the external, national system. But both local social change and nationwide ideology were themselves a direct response to material, economic conditions.

The third main cause was local-level organization, by which I mean the partially planned grouping together of individuals for the purpose of carrying out the ideology by political or military means. Such organization may be a preexisting one—a set of village factions or lineages with their leaders, which adopts an agrarian ideology—or the organization may be specially set up for agrarian ends, as is illustrated by the agrarian committees in Naranja. Clearly, the organizations may be motivated by other than agrarian sentiments, such as vendetta obligations or individual charisma, and the traditional or standing organizations may considerably antedate the material fact of agrarian inquiry. They enter into the causal sequence when informed by agrarian ideology.

In the present case, the first agrarian committees were followed in the 1920s by the far more militant and consistently organized factions, feminine leagues, agrarian executive committees, and "committees for material improvements." Their purposes were many: to oppose the landlords, expel the clergy, liquidate so-called reactionaries, obtain financial support for litigation at higher levels, and found schools. Pervading and dominating all these purposes was the fundamental political goal of taking over effective control of local government from the landed and conservative families that were collaborating with the clergy and landlords. The village committees were reticulated with statewide organizations, particularly the League of Agrarian Committees, and the entire complex was unquestionably stimulated by ideas about revolutionary undergrounds, labor unions, and village communes that had diffused from the anarchosyndicalism of the Flores Magóns. Many of the local participants were perfectly aware of the need for organization, and speak of "the party" and "shock brigades" as reasons for their success. Such local level organization, when conjoined with a revolutionary ideology and glaring economic inequities, might in theory have been sufficient to cause agrarian change, and surely the combination has generated it in other instances; a so-called revolt could be peaceful and more or less constitutional with, let us speculate, a gradual transfer of land. But most known history indicates that agrarian change is unlikely in such cases. In the present case, the outbreak of revolt unquestionably depended on the catalyzing effect of a fourth case.

The fourth case is physical violence; any revolt, including agrarian revolt, is normally preceded by violence, defined by violence, and accompanied and followed by a violence that is connected with the larger, encapsulating system. Threats to the status system, and economic inequity, and man's emotional ties to the soil are normally sufficient, when taken in conjunction, to precipitate physical aggression. Violence by itself, however, is never sufficient to precipitate revolt; in the absence of ideology and organization the most glaring inequities can coexist with violence for an indefinite period. And perhaps more than any of the first three causes discussed, physical violence is channelled and even prevented by the large political and cultural context. Ideologically motivated agrarian groups can work for decades or centuries in the face of agrarian inequity but be restrained from homicidal aggression and revolt by moral and religious sanctions.

I have demonstrated above that the Spanish capitalists initiated a vicious circle, going from their "rape of the pueblos," to the "predatory acts" of their foremen and hired hands, to retaliation by the Indians; by 1910, violence and murder had polarized the antagonists. The Mexican Revolution, dragging on for ten years between 1910 and 1920, weakened the fabric of peasant society and habituated many villagers to occasional executions, the intrusion of rival guerrilla bands and military detachments, and similar models of arbitrary violence and causes of social and moral disorganization. Many young Indians fought in Zapatista, Villista, and Carranzista armies. The assassination, in 1919, of the local agrarian leader Joaquín de la Cruz, by soldiers allegedly in the pay of the landlords, unquestionably encouraged the propensity to violence and its justification. But above all it was Primo Tapia, the ex-Magonista and ex-"Wobbly," who articulated violence as an idea, as an explicit concept, and as a necessary and concomitant method of agrarian revolt. Villagers agree that he was prone to violence and responsible for "bad acts" and had "obscure backgrounds." "Primo had good principles, but he was violent." During the actual struggle between 1921 and 1926, individual shootouts, ambushes, and firefights between *agrarista* militias and landlord forces—the latter often supported by troops—became a part of the local political culture; in the course of some of these years, 5 to 15 percent of the adult men perished or left the village. Such patterns were to live on with occasional flareups for many subsequent decades of factional strife. Patterns of local violence were reticulated with Tarascan and Mexican attitudes toward the inevitability and irony of death, and with Primo Tapia's obsessive premonition of his own violent end in 1926. Local violence, so distinctive of this political system, evolved into a complex of attitudes and sentiments, an inventory of methods, and a mode of action without which this particular agrarian revolt is difficult to visualize.

The fifth main cause is leadership in the specific sense of gifted or outstanding leadership, rather than of institutional changes, the normal routine of government, or the specific tactics required for litigating in the maze of superordinate structures. From the peasant's view, agrarian revolt is made by gifted leaders and ranks with the land question as a cited cause. Yet while the leadership must be gifted, it need not be charismatic; the crucial variable is the ability to mediate, arbitrate, communicate, and so forth, between the political systems of peasant village, the state, and the nation. In an analytical sense, gifted leadership is weaker than the other four causes in not being strictly necessary; revolt can and often does occur without it, and gifted leadership often fails to lead to revolt. But when gifted leadership is added to the four causes already cited, agrarian revolt becomes practically inevitable.

Two men were mainly responsible for the revolt in the Zacapu valley. Joaquín de la Cruz initiated the agrarian agitation, organized the early agrarian committees, and litigated in the state capital. But as local survivors emphasize, it was Primo Tapia who catalyzed and synthesized the preconditions of revolt into the realization of a revolt. I have sketched many of the traits of his character that exercised particularly strong symbolic effects: the mistreatment by his father, his superior education and linguistic skills, his sensitivity to local religious ritual, his ideological link with the Flores Magóns, and, finally, his sadistic "martyrdom" (i.e., lynching) after leading the villagers through the reconquest and first harvests of the ancient lands. Every one of these and other strands is vitally connected with the culture of the Zacapu valley Tarascans: patriarchy, ethnocentrism, bilingualism, and annual fiesta cycle, and attitudes about violence and death, land, and corn. As the villagers said, "Primo made bad mistakes, but he died to give us the land." "Without Primo we would never have won the land until the

Cárdenas administration." Primo Tapia, *simpático* and diagnostically violent, condensed and personified both local cultural and international revolutionary values, eventually becoming a symbol second only to land as an explicit and fundamental cause.

The sixth and seventh causes consist of the preexisting values and patterns for the interrelation of individuals and groups, which necessarily antecede, mould, and channel a revolt, no matter how inevitable its economic motivation or charismatic its leadership.

These limiting sociopolitical patterns were of two kinds. First, the indigenous institutions of land control, local politics, and kinship and the family. To begin with a negative example, the older traditions of informal control through consensus among the elders and the priest were contradicted by the agrarian executive committees under a thirty-four-year-old *cacique*, and it was this contradiction that conduced to open opposition, factionalism, political homicide, and even mass exodus. On the other hand, the preexisting system of communal use of marsh and mountain, together with the strong native value placed on communal usufruct, presumably facilitated the institution of communal *ejidos* and syndicalist organizations. Similarly, the foregoing study has shown how a program of economic transformation and even militant anticlericalism could be conjoined with considerable financial profit to the colorful and traditional forms of the annual fiesta cycle. But more than any other such formal cause, it was kinship, in a fairly inclusive sense, that tended to structure the forms of agrarian revolt. I have shown that Primo Tapia, even after fourteen years in the United States and his experience as a "Wobbly," still thought of the local revolt in terms of the attitudes and anxieties of his mother and sister, of the loyalty to his maternal uncle, from whom he had "inherited" the leadership, and of the large core of maternal aunts and cousins (mother's sister's sons) that was always the nucleus of his grassroots organization. Finally, the so-called political families (bilaterally extended name groups) became the maximal units within the opposing factions. Obviously, these patterns of family and kinship were neither necessary nor sufficient for revolt.

The revolt in Naranja was also determined in part by the administration, legislation, and power structure at the regional, state, and national levels. Some of this consisted of long-standing and even archaic patterns of personal relations and informal power and influence, but much of it was newly institutionalized, with a plethora of confusing rules, technical terminology, arbitrary deadlines, and vaguely defined offices. We have seen how Tapia's *relative* ability at coping with the superstructure facilitated the agrarian revolt, but also how his failure to cope with the contradictions of *Delahuertismo* contributed to his assassination. We have also seen how inadequacies in the legislation prevented or led to the protraction of the efforts of the first agrarian committees, but also how the improved legal machinery of the early 1920s, coupled with Primo Tapia's contacts and tactics, led rapidly to a land grant in 1924. In contrast, much of the later agrarian reform of the 1930s was carried through by the national government in regions where local leadership, organization, ideology, and even material conditions were insufficient. National policy and agency can precede or shape any of the preconditions to revolt discussed above; thus, national policy encouraged the expropriation by the Spanish capitalists, national conflicts directly contributed an anarchosyndicalist ideology, national statutes changed (shortened) the critical deadlines for agrarian litigation, national revolution introduced predatory, violent bands into Naranja, and state and (future) national leaders such as Lázaro Cárdenas affected agrarian revolt in Naranja at crucial junctures. On the other hand, we have also seen that agrarian revolt may evolve in partial independence from or even in partial opposition to the laws and policies of the state at some time; often revolt transpires in areas that are outside of or somehow shielded from national control and jurisdiction. In any case, the peasant tends to perceive the encapsulating national system as threatening, difficult to understand, and impossible to manipulate.

Let us conclude. I have restated my twin goals of (1) local ethnological history and (2) the elucidation of the preconditions of agrarian revolt in one historical case. Agrarian revolt in Naranja was found to have passed through several stages: from unrest, to focused and articulated discontent, to organization for change (which could have terminated with agrarian reform), to agrarian violence, often skillfully led, to full-scale agrarian revolt. These stages, incidentally, correspond in many essential ways to those for revolution in general that have already been established by social psychologists and political scientists. The preconditions or causes for agrarian revolt in Naranja were found to be: (1) inequity in land usufruct, clearly perceived and strongly appreciated; (2) an ideology of agrarian reform, and eventually, revolt; (3) local agrarian organization; (4) physical violence, both impinging from without and between local factions; and (5) gifted leadership. Local social structure—particularly kinship—functioned as a limiting cause. State and national policies and power structure also limited the revolt in diverse ways, but also positively determined the other preconditions and the overall course of the revolt itself. Some of the preconditions always overlapped, even in a purely diachronic sense, and in a synchronic sense they were all interrelated and fed into one another in a cybernetic fashion. In a purely logical and hypothetical model meant to hold for any pueblo, the seven preconditions for revolt could probably be ordered in terms of their relative power. The relation of logical power and chronological order can be further investigated "when we have cleared up the history" or typologically diverse local agrarian revolts in other parts of the world.

15

THE *CRISTEROS* OF SAN JOSÉ

Luis González y González

In 1926 the Church began to move against Calles to undermine the anticlerical program of his government. When the archbishop announced that Mexican priests would never observe the Constitution's regulation of religious activities, Calles accepted the challenge. He ordered priests out of the country and closed religious schools. The Church then went on strike and refused to give sacraments. From 1926 to 1929 violence raged across Mexico in the so-called Cristero War against the government. Cristero rebels were active in Morelos, Jalisco, Nayarit, Durango, and in the municipio of San José de Gracia in northwestern Michoacán.

In this selection from San José de Gracia: Mexican Village in Transition *(winner of the American Historical Association's C. H. Haring Prize, awarded every five years for the best book on Latin American history), Luis González, one of Mexico's finest historians, describes the Cristero rebellion in San José and its aftermath, from 1928 to 1932. Note the contents of the manifesto of the Liberation Movement. Does it indicate that its advocates were heirs of Zapata—that is, authentic peasant revolutionaries fighting an authoritarian state? Or were the Cristeros of San José a group of reactionaries, pawns of the hierarchy in its struggle with a reformist state? With the fighting over, were the Cristeros of San José history's losers or winners? San José witnessed violence; did it experience social change?*

At the beginning of the rainy season of 1928 there was a lull in the fighting. There were fewer federal incursions into Cristero territory; and it did not occur to the rebel bands (there were more of them now, but they were smaller and more poorly equipped) to

Reprinted by permission from Luis González, *San José de Gracia: Mexican Village in Transition*, translated by John Upton (Austin: University of Texas Press, 1974), pp. 165–67, 172–76, 179–80. Copyright 1974 by El Colegio de Mexico.

leave their "water holes." In Don Prudencio Mendoza's sector, from which Padre Federico was trying to coordinate the operations of the Cristeros in northwestern Michoacán and adjoining parts of Jalisco, half a dozen skirmishes took place after the storm on May 22. The *callistas* set fire to *rancherías* in the mountains; two days later, on July 15, Cristeros attacked the train from Los Reyes; there was action at Gallineros on July 18, at Lagunillas on August 12, and a battle at San Cristóbal on August 15. It was quiet enough for many of the hill people to return to tending their cornfields and milking their cows. Those who, like the San Joséans, were far from home spent their days and nights on horseback under the rain, receiving the encouraging news of the death of Obregón, taking part in religious services held by Padre Federico or some other Cristero chaplain, writing letters to their families and sweethearts, and celebrating at various times and in various places such events as the repopulation of San José.

When the rains had come that year, San José was still a pitiful spectacle: empty, blackened houses with fallen roofs; tall weeds and thistles growing in the streets and among the ruins; no sound but the howling of coyotes and cats. But the rains had hardly begun when the civil and military authorities (perhaps because the "concentration" had not had the desired effect, perhaps out of pity for the refugees) allowed the town and its surrounding *rancherías* to be reoccupied. Almost the entire population, lean and ragged, returned to the village. The women and children set to work making the houses livable, while the old men went out to replant the cornfields and round up and milk the remaining cows. They also returned to the practice of serving as spies and providing supplies for the armed rebels. There was an attempt to move them out again, but it could not be done; they now knew how to defend themselves against the government, how to turn politics against the politicians, and how to practice the art of dissimulation. During June and July more than half of the villagers came back to their homes.

Another piece of good news for those engaged in the revolution against Calles came when General Gorostieta was named supreme commander of the Liberation Movement on October 28, 1928. For some time people had been saying that he was an officer with excellent qualifications. He soon announced his manifesto, with its fifteen points, elucidating the goals of the Cristero movement; all the guarantees of the Constitution of 1857 "without the Reform laws"; refusal to recognize the authorities; adoption of laws based on the people's wishes and on tradition; votes for women; syndicalism; agreements between holders of *ejido* lands and property owners for the payment of indemnities; distribution "of rural properties in a just and equitable way after indemnification"; plans to make land available to the greatest number; baptism of the Cristero army as the "National Guard"; and adoption of the motto "God, Country, and Liberty." In line with these principles General Gorostieta would reorganize the Cristero revolution; he would unify the Liberation Movement without "flinching under the obligation imposed upon him by the will of the nation." Meanwhile, people were supporting José Vasconcelos in his campaign for the presidency of the republic, and the intellectual leaders of the Cristero movement were lamenting the poverty, disorder, and irresponsible behavior of their forces. . . .

Nineteen twenty-nine opened with severe frosts; the last of these, which did great damage to winter crops, struck on March 13 and 15. The years from 1930 to 1933 were cold and dry. For example, 1932 could not have been worse, with its niggardly summer rains followed by frequent bitter frosts. The corn withered in the hard earth and bent under the cold blasts of October. There was not enough of either corn or beans to satisfy local needs. Both had to be bought at terribly high prices: corn for 110 pesos a ton, and beans at 280 pesos. And, as if this was not enough, the cattle died in heaps during the frosts and drought that followed the meager harvest. The three or four thousand cattle that had survived the raids by federal troops and Cristeros were reduced to half that number in the drought of 1932. There was want even in the homes of the middle class. The moneylender (San José had never been without one) sank his teeth in. People were saying that there was a "crisis"; there was not enough food or clothing; families were living in houses that had been only half rebuilt. Ruined cornfields, decimated dairy herds, unemployment—these marked a period of widespread misery.

The political climate was not encouraging, either. General Calles was still ruling Mexico from his position behind the presidents, the governors, and the local puppets. The armistice was not entirely respected in all branches of the governmental machinery. The president demanded the banishment of Archbishop Orozco y Jiménez. On July 27 he made a declaration that did not square with the agreement that had been reached with the prelates, and, ultimately, he refused to return many of the churches. Don Pascual Ortiz Rubio, the second puppet president, revived the policy of limiting the number of churches allowed to remain open and returned to the old Calles brand of anticlerical statements. Some state governors continued religious persecutions. General Lázaro Cárdenas, governor of Michoacán, tolerated the burning of holy images by groups of "defanaticizers," but the aims of his government were far higher than the excesses of the "Calles gang." The governor's tolerance toward San José was at first so broad that the former seminary student and declared pro-Cristero Daniel González Cárdenas was appointed *jefe de tenencia*. Until 1930, local authorities had had complete control, but from that time on they were obliged to take orders from a military detachment under the command of Lieutenant "Ino," who owed his nickname to his inability to pronounce the word *himno* (hymn). Beyond making solemn public statements of all kinds, this man did no harm.

San José's social atmosphere was something else again. When the Cristero revolution ended, many soldiers in the army of Christ the King were no longer on friendly terms with their comrades, and some early sympathizers had turned against the Cristero movement. There was less unanimity in San José than there had been in 1927. Quarrels arose, and some of the politicians who were interested in getting rid of the ex-Cristeros fanned the flames. It is true that the San Joséans saw through these tricks, as the people of Cojumatlán did not, but that was not enough to restore harmony. In addition to personal quarrels, the town had to put up with exhibitions of barbaric behavior learned during the war: shooting off guns into the air, bullying, insults, gunfights, showing off, and drunken sprees. And then there was the robber band that seems to come along after every revolution. Manga Morada was their leader. One of his favorite amusements was sitting on the shoulders of his victims when they were being hanged. But personal quarrels, bad manners, and robbery were minor evils in comparison with certain emotional reactions to poverty and injustice.

Hatred was still the predominant emotion. On the eve of the revolution it had been the principal driving force behind the future rebels; throughout the struggle it had been responsible for the modest victories against the government. Before and during the war, anger played a role that was, if you wish, questionable; but it was not then useless or maleficent, as it turned out to be later. Targets of the postbellum wrath were—besides the machinery of government and the *agraristas*—the Mexican ecclesiastical hierarchy and anyone who had not supported the Cristero movement or who had obstructed it. Among the factors of this hatred were impotence, the bitterness of having been unable even to attack the enemy, let alone crush it, the helpless desire for vengeance, and a relentless fury. This rage led many men into pure iniquity, into "evil-heartedness," so that they were ready to lash out blindly. Others became merely irritable. Around 1930 there were plenty of vicious and rancorous people in San José. In general, they were not the old people or the more mature adults, but those of other age groups. This hatred was reinforced, accompanied, stimulated, and nourished by other violent passions that circulated through the village.

Once again, as in the prewar years, this hatred was a result not only of misery and injustice, but also of humiliation. The ex-Cristeros and their sympathizers felt doubly humiliated. They felt that the church authorities had laughed at them, and had not properly appreciated their sacrifice. Perhaps the behavior of Bishops Pascual Díaz and Ruiz y Flores, who had delivered them to their enemies tied hand and foot, had saddened and disappointed them most. The fiery Cristero Don Leopoldo Gálvez, the "Padre Chiquito," composed his "Great Offertory of Opinions." He searched in vain for a Catholic association that would pay to have it published. But no one wanted to hear his grievances, expressed in such terms as "The Mexican people have now indeed been humiliated. . . . I do not understand how the bishops had the heart to betray their children to their executioners without a second thought. . . . Why was Catholic worship suspended three years ago . . . if it was to be resumed under the same unacceptable conditions? . . . Did the heroic efforts of thousands and thousands of humble Christians . . . with weapons in their hands, mean nothing? Or is it that the common people were not intended to have figs and apples—only prickly pears and magueys? . . . Since not everybody was man enough to take up arms in the name of God, . . . God has humiliated us by ordering us to bend our necks under the yoke." Like the "Padre Chiquito," his neighbors and comrades in arms felt that they, too, had been humiliated—but they did not say so as openly.

Poverty, humiliation, and injustice produce fear and suspicion. The ex-Cristeros felt persecuted. "Many men have lost their lives in a mysterious fashion since the amnesty." "In Cojumatlán there is not a single ex-Cristero alive." "They will get us all in the end." Each of the survivors saw danger on every street corner, a man lying in wait to murder him in cold blood. Overcome by fear, many broke and ran. They saw no way out but to flee from their persecutors, and they could find no better hiding place than the cities. From 1930 to 1932 they went to Mexico City to lose themselves in the crowd. There was danger there, too, of course; ex-Cristeros were being slaughtered everywhere. The bad thing, the really bad thing was that this fear not only turned men into fugitives, but also turned the trusting village of San José into a nest of suspicion and a web of deceit.

Not only those who ran away, but also those who remained were suspicious. Needless to say, they had lost faith in the government long before, and after the Cristero revolution they no longer trusted the bishops, who "came out *con una y un pedazo, con arreglos a medias,*" as the "Padre Chiquito" said. In fact, the mistrust had extended to include all one's neighbors. Everyone was afraid to trust anyone else. The sin of suspicion took up residence in the hearts of most San Joséans, perhaps in the corners once occupied by love, perhaps in the little gardens where truth once grew. People were still saying that it was good always to speak the truth; but now they said it to protect themselves from the deceit of others, or to deceive others by making them believe that they were telling the truth. It was a climate of deception, a vast network of lies, and, at best, a conspiracy of whispers. If anyone had asked them why they had this ridiculous persecution complex, they would have replied: "The children of darkness are wiser than the children of light." . . .

By 1932 San José had inhabitants to spare—more than at any other time in its history. The destruction of the village had been like a good pruning. From zero (in 1927, when there had not been a single resident or an intact house) the town grew in a year and a half to 1,600 people (or 1,485, according to the national census of 1930), living in two hundred ruined dwellings in the process of reconstruction. After their exile and the Cristero rebellion the people who had lived on ranches tended to move into town. The rural population was only two-thirds of what it had been in 1921. The *tenencia* as a whole showed a considerable loss—490 inhabitants, according to the census, and a few more by other estimates. Many never returned after the revolution, and others lost their lives through war or disease. In short, the village residents increased by 55 percent, the rural settlements showed a population loss of 42 percent, and the area as a whole lost 15 percent of its inhabitants during the nine years between 1921 and 1930. The population of the *tenencia* was the same as it had been in 1890—numerically, if not structurally.

In 1930, females accounted for 53 percent of the inhabitants within the entire *tenencia*, and for nearly 60 percent in San José itself. Half were under fifteen, and about 7 percent were over sixty. There was a shortage of adolescents and young men—a shortage that had little effect on farming activities, and none at all on sexual ones. The birth rate, still taken care of by Doña Trina Lara, reached forty-four per thousand. Married couples were furiously engaged in making up for the lives lost during the war years. In addition to Don Juan Chávez, those dedicated to combating mortality now included Anatolio Partida (who had come back from his Cristero career with the prestige of a surgeon who had specialized in extracting bullets and setting broken limbs) and Don David Sánchez (who had returned from the United States with a general practitioner's talents, without ever having studied medicine). These three cornered the patient market; very few people could afford the luxury of bringing Dr. Sahagún from Sahuayo, or Dr. Maciel from Jiquilpan. Many resigned themselves to home remedies or to the herbs prescribed by popular tradition.

16

WHITE GUARDS

Gregorio López y Fuentes

In 1935 Gregorio López y Fuentes published what was to become Mexico's best-known and most influential novel, El Indio. It was awarded the National Prize of Literature, the first such award to be made in Mexico. It assured the novel a place in the history of Mexican literature akin to that of Azuela's The Underdogs *(see Reading 10) and Martín Luis Guzmán's* The Eagle and the Serpent. *Unlike López y Fuentes's earlier works that treated the Revolution itself (e.g.,* Campamento, 1931; Tierra, 1932), *this novel dealt with the problem of the Indian in a nonidealized, realistic way.* El Indio *reflects the indigenism, Indianism, and Indian nationalism of the 1930s. The values are traditional, rural, pagan, and Indian; not modern, urban, Christian, and European. Another indication is the author's interweaving of indigenous words, i.e., words from the Nahuatl language of the ancient Aztecs, with Spanish words. Indigenism was an idea that was an important part of the political and economic programs of the Cárdenas administration, especially the national plan for agrarian reform.*

In this selection, López y Fuentes describes the peons of the rancherías *and their sometimes reluctant participation in land-reform schemes and electoral politics imposed from outside and above the community. The* guardia blanca *or "white guards" were conservative peasants in the pay of the landlords. They specialized in the assassination of agrarian organizers and the destruction of crops and lands belonging to peasants bold enough to seek land grants under the agrarian laws.*

Everything that the leader had promised his people he got for them by tenacity and boldness. He relied most on the state deputy from his district who, as soon as he realized that the young Indian had the makings of an agitator, made a close friend of him. The deputy went with the leader and his delegation to the government palace, to the agrarian committee, and to every public man whose influence might be of advantage.

The leader had no sooner returned from his last trip to the city than instructions arrived to take his men to two rancherias near by, and there to organize the inhabitants for defense. A White Guard had just been formed to reoccupy the land that until a short time ago had belonged to the hacendado and had now been broken up according to the agrarian policy of the new government.

The defenders started eagerly, hoping for a chance to try out their newly acquired arms. If only they could have had them when the strangers outraged the girl and tormented the guide who took them to the hills in search of the mine and medicinal plants! All three adventurers would have been left in the canyon, not just one.

Now they were men: that is what a gun and authority will do. They went along jauntily, and when they met whites on the highway they looked them in the eye. Even the vehicles, which used to endanger their lives and cover them with dust, were now careful to slow down; the weapons were a warning. The troop, which included all the able-bodied men of the rancheria, was impressive. The Indians gave yells of pure savage joy. A few drinks at a roadside stand excited them more and more.

The other rancheria received them with enthusiasm. That same afternoon there was a meeting. Their young leader announced that he bore written orders from higher up; he expressed his friendship and loyalty for the deputy; and then asked for a detailed account of the quarrel.

It seemed that the inhabitants of this rancheria, who had been accustomed to working on certain haciendas, had occupied the land as he had told them to do. Then they had wanted other ground which they thought was better; and then the landowner had threatened them with his White Guard. They were ready to defend themselves, they added, but they had no guns. . . .

The old men and the leader talked things over. After that he said that at dawn he would give them the land himself. There was a big feast and a dance in his honor that night. They entertained him as the deputy himself had been entertained when he visited the rancheria.

At dawn the Indians began to come down from the hills, toward the valley. They came down as they had in other times, on their way to the river, to fish, or to search for wild fruits. But then they had carried net and spear; now it was rifle and machete. When they came to the hacienda, they cut the fence wires, made openings as boundary markers, and took possession. Just then a group of armed men appeared. It was the White Guard.

The shooting lasted twenty minutes. The natives and their attackers, shielded by tree trunks, had only two casualties. Both bands retreated cautiously, carrying their dead on improvised stretchers. The struggle had now actually begun. At a great mass meeting that night, the Indians decided to solicit more arms, and to ask the higher-ups—at least the deputy—for more positive instructions.

Then the economic problem came up; trips to the city cost money. The leader levied a quota on each head of a family. Some objected that the struggle was unnecessary, that they had enough with the lands already obtained. But the leader was upheld; he said that it was not just a matter of lands any more, but of principle. And he left, taking a large delegation along.

With the committee went Indians bearing presents for the powerful political supporters of the leader: one carried a big-crested turkey for three days to be given to his honor the deputy; another had fat hens for his honor the governor; the rest brought choice maize and new beans for other influential gentlemen.

In the old days, these same presents used to go to the local boss and the lawyer.

The landlord also, they heard later, went to the city to defend his rights. There being two different versions of what had happened, the authorities said that the case would be carefully investigated. The officials seemed to be sick and tired of conflicts like this. The deputy promised the committee to keep after the matter; and, in return, the leader would continue controlling the rancherias: the elections were approaching, and the deputy wanted a seat in the national congress.

Within two weeks orders came to organize all the people. The deputy planned to hold a great demonstration at the district seat to show his vast popularity, his identification with the humble, and to launch his electoral campaign. In the same letter the deputy said to the Indian leader that, considering his many qualities, he had taken the liberty of putting him on the ticket as his alternate.

With such prospects, the leader redoubled his activities. He told his people that this mere possibility was already a promise of betterment for all: to have a political representative of their own race. So now none of them would dream of refusing any commission, no matter how dangerous.

Indians converged on the town from all the sierras on the day of the demonstration. The roads were white with palm hats. They crossed the valley. They filled the streets. The crowd went through the middle of the town toward the other side, where the deputy, candidate for a seat in the federal assembly, was welcomed with fireworks and a blaring band.

The rival candidate, who had also organized a demonstration but could count only on the townspeople and some from the haciendas, had to retreat to the city hall. The first orator to address the throng was the Indian leader, who stood with the deputy at his right. He made a long speech in the tongue of his people: land, food, arms, agricultural implements, credit, et cetera.

A considerable number of the demonstrators were drunk by the afternoon, and the town looked as if it had been occupied by an army. The houses of the people supposed to be the leading citizens stayed closed. The multitude saw the deputy off, and left in an uproar.

Wherever the trails forked groups split off toward their own villages. Back in the rancheria, the leader frankly told his men, before they scattered, that his friend, the deputy, needed money to carry on his campaign; and that every head of a family would have to contribute his share.

The news alarmed them: the leader was notified that the land-owner's White Guard, in combination with the authorities of the town, intended to take the rancheria by surprise, burn the houses, and kill the new politician, who was now regarded as a real menace, in view of the demonstration of strength on the day of the parade through the streets.

The first step was to call a meeting. The leader said that the advantages they had gained had angered the old bosses; and that he was in the most dangerous position, as they intended to kill him; but he was always ready to sacrifice himself for his people — a phrase he had picked up faithfully from the deputy — and that now was the time when they all, with no exception whatsoever, must help to the utmost. He ended saying how much he regretted having to ask for more money to buy ammunition in order to be ready for a real battle.

The rancheria was transformed into an armed camp. Rock barricades, like trenches, were raised at the entrance. Advance outposts, also protected by stone walls, were put at strategic points on the roads, and those who had firearms were stationed there. The cripple, being insignificant, was sent down to watch from the bushes at the edge of the highway, and signal if the enemy approached. A lookout, who was on a ledge like a balcony at the highest part of the sierra, would pick up the signal.

Couriers went out daily in different directions: messages for concentration, orders, counter-orders, letters to the deputy, protests to the authorities. . . . Actually there were two fronts: the war on the White Guard, and the electoral campaign.

The *huehues*, spokesmen for caution, but also for weakness, advised flight as always: to take, as in other times of panic, the most tangled trails; seek safety in the ancient shelter of a cave or a hut deep in the forest. But the leader had his way.

In the end, word came that the White Guard had been notified from very high up, that in case of any more bloodshed, they would be held responsible, since they were attempting to undermine the strength of one of the candidates in the primaries. Besides which, it was already known that they had been the aggressors in the last encounter.

The essential idea of giving land to the majority, in order to help them economically, was being pushed to the background by politics. Long cordons of workers, native and mestizo, traveled all the roads, taken back and forth by leaders to show their strength to the politicians still higher up.

A whole pyramiding of interests: comings and goings of peasants to the meetings prior to the general elections; pilgrimages in support of the candidate for governor; fields abandoned because it was necessary to go to the seat of the district and give the candidate for deputy a rousing welcome; concentrations to defend the cause of the municipal president; groups supporting an alderman; committees to ask for another agrarian delegate; a trip to keep the precinct judge from being removed. . . . And, back of the peasants, the leaders driving the flock.

In the conflict of so many interests, a new style of attack arose: the ambush. The rancheria would hear every day of bloody and unpunished assaults: a volley from the forest, to obliterate an official, a landowner, or an Indian.

On election day, when long lines of Indians went through the fields on their way to town, the old men, as they passed the best lands, lamented not having had time to clear them, let alone to sow. The words *cintli* and *etl*, the maize and the bean, were pronounced with a certain fear: the traditional fear of a people that has suffered hunger.

17

STRIKES AND STRIKERS

Vicente Lombardo Toledano

Vicente Lombardo Toledano (1894 – 1968), born and raised in Puebla and educated in Mexico City at the National Preparatory School and the National University, was, after 1920, a leading figure in the political life of the emerging Mexican nation. His lengthy career included college teaching and administration, journalism, and public service as a governor of Puebla, alderman in Mexico City, and deputy to Congress. He was a key figure in the founding and organizing of the Party of the Mexican Revolution (PRM) in 1938. Lombardo is best known for his activity as a union activist and leader. In 1933 he organized the General Confederation of Workers and Peasants (CGOCM), and later, in 1936 after the dissolution of the CGOCM, he established a new union called the Confederation of the Workers of Mexico (CTM).

As a result of his college education, Lombardo considered himself to be a Marxist socialist. His Marxism was reflected in his actions and thoughts in 1933 when he first organized the CGOCM. At that time Lombardo hoped to unify Mexican labor into a single confederation that would be independent of state control, democratic in its procedures, revolutionary in orientation, and militant in its struggle with the capitalist class. He subscribed to Lenin's view that strikes were a "school of war" that resulted in the unmasking of paternalistic capitalists and the capitalist state.

After the CGOCM was formed, strikes became a common tactic for workers in Mexico. The year 1934 witnessed much labor unrest. In 1935 the number of strikes increased threefold over that of the previous year, with a tenfold increase in the number of strikers. The apex of Lombardo's career came in 1936 when the CTM was formed. With government backing, Lombardo was able to persuade thousands of workers to join unions and act together under the state-sponsored CTM. The electricians' strike of 1936 and the oil workers' movement in 1937 set the stage for the oil expropriation of 1938. (See Reading 18.)

Reproduced by permission from James W. Wilkie and Edna Monzón de Wilkie, *México visto en el siglo xx* (Mexico, D.F.: Instituto Mexicano de Investigaciones Económicas, 1969), pp. 311 – 13. Translated by W. Dirk Raat.

In the following interview, Lombardo describes to oral historians James and Edna Wilkie the conditions that gave rise to strikes in the 1920s and 1930s. He discusses the role of strikers and the CTM and the tactics of the leaders during the 1936 electricians' strike. He concludes by making brief mention of the 1937 oil industry strike and repeating his reasons as to how and when strikes can bring gains to the worker.

It is interesting to compare the ideas expressed by Lombardo in this 1960s interview with his earlier ideas outlined above. Note Lombardo's close association with government leaders, especially Lázaro Cárdenas, and his adoration of Alvaro Obregón. He appears to be suggesting that strikes can succeed only when workers form a partnership with the state.

It should be remembered that during World War II Mexican politics and politicians (including Lombardo) shifted away from the Marxian socialism of the 1920s and 1930s. During the war years, for example, Lombardo virtually prohibited CTM members from exercising their right to strike lest they jeopardize national security and the Allied war effort. Lombardo's career then reflects a major trend in the history of trade unionism in Mexico, the cooptation of autonomous unions by the state.

There are basically two reasons or conditions that explain the occurrence of strikes. The first is insufficient salaries, coupled with a decreasing purchasing power of the peso. The second relates to those times when a change in government presents the worker with a new opportunity for action. The workers, sensing and hoping that the incoming governmental leaders will be sympathetic to them, will take advantage of a change in regimes to make demands when the government, preoccupied with the problems of transition, cannot repress them with an iron hand.

It is quite understandable that during the years from 1920 to 1922 there would have been many strikes in Mexico. One can see that this period corresponds to the first implementation of the Constitution of 1917. General Alvaro Obregón . . . is for me the ultimate governmental leader; it was he who initiated and put into practice the principles and norms of the Revolution. It was only natural to believe that with his arrival in the office of the presidency the workers' confidence in his new government would be justified; Obregón would not only comply with the promises of the revolutionary movement, but would also put into effect the mandates of Mexico's new Magna Charta.

After this period the number of strikes continued to increase. In 1934 Cárdenas came to power, [and] a series of very important strikes took place. For what reason? you ask. Because when General Obregón was assassinated in 1928, the Mexican people lost six years of his potential leadership. There was a six-year gap that had to be filled by provisional presidents: Portes Gil, Ortiz Rubio, and Abelardo L. Rodríguez. But during the years of Abelardo L. Rodríguez, and even those of Ortiz Rubio, the government did not show any sympathy for the working class.... Abelardo L. Rodríguez had a very special concept of workers' rights. He affirmed that strikes were acceptable only during periods of economic tranquility, and that because we were then living in an era of prolonged economic crisis, which began in 1929–30 and embraced the entire world, a government preoccupied with crisis could not look with sympathy upon strikers' movements.

When Cárdenas came to power and even before, during his election campaign, the working class was mobilized, hoping that with his electoral victory he would be able to keep the promises he had made to the working class, and that is what happened. The most important strikes that have occurred in Mexico from 1910 until today were during the administration of Cárdenas. Why? In the first place, because the working class was unified. We formed the CTM in the year 1936. In the second place, we gave to the CTM a spirit of combat and struggle that it had not had before. And third, we unified the working class by creating labor unions in the most important industrial branches of the country: utilities, petroleum, and others.

The first strike really to attract attention in Mexico was the electricians' strike. This was started during the Cárdenas period by workers in the Mexican Syndicate of Electricians (Sindicato Mexicano de Electricistas). For the first time in my memory, Mexico remained without lights for almost a week. All electrical services were suspended, with the exception of emergency services such as pumping drinking water or hospital services. The strike was well prepared. The company argued that it did not have the resources to accept the demands of the workers, but we demonstrated that the company had recovered its invested capital many times over and had huge earnings. The movement was carefully planned, not only in the sense of withholding services, but also with one eye on the public reaction. It must be remembered that a suspension of public services can hurt the people if they are deprived of vital services. Therefore we conducted a major campaign among the citizens of the Federal District. We demonstrated that the company had an unjust attitude, and in a certain way was actually fighting against the rights of the workers as guaranteed in the Constitution of the country. In addition, when the electricians went out on strike, all of the factories were forced to shut down, resulting in the solidarity of all workers.

During the strike there developed a strong sympathy on the part of the public for the cause of the electrical workers. I remember that our preparation was solid, that I called a meeting of all the foreigners who happened to be in Mexico City at the time — North American tourists for the most part — in order to explain that we were going to suspend electrical services. This happened in a movie theater on Madero Avenue. There were more than three hundred North Americans, and we explained everything to them. We showed them the company books, their earnings, and the way the company recovered its capital. And even from the North Americans we received moral support.

Never before had the electrical services of the capital of the republic been suspended, and General Cárdenas was, of course, a little disturbed, and so I suggested to him the following: "Go away from Mexico City and leave us alone here, because otherwise you are going to receive a lot of pressure from all sides." And I was right. Then when we were left alone we resolved the conflict, obligating the company to accept the demands of the workers.

The other important strike, as you know, occurred in the oil industry in 1937. For more than half a year we negotiated with representatives of the Royal Dutch Shell Company and the North American companies. We talked until it was no longer possible to arrive at an agreement, and then a strike broke out. This strike was also carefully planned; not only had we done our research and had documents and proofs of excess profit taking, but also the strike received solid support from workers from all over the country and from people representing many sectors of Mexican society.

It needs to be said, then, that strikes produce results, as I said before, when there are unsatisfied demands and when, at the same time, the workers have confidence in the government because it plans to comply with the law. . . .

18

THE MEXICAN REACTION TO THE OIL EXPROPRIATION

Josephus Daniels

In 1933 Josephus Daniels (1862–1948), a newspaper editor from North Carolina and former secretary of the navy during the Woodrow Wilson administration, was appointed by President Franklin D. Roosevelt ambassador from the United States to the Republic of Mexico. Daniels's friendship with Roosevelt dated back to the time when Roosevelt worked with him in the navy department as assistant secretary. Daniels, a competent and intelligent public servant, served as ambassador to Mexico for nine years, from 1933 to 1941. His earlier friendship with Roosevelt continued throughout the 1930s, with Daniels making Roosevelt's "Good Neighbor" policy his personal mission. On more than one occasion he would bypass Cordell Hull, Sumner Welles, and the State Department to bring Mexican affairs directly to the attention of the president. During the period of the oil expropriation, Daniels almost singlehandedly prevented a diplomatic rupture between the two countries.

In the following selection from his autobiography, Shirt-Sleeve Diplomat, *Daniels describes the Mexican reaction to the oil expropriation of March 18, 1938. Note how the occasion of the expropriation became a kind of national religious cause and a day of celebration for Mexicans (a national holiday and fiesta). The reader should especially pay attention to the role of women. Note also the themes of economic warfare, which include boycotts and a discontinuance of silver purchases, and a split among American investors in Mexico concerning the wisdom of United States policy. Finally, Daniels suggests that fear of German intervention, as personified in the William Rhodes Davis matter, was a major factor affecting the change in the United States position.*

Reprinted from *Shirt-Sleeve Diplomat* by Josephus Daniels, pp. 246–54. Copyright 1947 The University of North Carolina Press. Used with permission of the publisher.

With the expropriation of foreign oil properties, a wave of delirious enthusiasm swept over Mexico, heightened by bitter denunciations from other countries, as the people felt that a day of deliverance had come. On March 22, upon the call of the Confederation of Mexican Workers, some two hundred thousand people passed in compact files before the National Palace acclaiming President Cárdenas and carrying banners such as: "They shall not scoff at Mexican laws." Old inhabitants said there had never been such manifestations of the unity of the Mexican people in the history of Mexico as followed the appeals to the people to uphold the Constitution and the sovereignty of Mexico. It was shared by people who lost sight of oil in their belief that Mexicans must present a united and solid front.

Closing his address to the multitude, Cárdenas told labor men they deserved the support of their government, and counselled them to discipline their ranks, increase production, and avoid insolent attacks—"to prove there is a real, individual liberty justly demanded by the Mexican people."

Many thousands of students in the Mexican University organized an enthusiastic parade. Its Rector, speaking to President Cárdenas, said: "The University offers you its solid support in this moment when the fatherland requires the unity of its sons. It comes to offer the youth of Mexico to be with you as you are with the honor of Mexico."

Catholics Raise Funds

Noticeable was the enthusiasm of Catholics, many of whom had been critical of the Cárdenas government, in raising funds to support his expropriation move. On Sunday, April 30, the Archbishop of Guadalajara advised from the pulpit that it was a "patriotic duty to contribute to this national fund." It was announced (April 3) that Archbishop Martínez had promised a "letter on the oil controversy during Holy Week." On May 3, a circular, approved by archbishops and bishops, was published, exhorting Catholics to send contributions. All over the country in churches collections were taken to help pay for the seized oil properties.

Women Make Expropriation a "National Religion"

Women in Mexico have generally followed an old slogan: "The place of woman is in the home." That was the attitude of women in the early part of April, 1938. Then, as by a miracle, suddenly they became vocal in their patriotism. Cárdenas had made approval of the expropriation of oil a sort of national religion. The people believed—and had grounds for their opinion—that their patrimony had been given for a song to foreigners who refused to pay living wages to the men who worked in the oil fields. When the men gathered by the hundred thousands to show allegiance to Cárdenas after the oil expropriation, the women poured out of their homes by the thousands to voice their ardent support of the leaders who had somehow made the people feel that the oil exploiters were the enemies of their country. What could they do? President Cárdenas had given his word to me on the day after the expropriation that payment would be made. The people were zealous to see that his pledge was kept. What could the women do? Pitifully little toward the millions needed, but all Mexico in a day was full of the spirit of the widow who gave her mite and was commended, having given her all as giving "more than all the rest."

Something the like of which has rarely been seen in any country occurred on the twelfth day of April. By the thousands, women crowded the Zócalo and other parks and in companies marched to the Palace of Fine Arts to give of their all to the call of their country's honor. It was a scene never to be forgotten. Led by Señora Amalia Solórzano de Cárdenas, the president's young and handsome wife, old and young, well-to-do and poor—mainly the latter—as at a religious festival gathered to make, what was to many, an unheard-of sacrifice. They took off wedding rings, bracelets, earrings, and put them, as it seemed to them, on a national altar. All day long, until the receptacles were full and running over, these Mexican women gave and gave. When night came crowds still waited to deposit their offerings, which comprised everything from gold and silver to animals and corn.

What was the value in money of the outpouring of possessions to meet the goal of millions of pesos? Pitiably small—not more than 100,000 pesos—little to pay millions—but the outpouring of the women, stripping themselves of what was dear to them, was the result of a great fervor of patriotism the like of which I had never seen or dreamed. It was of little value for the goal. It was inestimable in cementing the spirit of Mexico, where there was a feeling that the Cárdenas move was the symbol of national unity.

American Concerns Boycott Mexican Oil-Producing Organizations

Two American acts after expropriation especially offended Mexicans. In this situation in which all indignation was not on either side of the border, these acts seemed items of tough economic pressure from north of the Rio Grande.

Not long after the Mexican government expropriated the oil properties, the government needed to buy pumps and parts for machines made in the United States to operate effectively. Their order was refused. I was told of the boycott, as I wrote home (October 29, 1938):

> Thursday, when I was at the Foreign Office, Mr. Beteta, the Undersecretary, told me that he was very much concerned. The night before he had attended a meeting with reference to the petroleum situation, and the head of the government organization said he had sent orders to a number of manufacturers in the United States who had been furnishing pumps and all sorts of machines and parts to the Standard Oil and other companies which had been operating in the Federal Petroleum District; but that the American companies sent the money back and would not fill the orders. They regard this as a boycott by American manufacturers in retaliation for the government's expropriation of the oil fields. Beteta said that the government had expropriated the oil fields for good and sufficient reasons and intended to pay for them; but they would not be returned. He said: "I am chiefly concerned because if United States manufacturers and dealers refuse to sell us the essentials for carrying on the oil work, they throw us into the arms of Germany, where we can swap oil for this machinery, etc., that we need."
>
> He felt very strongly about it, and said he would send me a list of the orders which had been rejected. "If we were asking any favors," he said, "as to credits, etc., we would not feel bad about it — but when we offer the cash and then the manufacturers who have the material for sale reject the orders, it looks as if the oil companies are dominating to such an extent that the manu-

facturers will sell to everybody in the world except Mexico." He added: "It seems that your country objects to our selling oil to Germany, Italy, and Japan; but the Standard Oil is selling all the time to these countries without any protest and with the consent of the government. We wish very much we could sell our oil to democratic countries; we have no sympathy with the totalitarian policies of Italy and Germany; but if the United States and England boycott us we shall have no alternative but to trade where we can.

Mexicans Incensed at Blow to Silver

The sudden discontinuance of buying Mexican silver by the United States a few days after the oil expropriation was received by Mexicans as a punishment for the expropriation and as a plain threat: "Return the oil properties or take the consequences."

It was a severe blow to the Mexican treasury, for the silver export tax was sorely needed, and at the time I wrote Washington that the question of purchasing silver should be considered on its own merits and should certainly not be made to seem a device for punishment.

In 1933 Mexico was receiving 26 cents per ounce for its silver and in 1933–34 exported 95 million ounces in various forms for which it received 24 million dollars. Later (in 1938) the prevailing price reached 70 cents, which for the full production of the mines would have brought the mine owners 66 million dollars, with increased taxes to the treasury.

The effect of stoppage was serious because 100,000 heads of families were employed in silver mines; the government received 10 percent of its revenue from it; the National Railways received 17 percent of its income from that source; and silver provided the major source of foreign exchange. As against silver mining giving employment to 100,000 heads of families, the oil industry employed only 16,000.

Not only were officials of the Mexican government indignant at the body blow, but the silver mine owners, mostly Americans, who felt they were being made to suffer for the deeds of the oil companies, were also infuriated. They owned 80 percent of the Mexican mining industry which spent millions in the United States for mining equipment.

I talked to some silver mine owners who felt that they were being made the goat. They said it would deny many workers employment and would distress all the mining districts. The protests of the American mine owners were carried to Washington and the discontinuance of the purchase of Mexican silver was of short duration. The effort of the stoppage increased the determination of Mexicans not to be influenced by any outside pressure. However, one silver mine operator had a different opinion, about which I wrote home (November 19, 1938):

> This is a queer world. Mr. and Mrs. Lockett were in Pachuca last week and were entertained at luncheon by Mr. Kuryla, of the Real del Monte mine. When he returned Mr. Lockett told me that he had never in his life heard people so violent in their denunciation of President Roosevelt. Mr. Lockett told Mr. Kuryla that if anybody in the world ought to be grateful to President Roosevelt it was the silver mine owners. Lockett told him: "Before Roosevelt began to buy silver you were getting 32 cents. Now you are getting 42 cents and at one time you were getting over 50 cents. You are enjoying the best subsidy of any people in the world and yet you are more against his policy than anybody else. Why is it?" Of course there was no answer. When people are very partisan in their politics they are not very reasonable, as we have found out at home as well as in other countries.
>
> The last time I saw Mr. Kuryla he asked me what I thought was going to be the future policy about silver in the United States. I told him I thought the government would continue to buy silver, but that whether they would continue to buy except from mines in the United States I did not know; that there was a strong sentiment against buying it from Mexico, Canada and other countries. I told him I did not know whether that would materialize but that he knew as well as I did that Americans (in fact 90 percent of the mines in Mexico are owned by Americans) get the cream of the money paid from the United States Treasury for silver, though of course Mexico was benefited because the mines gave employment to thousands of workmen and brought taxes into the treasury.
>
> Mr. Kuryla said to me: "Though I am a silver miner, I am troubled about silver in the future, because all of this silver is being put into the ground in the United States and not used. My experience in life and my reading show that when there is no use for any product it loses its value and as years go by and the millions of pounds of silver are dumped in the ground and

locked up and soldiers are engaged to protect it, it loses its value.
Is that to be the future of silver?"

In every drama there must be a heavy villain, just as they say
that in all successful business enterprises there must be a wicked
partner and in politics a crooked politician. Before the oil expropriation, the Mexicans named the foreign oil magnates as the heavy
villains, while the oil men gave that place in the case to Cárdenas
and Toledano, and staged William Rhodes Davis as accessory after
the fact. Davis appeared on the scene not long after the expropriation. Little was known of him except that he had roamed the world
on what he thought would be a sea of oil. He loomed upon the
center of the stage, taking two parts: to the big oil companies, after
expropriation, he was the heaviest of heavy villains; to the
Cárdenas administration, the deliverer in the time of need. Out of
resentment for the expropriation and the hope that Mexican operations would fail, markets for Mexican oil in the United States and in
Britain suddenly dried up. Without markets the Mexicans would be
drowned in their oil, and the expropriation would fail. Some people
regarded Davis as a Mulberry Sellers; others, as a rich oil promoter
who would furnish needed markets for Mexican oil; and others as a
glad-hand Nazi agent or as a crook. He was a composite.

The Mexican government had no market for its flowing oil
except for domestic consumption and the dribbles they could sell in
such Pan American countries as were not under obligation to buy
from the old oil companies. In that critical situation Davis dropped
down as if from the skies, as the Mexican oil administration saw it.
But, to the old oil companies, he came as a devil from other regions.
He had been an oil operator in England until, having clashed with
the big oil companies, he lost out. Then he went to Germany. The
First National Bank of Boston backed Davis to use blocked markets,
which the bank had in a German account to help build a refinery.
Germany was in desperate need of oil, and so was Italy. The
Mexican government oil concerns were in sore need of a purchaser
for their surplus of oil. In that situation Davis arrived in Mexico and
quickly made arrangements to buy Mexican oil for Germany At
once the oil interests of Britain and the United States said that Davis
was a Nazi agent and that if Mexico had dealings with him it would
demonstrate that it [Mexico] was a Nazi sympathizer and against
the countries which were at war with the Nazis and the Fascists. As

giving proof of this charge, Jean Schacht, son of Hitler's former head of the Reichsbank, Hjalmar Schacht, appeared in Mexico. He was seen much with Davis, though he asserted he came to Mexico on a pleasure trip.

The Mexicans welcomed any purchaser of their oil. They were ruined without an outlet for the supply. Davis made a contract to supply the Nazis with Mexican oil. Associated with Davis was Joachim Hertslet, who worked in engineering deals that made it possible for the Nazis to get oil out of Mexico. Long after, Marquis Childs wrote of seeing Davis in Mexico City at that time:

> When I saw Davis in the blue-and-gold presidential suite of the Hotel Reforma in Mexico City in 1938, he still talked of the far-reaching international trade he was directing. While he talked, telephone calls came from London, Hamburg and Washington.
>
> In reality he was a ruined man, intriguing with the evil force of nazism out of the bitterness of his resentment and frustration. And always he and his associates talked of how much more oil the Germans had got, in the years of preparation for conquest, from the big British and American combines than they got from Davis.

Was Davis a Nazi agent? He was shadowed by the British secret service in Bermuda and Portugal on his way to Berlin in 1939. Whether the British were trying to prevent Davis from buying oil from Mexico or suspected him to be in league with the Nazis is not known. It may have been both, but it has been stated that Davis arranged for the payment of a $5,000-radio-hook-up in 1940 when John L. Lewis delivered his bitter attack on Roosevelt and tried to get Labor to oppose Roosevelt's reelection that year. Davis did not use his own money, if at that time he had money to spare. And it is not known that Lewis was informed that friends of Davis paid the bill, though Drew Pearson has said that John L. Lewis complained to Assistant Secretary of State Berle because FBI men covered Davis's apartment in the Mayflower Hotel.

Many years afterward it was revealed in investigation by the United States Department of Justice that Davis was used by Foreign Minister Joachim von Ribbentrop in the Nazi organized effort to defeat President Roosevelt for reelection in 1940. The German Foreign Minister explained that it was "essential to defeat Roosevelt because he, more than any other American, was capable of making sweeping political decisions" that would not be pleasing to the Nazis. To this was added testimony that in 1939–40 the chief objective of the Nazis was to defeat President Roosevelt in 1940. In 1936 when Davis was trying to organize a big oil company, he was quoted as claiming to have "made available" $291,286 to an amount to elect Roosevelt and certain senators. If so, it was without the knowledge of the White House and if and when he sought White House favor, Davis got no recognition. Davis was also said to be trying to put on a three-cornered deal between Mexico, Germany, and the United States involving surplus cotton. No "pent-up Utica" contracted his soaring adventures.

Celebration of Anniversary of Expropriation

On the anniversary of the expropriation (March 18, 1939) two thousand people attended a banquet in the bull ring in celebration, and on Sunday seventy-five thousand people gathered in the Zócalo with banners, and heard speeches by President Cárdenas, syndicate workers, and others to celebrate "the historic decree." The ringing of the Hidalgo bell was said to be the signal for throwing off the foreign yoke. The syndicate workers and Señor Rodríguez, president of the Mexican Revolutionary party, created great enthusiasm by their attacks on imperialistic policies. President Cárdenas's speech was mild in comparison, but he upheld the course he had pursued, said that no backward step would be made, and indicated that the negotiations going on between him and Mr. Donald Richberg, attorney for the oil companies, would be successful, leaving operation in the hands of the government.

His speech was enthusiastically received, particularly when he denounced the oil companies for launching a fiery campaign through the foreign press in an endeavor "to crack the domestic economy." He defended "the reincorporation of the oil subsoil rights to the hands of the nation." He declared that the oil companies had "made it a practise to obstruct the enforcement of the most fundamental laws by way of diplomatic coercion or mercenary revolt." He declared, "The potential wealth of Mexico, purely hard Indian labor, exemption from taxes, economic privileges and tolerances on the part of government constitute the essential figures of the great prosperity of the petroleum industry in Mexico."

At the same time flags were flown on the towers of the Cathedral which faces one side of the Zócalo. On one of the towers was a large Mexican flag with the eagle and snake. On the other tower was a great flag of the Mexican Revolutionary party, and high above all was a banner reading: "The PRM extends greetings to President Lázaro Cárdenas, Redeemer of Economic Independence." I do not recall ever before seeing a political banner on the Cathedral.

19

TARAHUMARA HERBS

Alfonso Reyes

The theme of indigenism (see Reading 16) is expressed in this poem entitled "Tarahumara Herbs" ("Yerbas del Tarahumara," 1935) by Alfonso Reyes (1889 – 1959), Mexico's great humanist, philosopher, man of letters, and prose stylist. Son of the porfirista general Bernardo Reyes, he spearheaded in 1909 a radical shift in Mexico's culture and philosophical orientation as a leading member of the antipositivist Ateneo de la Juventud. Combining Mexican nationalism with an appreciation for the Spanish Masters of the 1898 Generation (Miguel de Unamuno, José Ortega y Gasset, et al.), Reyes created universal works of art from native themes.

"Tarahumara Herbs" refers to the Tarahumara Indians, who live in the Copper Canyon country of Chihuahua in northern Mexico, and who are often seen by tourists and others on the streets of Chihuahua City. They are famous for their physical prowess, stamina, and ability to run long distances. They are especially important as survivors — people who in the face of "modernization" and the expansion of western civilization have been able to maintain an indigenous culture of pagan beliefs, herbal medicine, and a native diet of pinole, maize, and chicha beer. Indigenist writers tend to glorify the Indian past and culture, and are fond of contrasting Indian values with non-Indian ones. The reader should decide whether Reyes does this.

The Tarahumara Indians have come down,
sign of a bad year
and a poor harvest in the mountains.

Reprinted by permission from *An Anthology of Mexican Poetry*, edited by Octavio Paz and translated by Samuel Beckett (Bloomington: Indiana University Press, 1973), pp. 188–90.

Naked and tanned,
hard in their daubed lustrous skins,
blackened with wind and sun, they enliven
the streets of Chihuahua,
slow and suspicious,
all the springs of fear coiled,
like meek panthers.

Naked and tanned,
wild denizens of the snow,
they — for they thee and thou —
always answer thus the inevitable question:
"And is thy face not cold?"

A bad year in the mountains
when the heavy thaw of the peaks
drains down to the villages the drove
of human beasts, their bundles on their backs.

The people, seeing them, experience
that so magnanimous antipathy
for beauty unlike that to which they are used.

Into Catholics
by the New Spain missionaries they were turned
— these lion-hearted lambs.
And, without bread or wine,
they celebrate the Christian ceremony
with their chica beer and their pinole
which is a powder of universal flavour.

They drink spirits of maize and peyotl,
herb of portents,
symphony of positive esthetics
whereby into colours forms are changed;
and ample metaphysical ebriety
consoles them for their having to tread the earth,
which is, all said and done,
the common affliction of all humankind.
The finest Marathon runners in the world,
nourished on the bitter flesh of deer,
they will be first with the triumphant news
the day we leap the wall
of the five senses.

Sometimes they bring gold from their hidden mines
and all the livelong day they break the lumps,

squatting in the street,
exposed to the urbane envy of the whites.
Today they bring only herbs in their bundles,
herbs of healing they trade for a few nickels:
mint and cuscus and birthroot
that relieve unruly innards,
not to mention mouse-ear
for the evil known as "bile";
sumac and chuchupaste and hellebore
that restore the blood;
pinesap for contusions
and the herb that counters marsh fevers,
and viper's grass that is a cure for colds;
canna seeds strung in necklaces,
so efficacious in the case of spells;
and dragon's blood that tightens the gums
and binds fast the roots of loose teeth.

(Our Francisco Hernandez
—the Mexican Pliny of the Cinquecento—
acquired no fewer than one thousand two hundred
magic plants of the Indian pharmacopoeia.
Don Philip the Second,
though not a great botanist,
contrived to spend twenty thousand ducats
in order that this unique herbarium
might disappear beneath neglect and dust!
For we possess the Reverend Father Moxo's
assurance that this was not due to the fire
that in the seventeenth century occurred
in the Palace of the Escurial.)

With the silent patience of the ant
the Indians go gathering their herbs
in heaps upon the ground—
perfect in their natural natural science.

ART AND INDIGENISM

Diego Rivera. The Great Tenochtitlán. Ancient Indian Market. National Palace, Mexico City. Panorama Editorial.

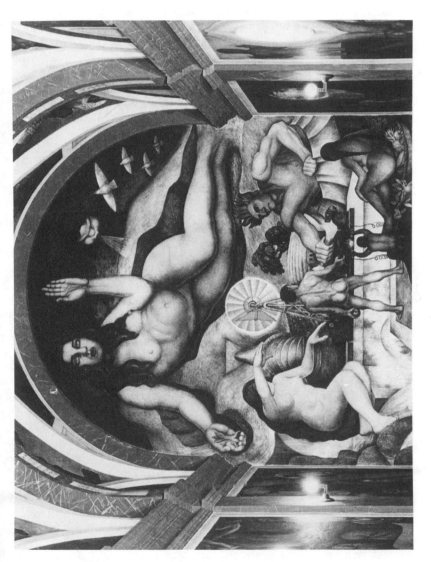

Diego Rivera. The Liberated Earth. Indian family in foreground, Earth goddess figure in background. University of Chapingo, State of Mexico. Panorama Editorial.

Not since the military uprising against Madero led by Victoriano Huerta in 1913 had there been anything that had damaged our image as much as Tlatelolco/October 2, that had so defiled us, that had so stunned us, that had filled our mouths with the taste of blood, the blood of our dead.

Isabel Sperry de Barranza, mother of a family from Elena Pointowska, *Massacre in Mexico*

PART IV
MEXICO SINCE CÁRDENAS

Visitors to Mexico in 1940 heard the rhetoric of revolution but saw few results. The country and the people looked much the same as they had three decades earlier. The countryside still offered the incongruity of natural beauty and human poverty. Mexicans remained Catholic, rural, and poor; Mexico comprised mestizo villages. Visitors saw little evidence because the Revolution combined sweeping idealism and small improvements for villages. The cataclysm of war shattered revolutionary visions after 1940.

World War II threatened world civilization; for Mexicans it meant tremendous profits in dollars for raw materials and manpower provided to the United States. Already committed to a slower pace in revolutionary programs by the selection of Manuel Avila Camacho as president in 1940, the ruling party recast its programs into industry development programs. Avila Camacho laid the groundwork, and Miguel Alemán molded the new Mexico. Above all, Alemán was a bureaucratic spokesman for business. He brought a change in mentality and style, ending the "revolution of small things" and launching the revolution of the grandiose. His concern for gross national product and gaudy public works stripped the Revolution of its essence. The official party was the mainspring of centralization, and shortly after the selection of Alemán, the party was reconstituted as the PRI, the Institutionalized Revolutionary Party. (For this development and a discussion of the PRI since its inception, see Reading 20.)

Gradually Mexicans began to recognize that the Revolution had disappeared into annual reports, government accounts, balance of payments, and, above all, averages. Few found comfort in the median increase in income, education, housing, and diet of the average Mexican. The suspicion grew that in real life this statistical improvement represented only mushrooming profits for the elite. The new rich, caricatured by Abel Quezada (Readings 21 and 22), raced fast cars around the capital, entertained in palatial houses in Lomas, dashed to weekend homes in Acapulco, and recited revolutionary rhetoric all the way to the bank.

The post-1940 regime moved to coopt the powerful interest groups that opposed it. The longstanding revolutionary program against the Church was suspended, and a rapproachement with the Church hierarchy was arranged. (See Reading 23.) Other interest groups soon fell under the sway of the regime, giving the PRI increased social control over dissenting factions. (See Reading 24.)

Mestizo Mexico huddled on society's edges. Here marginal men rejected this revolution for statistical phantoms. But without leaders or organization they could do little to protest. Then in 1959 the dizzy rate of inflation pushed them to desperation. These forgotten Mexicans challenged the government in a wave of strikes. President Adolfo López Mateos used troops to break demonstrations and the wartime antisocial disruption law to arrest leading labor leaders. Among the first to be imprisoned was the chief of the railroad workers, Demetrío Vallejo Martínez, and he was soon followed by the internationally famous muralist, Dávid Siqueiros. The government ended the radical movement in the countryside in May 1962 with a series of assassinations. Ruben Jaramillo, his wife, and his two sons were shot to death in 1962. When cooptation failed, the government rarely hesitated to use violent methods. (See Reading 25.)

The success of the PRI modernization programs earned Mexico the recognition of the industrial nations as it was named host of the 1968 Olympic Games. Just prior to the lighting of the Olympic torch, students demonstrated in Mexico City, raising questions about the integrity of the government and the nature of the Mexican Revolution. The president was determined to prevent any disruption of the Olympics; the result was a massacre at the Plaza of Three Cultures. (See Reading 25.) The world saw modern, peaceful, urban Mexico on color television. But the massacre lingered in Mexicans' minds; the episode brought them face to face with themselves.

Mexicans had to reflect on what the country had become. For workers, peasants, students, and intellectuals such as Octavio Paz, the massacre confirmed that the PRI had discarded the Revolution for profits. Other Mexicans suddenly grasped that glamorous statistics could disguise morbid reality. Modernization also meant low wages, zooming birth rates, burgeoning slums, increasing food imports, and stupefying pollution. (See Reading 26.) Even those who praised the government for its handling of the demonstrations received two jolts. First, the country faced overwhelming population problems—a staggering rate of birth, an even higher rate of urbanization, and a shortage of food; and second, and more serious to businessmen, the economic growth had begun to wither.

Mexico has yet to resolve either of these problems that became apparent after Tlatelolco.

Throughout the twentieth century, the United States has represented an enduring presence in Mexico. The different images of the United States held by distinctive groups in Mexico help explain the formulation of Mexican foreign policy and reveal conflicting attitudes toward modernization and progress. (See Reading 27.) There are many images of the United States because there are many segments of the Mexican society.

Mexicans today compose a cultural mosaic that portrays jet-set sophistication, centuries-old tradition, astonishing wealth, grinding poverty, and middle-class complacency. The Revolution appears in name only because it is over. For Mexicans to overcome modern problems they must discard the dead weight of a movement long past. This does not mean discarding the heritage, for while it lasted it was a glorious Revolution.

20

MEXICO SINCE CÁRDENAS

David G. LaFrance

In the decades since 1940, Mexican leaders and foreign observers have proclaimed the "Mexican miracle" of political stability, industrial growth, and beneficial urbanization. But David LaFrance, research professor in the department of history, Universidad Autónoma de Puebla, shows that these indicators measure only appearances. Stability did not provide democratic participation, industrialization did not yield widespread distribution of wealth, and urbanization did not mean that those who came to the city for a job actually got one. Urban migrants became firsthand witnesses to the labyrinthine bureaucracy that managed politics and the increasing disparity between the industrial rich and the marginal poor. Lofty statistics and stark, visible reality clashed when student demonstrations in 1968 challenged Mexico's "PRI-modern" society. Combat troops smashed the demonstrations in the massacre at the Plaza of the Three Cultures but provoked a general disillusionment with the government that remains today. Although LaFrance gives a grim account of Mexico since 1940, he concludes with an assessment of the regime's achievements. Most Mexicans are better off—in personal freedom, economic well-being, and broadbased opportunities—than their parents. Yet today most Mexicans do not measure their lives against the past, but compare them to other Mexicans and to what the ruling party has promised. The gap between increasing expectations and the actual satisfaction of need has, unfortunately, increased since 1970.

Historians, in order better to analyze and make sense out of the past, divide it into periods. These arbitrary divisions are based on any number of criteria, from presidential terms to revolutions. Accordingly, Mexico's recent history is often broken into time frames. One of these, the topic of this essay, begins in 1940 with the presidency of Manuel Avila Camacho and World War II and ends in 1982. In most respects, this chronological division is a justifiable one. Since the end of the presidency of Lázaro Cárdenas in 1940, Mexico has undergone a series of profound changes that have perhaps altered the country more than in any other period in its history save the first decades following the Spanish conquest in the early sixteenth century. It should be made clear, however, that these modifications did not begin in 1940. Indeed, they originated during the second half of the nineteenth century. In the post-1940 period, however, they accelerated and consolidated, resulting in great impact on the country.

Political centralization, economic development based on industrialization, and urbanization are the three most salient features of Mexican life during the past forty years. For most Mexicans these characteristics of their country's experience have been seen as positive, and to most they are still viewed in such a light. Government-imposed stability following the upheavals of the 1910 Revolution and its aftermath, the availability of a wide range of consumer goods, and the growth of large congested urban areas are generally viewed as necessary and correct steps in the process of creating a modern and prosperous nation. Such an outlook has come under increasing scrutiny in recent years, however, as the image of a Mexico with a limitless future has slowly become tarnished. This changing attitude, increasingly evident following the political movement of 1968 that ended in the massacre of Tlatelolco, has recently been reinforced by the most serious economic crisis since the Revolution. Again, Mexicans are being forced seriously to examine themselves and their institutions. Whether this process begun in 1968 will result in any significant changes in the nature of the political centralization, economic development, and urbanization that has taken place since Cárdenas remains to be seen. Nevertheless, the student of Mexico should realize that what the casual observer may perceive as a nation that is calm and prosperous is, underneath, one ill at ease.

Political Centralization

It took Mexico more than one hundred years following indepen- dence from Spain in 1821 to create a workable political system. Porfirio Díaz (1876–1911) went a long way toward centralizing the nation's political institutions during his long dictatorship. His heavy hand and exclusion of important sectors of the population from the system, however, undermined its legitimacy, resulting in the 1910 Revolution. In the aftermath of the violence of the decade from 1910 to 1920, revolutionary leaders turned presidents — Alvaro Obregón and Plutaro Elías Calles — slowly pieced together a viable system. Rhetorically, the new creation was designed to carry on the ideals and programs of the Revolution; in reality, its principal aim was to consolidate the political power of this new revolutionary elite.

In 1929 Calles formed the National Revolutionary Party (PNR). President Cárdenas then changed the party's name to the Party of the Mexican Revolution (PRM) in 1938 and strengthened it by incorporating into its ranks confederations of laborers and peasants. Soon after, a mostly middle-class group, including bureaucrats and the military, was added to the party. Resting on its broad-based institutional support, its identification with the Revolution and therefore the nation, and a sophisticated ability to coopt opponents (see Reading 24), the party soon became the only viable show in town. By 1946, when President Miguel Alemán again changed the party's name to the Institutional Revolutionary Party (PRI), the opposition held only a handful of elected offices in the whole country. The inclusion of the term *institutional* in the party's new name was exceedingly appropriate.

While the PRI serves as the political mobilizer and base for government candidates, the most powerful element in this highly integrated system is the national executive, especially the president. Although few of the presidents since 1940 stand out as individuals, the influence they wield over the political machine they have helped to create and ultimately the nation they lead is overwhelming. In fact, the president is the keystone of the system, since he is head of both the party and the government. Despite the facade of democratic institutions such as parties, elections, and a constitution, Mexico is really a dictatorship of the presidency, albeit one that rotates every six years. There is little of significance that occurs throughout the political system that has not been initiated or does not have the approval of the president. The national congress, for example, seldom acts on legislation that has not been proposed first by the executive, and it always rubber-stamps the president's wishes. He enjoys the power to name and remove officeholders and, as a last resort, has the army and police forces at his disposal as well as the right to suspend constitutional guarantees (with congressional approval). Indeed, so intimidating is the presidency that the press dares not directly criticize the man. (It should be noted that the government controls the distribution of newsprint, upon which the press is dependent.) His motives and actions are always correct; if something goes amiss, his underlings have misinterpreted and mismanaged the execution of his orders.

This combination of an official party that embraces and coopts important sectors of the society linked to an all-dominating executive who has the power even to interpret the Constitution to his benefit has controlled Mexican political life since 1940. Nevertheless, especially since 1968, this nearly monolithic system has begun to show signs of stress. In response, the government has initiated a limited set of reform measures that it hopes will satisfy its critics yet not yield any of its power over the political life of the country.

One serious problem that has emerged is the tendency of government operations to stagnate from the time a presidential successor is named (the current president, of course, selects this person) to the time of his official inauguration, generally fifteen months later. Presidential power is almost absolute and so personalized that once the sitting chief executive names the man to replace him, he loses a great deal of his clout. Bureaucrats, favor-seekers, and others see little need to deal with the current president, since he is on his way out; and while they scramble to join the political bandwagon of the future president, the candidate does not yet have the formal power necessary to see that the system carries on as usual. Hence, all types of important as well as mundane governmental decisions and functions are postponed or reduced until inauguration day. This cyclical stagnation caused by the nature of the political system also has serious economic consequences. The speculation and uncertainty over who the candidate is and what his policies will be, as well as the cutthroat maneuvering designed to curry the favor of the new man, create an air of instability. This situation is reflected in the business community's and government's unwillingness to invest and undertake other positive economic measures during this period. The seriousness of this situation can easily be turned into a disaster if it coincides, as in 1981–82, with a downturn in the international economy upon which Mexico is so dependent for credits and exports.

A second problem inherent in the nature of the political system since 1940 is the increasing conflict between politicians and technocrats. One of the foremost strengths of the PRI over the years has been its ability to recruit competent people at the local and state levels, who, by dint of hard work within the official ranks, are guaranteed the chance to rise to influential and generally lucrative positions in the government and the party. Now, however, as the economy and society become increasingly complex, there is a tendency to bypass political stalwarts for technocrats with little, if any, experience in the rough-and-tumble political school of the PRI. This practice not only creates tension within the government between the two groups but also reduces the PRI's appeal to aspiring young politicians.

A third serious problem facing the PRI and government leadership in recent years has been the growth of both passive and active resistance to the system. Large numbers of Mexicans, whether progovernment or not, see little use in concerning themselves with a political system that is so self-contained and all-powerful. Abstentions, which run as much as 40 percent in national elections and even higher for local contests, have become a threat to the PRI. In order to maintain its legitimacy, the official party must attract large numbers of voters. Indeed, during the 1982 presidential campaign, the candidate, Miguel de la Madrid, ended the effort on his own behalf several weeks early in order to travel around the country urging people to vote. And on election day the World Cup soccer matches from Spain were tape-delayed from the morning to the evening so that Mexicans would not remain in front of their television sets rather than vote. Given the fact that most of the opposition is much less known to the population than the PRI, officials reason that any increase in voter turnout will accrue to the latter's benefit.

While the apathy of the electorate poses an indirect threat to the regime, its active opponents offer a more direct one. Armed rebellion during the late 1960s and early 1970s proved to be a serious though hardly threatening challenge to the government. The rural guerrilla movement led by Genaro Vázquez and Lucio Cabañas in the southwestern state of Guerrero was put down following the dispatch of tens of thousands of army troops. Guerrero is the state in which the resort of Acapulco is located and one of the poorest in Mexico. During these same years, an armed urban movement also erupted that was efficiently and at times brutally subdued. Most observers agree that political prisoners remain (although not officially admitted by the government) from the campaign against the guerrillas while the bodies of others, evidently dumped from helicopters, have been found washed up on the beach around Acapulco Bay.

Nonviolent opposition to the PRI has also increased in recent years. The main group on the right is the National Action Party (PAN). Founded in 1939, the PAN has outlived charges of being financed by the PRI (in order to legitimize the government's claim that a real opposition does exist) and is no longer seen as a ludicrous, outmoded, reactionary Catholic vestige of the nineteenth century. The party has gained a modest following (although some would charge that its appeal is not because people favor the PAN but because they oppose the PRI) and has managed to challenge the PRI successfully in local contests in scattered areas of the country. In the 1982 presidential election, it came in second to the PRI with more than 16 percent of the vote.

The next most important electoral challenge to the PRI comes from the left of the political spectrum. For many years that honor had been held by the Popular Party (later Popular Socialist Party, PPS), founded in 1948 by the labor leader, Vicente Lombardo Toledano. The PPS's inability to distinguish itself from the PRI and its backing of the PRI candidates in most major elections has reduced its influence in recent years. To replace it, a coalition of several other leftist parties, including the Mexican Communist Party, has emerged. The new grouping, called the United Mexican Socialist Party (PSUM), has attracted a significant amount of intellectual and dissident *campesino* and worker support. Whether this still unsteady merger (which garnered 3.5 percent of the vote in the 1982 presidential election) will survive or, as has often been the case within the Left, break up in quarreling factions, remains to be seen.

These challenges to the PRI, both violent and nonviolent, have forced the party and government to initiate modest reforms. Changes in the system do not come easy. The left-leaning *cardenista* wing of the party found this out after 1940, as did the reform-minded president of the PRI, Carlos Madrazo. He was fired by President Gustavo Díaz Ordaz soon after trying to democratize the selection of PRI candidates at the local level in 1965. The very essence of the PRI's power is the fact that it offers the only viable alternative. Hence, the reforms undertaken have deliberately not been sweeping enough to provide the opposition with a real chance to capture a major post such as the presidency or a governorship or to control the national legislature. Beginning in 1962, with changes and additions in 1973 and 1977, the government facilitated easier registration of political parties. It also provided for the seating of up to one hundred losing opposition deputies in the four-hundred-member federal chamber, based on the parties' national vote percentage. With such schemes, the government hopes to protect the PRI's dominant position by encouraging the opposition's participation in the system without really giving it a chance to compete on an equal basis.

Political centralization under the combined guidance of the PRI and the government (especially the executive) has been an important feature of Mexican life since 1940. This system has provided a great deal of stability to once very shaky political institutions. The arrangement has in recent years, however, been less capable of satisfying the democratic aspirations of an increasing portion of the Mexican populace. Limited reform may provide momentary relief, but for real democracy to develop, the PRI will have to compete on an equal basis with other political groups.

Economic Development

To claim that Mexico's economic development based on indus-trialization began after 1940 would be an outright falsehood. Nevertheless, most historians and economists would agree that the country's economic performance during the past forty years has outpaced any previous period in its history. Only two decades, 1885 to 1905, of the Porfiriato can compare to the post-1940 period.

The extent of this economic surge can be seen in a wide range of indicators. Growth rates since World War II have averaged 6 to 7 percent per year—one of the highest and most sustained per-formances of any country in the world for the same period. Agricultural production, for most of this time, kept up with and in some sectors even outpaced the population growth, which was doubling nearly every twenty years. Mexico has become an industrial power, supplying its own needs not only in a broad spectrum of consumer goods but also in such strategic items as iron, steel, and oil. Indeed, illustrating the shift from a predominantly agricultural economy to an industrial one is that in 1940, agriculture occupied 67 percent of the population and represented 18 percent of the gross national product (GNP); in 1970, 50 percent worked on farms, accounting for 11 percent of GNP. In 1940, 13 percent of the workforce had jobs in manufacturing, which provided 19 percent of GNP, while in contrast the figures for 1970 were 16 and 26 percent, respectively. To go along with these impressive growth rates was an inflation that averaged only a little more than 7 percent during the 1950s and less than 3 percent for the 1960s.

The results of this sustained boom were seen not only in the realm of abstract statistics, but also in large public works such as the new national university, the modern subway, super highways leading from Mexico City, and the world-famous museum of anthropology. The middle and upper classes grew and flourished along with their consumption of automobiles, comfortable homes, vacations abroad, and private schools for their children. Along with economic prosperity came international prestige and confidence as Mexican bonds sold on the United States and European markets in 1963 for the first time since the Porfiriato, and the country hosted the Olympics in 1968.

What was the strategy behind this economic success story? The first element was the industrialization of the country. Although significant progress was made during the Porfiriato in this direction, especially in the production of textiles, beer, glass, and other consumer goods, the revolutionary leadership of the 1920s and succeeding years saw the need to build upon and expand this earlier effort. Not only were they motivated by the desire to make Mexico economically strong and to provide material benefits to the Mexican people; but given their political control of the nation, these leaders also saw the opportunity to use their power to move into parallel personal economic pursuits. A policy of economic expansion under their control would not only enrich themselves, they reasoned, but also ensure the official party's ability to coopt its opponents economically. Consequently, the country has enjoyed rapid industrialization but at the cost of high levels of official corruption. In fact, so corrupt was the Alemán administration that one street in the resort city of Cuernavaca along which many of the president's top aides had mansions was called the Avenue of the Forty Thieves.

Coupled with the program of industrialization has been a strategy of encouraging foreign investment, exports, and tourism.

Mexico has a large and capable labor force and most of the necessary raw materials for industrialization, but it lacks sufficient investment capital, technology, and certain manufactured goods to round out the process. Mexican economic planners calculate that foreign investments can provide needed technology and some capital. Exports generated from this very industrialization process and the agricultural sector, along with tourism, pay for needed imports, including foreign loans.

The third major element in Mexico's development plan since 1940 has been the government's participation in the economy. As mentioned above, the revolutionary leadership saw its role in the economy as both promoter and beneficiary, and these leaders have actively carried out these objectives. Since the creation of the national bank in 1925, the government's economic role has grown and diversified. It provides credit and financial expertise through a multitude of banks, builds and operates the infrastructure (roads, electrical system, ports) to facilitate the development of private enterprise, controls foreign investments and imports, and even takes over or creates industries to make products or provide services that the private sector does not find financially attractive. So pervasive is the government in the economy that the public sector is estimated to account for as much as 75 percent of the GNP.

Finally, Mexico's economic plan has called for a controlled labor force — one that will not pinch the profit margins of the owners or threaten the economic or political status quo. The nation's largest labor confederation, the Mexican Confederation of Workers (CTM), is part of the PRI. Its long-time leader, Fidel Velázquez, cooperates closely with the government, as do most other labor officials. It is often the case that they hold government posts and their labor positions at the same time. Consequently, the labor hierarchy is well taken care of while the union rank and file are forced to accept wages and benefits that fit the government's and private sector's development strategies. While the unionized workers in Mexico do better than their unorganized colleagues, they nevertheless have benefited only marginally from the country's economic success.

Mexico's economic performance over the past forty years has been a success if one measures growth in the GNP, tons of steel produced, and so forth. Nevertheless, the fruits of this boom have not been shared equally by all, and in the past decade, especially, this model, as described above, seems to be floundering. Equally important, just as the events of 1968 forced a new and critical look at the political system, this examination has spread to the closely linked economic system—a process that has intensified with the crises of 1976 and 1982.

Full-scale industrialization such as Mexico has attempted over the past forty years is a long and complex process subject to many pitfalls. The construction of steel mills, petrochemical complexes, national electric grids, and the like are extremely expensive. The country's income (both private and public sectors) from tourism, exports, taxation, foreign investment, and profits is not enough to finance such projects and meet the other needs of the populace, such as education, housing, health care, and wages. Consequently, Mexican businessmen and government officials have resorted to using foreign loans to make up the difference between the cost of their spending plans and their income. As a result, Mexico's foreign debt (both public and private) increased from approximately $150 million at the end of World War II to more than $80 billion in 1982, making Mexico the most indebted nation in the world. Most of the increase took place during the 1970s and early 1980s. While the economy managed to absorb the increased spending on large-scale projects during the 1950s and 1960s with only moderate inflation (the higher inflation of the 1940s was primarily due to the special circumstances caused by World War II), the accelerated spending of the 1970s, spurred by foreign borrowing and the printing of money, aggravated the situation. Also, much of the money that should have been directed toward improving the infrastructure in order to increase the system's ability to produce efficiently was instead spent on luxuries and superfluous imports, sent abroad, or siphoned off through corruption. Inflation increased to the 20 percent range by the mid-1970s and the 30 percent range by the end of the decade. Mexico's balance of payments worsened as exports became more expensive, tourists found Mexico less of a bargain, and imports cheapened. As a lack of confidence in the overvalued peso deepened, speculators as well as ordinary citizens began putting their money into other currencies, mainly dollars. Lacking foreign reserves to defend the peso any longer, the Mexican government was forced to devalue the peso in 1976 and again in and after 1982. It slipped from 12.5 to 200 to the dollar in eight years.

As a result of the sharp devaluations of 1982 (27 to 150 to the dollar), imports have become prohibitively expensive, crippling the purchase of needed goods from abroad and helping to push the inflation rate to 100 percent. With the shocks of 1976 and 1982, especially in the aftermath of the optimism creased by the oil boom of 1978 – 81, it will take a long time before Mexicans again feel confident in the economy and their government's ability to manage it.

The borrow/inflation/devaluation syndrome that affects the Mexican economy is only one problem area that merits attention. Mexico's close economic relationship with the United States, too, bears examination. Such a relationship is not always beneficial to Mexico and certainly elicits a great deal of criticism from nationalists and leftists. The United States does provide Mexico with a market for its exports and is a major source of credits, investment capital, and technology. Nevertheless, United States investments in Mexico, which increased from $286 million in 1943 to almost $2 billion in 1972, have come in many cases at the expense of Mexican firms, have dried up local sources of credit, have introduced capital-intensive technology that does little to ameliorate Mexico's chronic unemployment problem, and have decapitalized the Mexican economy through purchases abroad and remittances to parent firms. Also, 60 to 70 percent of all Mexican exports and imports during the entire postwar period have been with the United States. As a result, when the United States changes its trading laws or the United States economy slows down, the consequences for Mexico can be disastrous.

Another extreme problem area is the "petrolization" of the economy at the expense of other sectors, especially agriculture. By the early 1980s, nearly 80 percent of Mexico's export earnings were provided by oil exports, while such traditional foreign exchange earners as cotton and coffee, as well as a range of manufactured goods, had decreased not only relatively but also absolutely. The dependency on petroleum also accelerated the decline in agricultural production for the domestic market. Although Mexico had relative success in feeding itself until the 1970s, that decade witnessed a decline in production. Investments shifted from the agricultural sector to more lucrative ones such as commerce and speculative endeavors. The main reason for the decline in the profitability of agriculture is the government's attempt to hold down food costs for the growing number of poor urban dwellers by placing price ceilings on such staples as corn and beans. The oil boom only accentuated the trend by providing even more profitable investment opportunities outside of agriculture as well as the foreign exchange that the government needed to import foodstuffs. Instead of tackling the problem directly, the government took the easy way out by importing food to cover the increasing gap between production and consumption. As a result, Mexico spends a significant share of its foreign-exchange earnings on importing food that could be produced domestically. Walking along the streets of any Mexican town, it is common to see in the stores beans and eggs from the United States and powdered milk from Canada and New Zealand. Even corn, the traditional staff of life, is imported in large quantities, provoking complaints that today's tortillas no longer taste like they used to.

Another concern of many observers is the increasing state control of major sectors of the economy. Although Porfirio Díaz paved the way by nationalizing part of the railroad system in 1908, it was not until the presidency of Cárdenas that this trend was fully established. Following Cárdenas's expropriation of the railroad and petroleum industries, succeeding governments have taken control of the electrical system, the film industry, the telephone network, the manufacture and distribution of newsprint, and others. Not only does the government take over existing industries, but it also creates entities that it feels make up for a lack of private-sector initiative. Such endeavors include the National Fianciera (NAFINSA), an investment bank; National Diesel (DINA), a maker of heavy motors as well as trucks and buses; and the Mexican Coffee Institute (INMECAFE), which buys and markets coffee. The most dramatic example of the government's intervention in the economy in recent years was the 1982 nationalization of the banks by President José López Portillo. This move against one of the most powerful groups in the nation provoked emotional reactions, both for and against. Even among many of those who applauded the action, however, there existed an underlying note of caution. They argued that although the intentions of the government were laudable (to reduce interest rates, stop the flow of dollars abroad, channel money into needed domestic investments, and in general benefit the Mexican people as a whole), the chances of creating another corrupt, bureaucracy-heavy state enterprise like the national oil company, Mexican Petroleum (PEMEX), was also a real and sobering possibility.

Finally, it is important to note that the share of the Mexican population (50 to 60 percent) that has not fully shared in the fruits of their country's economic miracle are showing signs of increasing unrest, despite their reputation for unlimited patience. Mexico has one of the most unequal income distributions in Latin America. In 1969, for example, the bottom half of the population received 15 percent of national income, while the top 20 percent received 64 percent. (In the United States it was 17.2 and 41.1 percent, respectively.) Although the buying power of most Mexicans has increased since 1940, the gap between the rich and the poor has widened. Today's generation may be better off than their parents, but most people compare themselves to their neighbors, not the dead. Consequently, many feel frustrated at not being able to "keep up." This frustration will only increase as the zooming inflation rates of the past decade and government austerity measures have begun to cut real earnings for the first time in memory. The strikes and protests of organized labor and some peasant organizations are only the most salient manifestation of this growing unrest. Unease among the less vocal elements of the population can also be seen in the sharp rise in street crimes, panic buying, increasing vote totals for opposition parties, and the complaints and grumbling one hears whenever the topic of the economy and government are mentioned.

Urbanization

Concomitant with and partly as a result of political centralization and economic development, Mexico has also experienced a sharp rise in urbanization since 1940. In 1900 Mexico was an overwhelmingly rural country in which only 19 percent of its population lived in towns and cities. Forty years later, this figure had increased to 35 percent, and by 1970 it had reached 59 percent.

There are several reasons for this shifting population trend. The growth of centralized government has meant the expansion of the bureaucracy, which in turn has tended to attract and concentrate people in urban areas. Also, Mexico's emphasis on economic development in recent decades has focused on those activities, industry and commerce, that are most efficiently undertaken in urban areas, where there is an adequate supply of labor, credit, transportation, and communication, and a nearby market. The deemphasis on the agricultural sector has meant that opportunities on the farm have diminished in comparison to the expanding cities. Finally, the lure of urban life, enhanced by radio and television and made more accessible by modern means of transportation, has persuaded many that their future lies in one of Mexico's rapidly growing cities.

All these factors would be sufficient to encourage urbanization, but in Mexico's case an exploding population has intensified the process. With a falling mortality rate and a birth rate that has averaged between 3 and 3.5 percent for the past three decades, Mexico's population increased by 3.5 times between 1940 and 1980, from 19.7 to 69.3 million inhabitants. This phenomenon has accentuated the urbanization process, especially since it is in the rural areas where birth rates tend to be the highest and economic opportunities the least. In decades past, many rural dwellers and their offspring remained on the farm in hopes of benefiting from the government's land-reform program. Even this slim hope vanished, however, when President López Portillo declared that there were no longer any plots to be distributed.

The move from the land to the city has dramatically changed the character of Mexico and at the same time created a number of serious problems. The travel-poster image of a Mexico populated by white-clad, sombrero-wearing peasants sleeping in doorways or riding burros is now very much the exception. More likely today's visitor will find large, congested urban areas where the smartly dressed pedestrians could easily fit into the street scenes of New York or Los Angeles.

On close look, however, one will soon detect signs that contradict this image of modernity, progress, and prosperity — the ragged and dirty shoeshine boy, the adult male selling tissues in the intersection to motorists, the seated Indian woman, surrounded by several children, selling gum and candy on the sidewalk, the prostitute in the seedy hotel doorway, the traffic cop taking a bribe from a truck driver, and a passing city bus belching clouds of choking diesel exhaust and waves of earsplitting noise. These images, too, are the reality of urban Mexico. The nation's cities certainly are the showcases of the "Mexican miracle," but they also contain severe problems and the seeds of potential social turmoil.

Government efforts to provide basic public services as well as jobs have not been anywhere near adequate, given the rapid growth of the cities since 1940. The unemployment rate, which hovers around 10 percent, does not reflect the seriousness of the problem, since up to 50 percent of the workforce is under-employed. Even if a worker has a full-time job that pays the minimum wage (currently about $3.50 per day in Mexico City), it is estimated that two-thirds of this amount is needed merely to feed a typical household of five people. Consequently, all members of many families, including the children, must work to contribute to the family's sustenance.

Children who are undernourished (some estimate that half the country's children receive inadequate diets) and work have little time or ability to attend and do well in school. Only one in one hundred persons who starts primary school continues to the university level, and the average per capita number of years of schooling for the population is 3.5.

Not only has the urbanization process concentrated into small areas large numbers of people who need services and jobs to be able to participate fully in and contribute to Mexico's development; it has also created an environmental crisis. Most observers point to the severe air and noise pollution (not to mention contaminated drinking water, garbage-strewn, unpaved streets, and the like) in Mexico City with its crushing population of fifteen million. Other cities, too, have serious problems, but they seem miniscule when compared to the capital. Not long ago considered one of the most beautiful cities in the world, with clean air, a spring-like climate, and a ring of snow-capped mountains, Mexico City is now an environ-mental nightmare. It regularly has pollution levels, for example, two and three times the amount at which New York authorities begin closing factories and warning people with respiratory prob-lems to remain at home. Faced with such conditions, it is little wonder that millions of Mexico's city dwellers question the validity of the "Mexican miracle."

Conclusion

This description of Mexico since Cárdenas may seem over-pessimistic and subjective—akin to looking at the yellowish-brown cloud that almost daily covers Mexico City and claiming that that situation represents the entire country. It would create a false impression not to recognize that Mexico has made significant strides in the past forty years. Its centralized political system has created a great deal of stability, at the same time allowing a large degree of personal freedom. Its economic advances have helped ensure the stability of the political system and made Mexico a regional power. Now, with its oil riches, it may be on the verge of becoming an important actor on the international stage. Also, the economic boom has improved the lives of most Mexicans in many ways. Finally, the urbanization process has provided new and varied opportunities for millions of Mexicans—options that they would never have even dreamed about if they had remained on the farm.

Nevertheless, Mexico's success story has come at great expense—a cost that if ignored means perpetuating a system that prevents the development of full democratic participation by its citizens in the political and economic life of the country, and that condones a life of poverty, ignorance, and ill-health for millions. The system thus far can be judged a qualified success; however, unless it finds the dynamism and flexibility to reform in order to benefit more of the nation's people as well as deal with other problems such as the negative effects of urbanization, the questioning of the system that began in 1968 will become more than an exercise in passive self-examination.

BIBLIOGRAPHICAL NOTE

Bazant, Jan. *Historia de la deuda exterior de México, 1823–1946.* Mexico City: El Colegio de México, 1968.
Gollás, Manuel, and García Rocha, Adalberto. "El desarrollo económico reciente de México." In *Contemporary Mexico: Papers of the IV International Congress on Mexican History,* eds. James W. Wilkie, Michael C. Meyer, and Edna Monzón de Wilkie, pp. 405–440. Berkeley: University of California Press, 1976.
Hansen, Roger D. *The Politics of Mexican Development.* Baltimore: Johns Hopkins University Press, 1971.
Levy, Daniel, and Székely, Gabriel. *Mexico: Paradoxes of Stability and Change.* Boulder: Westview Press, 1983.
México demográfico: Breviario, 1980–81. Mexico City: Consejo Nacional de Población, 1982.

Niblo, Stephen R. "Progress and the Standard of Living in Contemporary Mexico." *Latin American Perspectives* 2 (1975): 109–124.

Paz, Octavio. *The Other Mexico: Critique of the Pyramid.* New York: Grove Press, 1972.

Russell, Philip. *Mexico in Transition.* Austin: Colorado River Press, 1977.

von Sauer, Franz A. *The Alienated "Loyal Opposition": Mexico's Partido Acción Nacional.* Albuquerque: University of New Mexico Press, 1974.

Semo, Enrique, coord. *México: Un pueblo en la historia.* Vol. 4. Mexico City: Editorial Nueva Imagen, 1982.

Vernon, Raymond. *The Dilemma of Mexico's Development: The Roles of the Private and Public Sectors.* Cambridge, Mass.: Harvard University Press, 1965.

21

THE MEXICAN REVOLUTION AND THE CARTOON

Víctor Alba

A Mexican journalist of Spanish origin, Víctor Alba has had a lifelong fascination with Mexican culture that he has discussed in numerous periodicals and books on his adopted people. When he is not practicing his profession, writing volumes such as The Mexicans, *he serves a stint as a visiting professor of political science at a North American university. In the following essay, he discusses the nature of political cartoons, the distinctive qualities of Mexican cartooning, and the impact of the Revolution on this form of satire. Abel Quezada wrought the greatest changes in the cartoon, Alba tells us, when he dismissed the nineteenth-century symbols of the charro, priest, and general, and created caricatures of Mexico's pervasive machos and arrogant new rich. Quezada and others have abandoned political themes to examine Mexican society; they display everyday habits of Mexicans with wit and satire, exposing aspects of the culture that often escape professional investigators. When Quezada uses his cartoons to confront the Mexican with himself, Alba argues, he is helping to create the Mexican nationality, whether intentionally or not; establishing the national identity was also the goal of the Mexican Revolution. An example of Quezada's work follows Alba's essay.*

The cartoon had a considerable influence on the political life of Mexico in the period immediately prior to the Revolution. This influence continues in contemporary Mexico, but with a completely different character. This brief essay proposes to examine the

From Víctor Alba, "The Mexican Revolution and the Cartoon," *Comparative Studies in Society and History* 9 (1966): 121–22, 128–33, 136. Reprinted by permission of Cambridge University Press.

causes of this change of attitude in the Mexican cartoon, for its measure reflects the transformation of the country. To do this, let us begin with a summary analysis of the nature of the cartoon in independent Mexico.

Symbol or Portrait?

The cartoon is probably one of the mediums of expression that has changed least in history, both in form and in procedure. The cartoonist has always tried to attain a synthesis of various ideas: to ridicule someone or something, to provoke in the spectator a sentiment hostile to the thing ridiculed, and to bring out in the spectator certain tendencies that might be called "natural" and that do not generally change with time. In short, the cartoonist wants to irritate, and at the same time to satisfy others who also want to irritate.

This synthesis is not extraneous to the purpose. On the contrary, it proposes to exercise a certain influence on the spectator, inducing him to oppose those whom the cartoonist ridicules, while persuading him to divorce himself from certain ideas that the cartoonist satirizes.

In theory the cartoon should contain an ingredient of humor, but this is achieved by only a few cartoonists. The majority of those who practice the trade limit themselves to attack, satisfied that some of their readers will laugh or smile, not because the cartoon has humor, but because they will be pleased that someone has expressed their own desire to attack. If the cartoonist is very capable (as a cartoonist, not as an artist), he can even provoke the sentiment of ridicule in those who do not share his desire to criticize or attack. It is then, and only then, that the cartoon is successful in achieving its purpose — influencing the spectator.

There are various means to this end, but they can all be reduced to two; the symbol and the portrait of reality.

The cartoon that uses symbol is found particularly in societies or social groups of less cultural refinement; it is the most common form of cartoon. Because of the audience it reaches, auxiliary markers to guide the spectator, to explain meaning, and to avoid the danger of erroneous interpretation are frequently required. The spurred boot treading on a newspaper seems sufficiently symbolic of the military dictator's treatment of the press. But many cartoonists still support their effects by hanging a sign on the boot that says "dictatorship" and another on the newspaper that reads "freedom of the press."

This is the kind of cartoon most abundant in the camp of political criticism. On the other hand, although less prevalent generally, the portrait of reality is the most common form of cartooning among those interested in social criticism. It is directed toward spectators of more intellectual refinement, who are capable of grasping the ridicule without needing signs and symbols. Political criticism in cartooning, simple and direct in form, has had a long history in Mexico before and during the Revolution; social criticism through realistic cartooning is of recent origin. . . .

The Revolution

The cartoons of the revolutionary period are essentially political, the majority of them directed against President Francisco I. Madero, as well as against the popular revolutionists Emiliano Zapata, the agrarian leader, and Francisco Villa, the guerrilla leader of the North. One might think that this was due to the presence in the final stages of the Díaz regime of a group of Spanish cartoonists who defended the dictator and attacked his opponents. But we have to look deeper for an explanation. In fact, this lack of social expression in what started as a political revolution against reelection, and only later evolved into a social revolution (for the land), and nationalistic revolution (for nationalization of the mines and for Mexicanization of the Church, in which Spanish clerics had predominated), occurs not only in cartooning, but also in other forms of popular expression and folklore. In the revolutionary songs, for instance, military and lyrical themes predominate. (The most popular of them all, *Adelita*, sung by Villa's soldiers, is a song of love and jealousy.) There were some songs with political themes, but very few with social ones. The peasants who followed Zapata, and who killed and were killed in the effort to recover their land, sang of their sweethearts and of their heroes, but did not put their desire for land into music or verse.

Perhaps this can be explained by the fact that the Revolution was not the result of preconceived theories; the doctrine came later, with the writing of the Constitution of 1917, when the achievements of the Revolution were legalized. A complementary explanation might be found in the possibility that the fighting masses, apart from their primary thirst for land, had only a vague conception — or none at all — of their own aspirations; perhaps they went to war as a reaction against their way of life, not knowing clearly how they wanted to live, but only that they did not want to continue as they were. They felt no need to describe in their songs the mode of living that they had rejected, because it was known to them all. This being the case, it is logical that the cartoonists, who reflected the sentiments of their readers and not of ideologists, should show no interest in social themes. On the other hand, it should not be forgotten that the great cities, especially the capital, where the majority of dailies and weeklies appeared, were never revolutionary and looked without confidence upon the revolutionary leaders and with terror upon the provincial revolutionary masses.

This situation continued until the Revolution became settled, secured, and institutionalized. Although the presidents (Obregón and Calles) were soldiers of the Revolution — a period of very active political struggle, characterized by the frequent opposition of the parliament and the executive, a great diversity of parties, general strikes, conflict between Catholics and Liberals, and foreign pressures — the cartooning we find in the Mexican press is not fundamentally different from that of the prerevolutionary period. It is political cartooning, concerning the personalities of the movement. The cartoonists employed the traditional techniques and styles. There were no innovations at all, either in theme or in treatment. One would think that for the cartoonists the Revolution had been a completely alien movement. Not even the muralists, who, as has been noted, treated epic revolutionary themes, and who denounced colonial exploitation and the then-past dictatorship, made any innovations in their cartooning.

One had to wait for the Revolution to be converted into something irreversible, accepted by almost everyone, to find a change of direction in Mexican cartooning. The first change was thematic. Manual Cabral and Antonio Arias Bernal began it, with photographic "cartooning." This found wide popularity in a short-lived weekly called Rotofoto, immediately before and during the Second World War. Here the indiscretions of the camera were used to satirize public figures and, occasionally, customs and social habits.

It has only been with Abel Quezada, in the period of civilian presidents since 1955, that a new kind of cartoon has appeared. Quezada is not alone, but without doubt he has had the most influence and has carried social criticism the furthest.

The Social Cartoon

The Mexican Revolution was many things. Even today, at the end of almost half a century, the significance of the Revolution is still a matter of discussion. Was it solely political, or was it also social? And was it nationalist? In any event, it occasioned a profound transformation of the social structure. Even if *latifundia* did not completely disappear, the great landed proprietors lost their political influence. New social groups were formed, or if they had existed before, they grew and acquired power. Above all, the middle class grew. One can say that today there are only middle-class groups and the masses. True, there are some very wealthy people — bankers, great landowners, politicians, and some industrialists — yet in their mentality and their behavior they belong to the middle class. The growth of Mexican capitalism has not created an upper bourgeoisie, nor an aristocracy of the Revolution. The party that has held power, under one name or another since 1917, that is to say, since the Revolution triumphed and became institutionalized, is a party directed by members of the middle class that also includes organizations of workers and peasants.

This development of middle-class groups has had cultural and social consequences. The old Victorian morality has little by little given way to new ideas, in which the influence of industrialized countries is marked. The cultural nationalism that followed the Revolution has been succeeded by a more open culture, to a certain degree imitative of industrial societies. It is as though the middle-class groups, which are the only ones culturally active, try to live a kind of "future" existence, try to conduct themselves and react as would be normal in an industrialized Mexico of the future. Yet all of this is taking place in a country still on the road to industrialization.

Naturally, this produces maladjustments that are reflected in prejudices, taboos, and collective customs. Cartooning today — especially in the style of Abel Quezada — is essentially devoted to fighting these customs, prejudices, and taboos. It is therefore fundamentally social, although the cartoonists clearly do not ignore political themes. Nevertheless, the present norm, which sets the tone for Mexican cartooning, is social criticism, rather than criticism of a given person, party, or decision.

This has led logically to the need for replacing old symbols with new ones. The *charro*, a facile symbol more a product of folklore than of any social reality, the fat, greedy and lustful priest, or the strutting general with trimmed mustache and unsheathed sword, are no longer representative Mexican symbols; they have no counterparts in everyday life.

Abel Quezada has created two symbolic figures that are undoubtedly the basis of his success as a cartoonist and of the popularity of his work (apart, clearly, from his talent, unless one says that his talent lies precisely in having created these symbols).

In the past the cartoonist tended to contrast the people — in the figure of the *charro* — with the pompous cleric and the arrogant general. Today Quezada views Mexican society not as a struggle of the people against its enemies, but as a series of attitudes common to high and low alike, attitudes on which he declares war.

We may therefore say that the cartooning of Quezada, and of others who work along the same lines, reveals the realities of Mexican life far more faithfully than did prerevolutionary cartooning. Abstract ideas are related to concrete situations. In the new cartooning, actual customs are handled independently of ideologies and general ideas. While the cartoons of the age of Díaz and Madero needed Díaz and Madero, today's cartoons do not need any president at all. It is clear that the intangible, almost sacred, aura that has surrounded the office of president of the republic since the Revolution has played no part in this evolution of caricaturing.

The cartoonist, while he does not attack the president (not because the law prohibits it, but because it is not a part of the mental habits of present-day Mexico), has sought a theme that is not protected by any general taboo; the customs of the society in which he lives.

Spoken Humor and Printed Humor

This leads us to point out a very interesting characteristic of Mexico, one that does not occur in any other Latin American country with an equal liberty of expression: the distinction between spoken humor and humor in print.

Although it extends to all public figures — political, cultural, even to those of the cinema — this characteristic is seen primarily in the unique treatment of the president of the republic, in what is written, drawn, and spoken about him. The jokes that pass from mouth to mouth about the president are legion, and are not generally adapted from foreign jokes, as they are frequently in other countries; they are newly invented stories and excellent verbal cartoons, usually portraits of the first magistrate as the public sees him. They are frequently facetious, not rarely coarse, and almost always devastating, but they refer to the man and not to his office. On the other hand, sarcasm about the president never appears in the press. There is no censorship in Mexico. Hostile criticism of the president appears frequently, particularly in the political press, but not in cartoons.

Perhaps the explanation of this difference lies in the popular saying, "Words are gone with the wind, but papers remain." But perhaps the explanation should be sought in the extreme sensitivity of today's Mexican, who is not the same as the Mexican of the past, when cruel cartoons of the first magistrate abounded. He does not tolerate public burlesqueing of the president. It is relevant also to note that while there always used to be satirical weeklies, none has existed for the past thirty years. The satirical weekly in the style of Punch or Le Canard Enchaîné is unthinkable in Mexico today. Some people say this is owing to the sensitivity of the new rich, and every comfortable Mexican today is in some measure newly rich, although we are increasingly dealing more with the second generation. Others affirm that it is a consequence of the unique political system in which a single party, incorporating all the important figures, has governed since the Revolution, has won all the elections, and has proportioned the presidents among the various factions of the party. In such a regime, it is said, criticism of ministers, institutions, laws, and customs is acceptable, but the president, who is the catalyst of the system, must not be touched.

Whatever the explanation, and it is possible that it is a mixture of the above points, it is certain that political caricature is declining in Mexico, while social caricature is springing up in the whole of the press. It is curious also how opposite the positions of social caricature and political cartooning are. While the latter has abandoned the press and taken refuge in the spoken political joke, social caricature and the criticism of customs, though freely printed, are not found in such verbal joking. It seems that the Mexican tolerates social criticism in the press, but does not indulge in it himself; at the same time, he disapproves of printed satires of his president, although he delights in speaking ill of him.

The New Rich and El Macho

As we remarked above, Abel Quezada created two new symbols to replace the obsolete figures of the *charro*, the fat priest, and the swaggering general. His two figures are the new rich man and the distinctively Mexican *macho* (the self-conscious he-man).

Quezada found a symbol of great satirical strength for characterizing the new rich: a man wearing a ring set with an enormous solitary diamond — in his nose. In a country where the men are very fond of jewels, the new rich do not discreetly refrain from display; they cannot refrain from a conspicuous show of wealth. For example, rings with large stones on the little finger are favored. Quezada gave his new character a ring, but cruelly; he made the savage's nose-ring the mark of the new rich.

As for the figure of the *macho*, Quezada gave him certain touches that make him a perfect vehicle for social criticism. In Mexico, as in many other Latin American countries, there is a popular idea that men ought to be "very masculine," quick to take offense and ready for violence, dominating and tyrannizing their homes, disrespectful to women and aggressive to men. Naturally, as with all types of bullies, the *macho* is a coward who conceals his cowardice behind his swagger. Quezada employs his *macho*, whom he calls Charro Matías, to criticize political customs. His Charro Matías wears an enormous hat, on the brim of which always appear phrases or proverbs invented by the cartoonist that contradict the actions of the figure in the drawing. In this way Quezada criticizes the very Latin American habit of living on two distinct levels, those of words and actions: Charro Matías says one thing and does another. He is thus the personification of all the habits that the cartoonist criticizes. Sometimes, looking for a job, he flatters a successful politician. Sometimes he is the politician himself, a representative eager to exercise privileges. Sometimes he is the man of influence who, in one way or another, charges for the recommendations he gives. Sometimes he is the provincial, startled by the big capital city, who compensates his timidity with bravado.

As can be seen, Quezada's devils are, on the one hand,

machismo and, on the other, the poor taste and conventionality of "distinguished" members of the new-rich society taking form in postrevolutionary Mexico. Quezada does not limit his criticism to those two areas of social behavior, but implacably makes fun of other Mexican habits. For example, he keeps up a running fight against the trimmed mustaches that are so common.

Mexicans speak a peculiar Castillian, in which are words that come from Nahuatl, spoken before the arrival of the Spaniards, and words and phrases that the Spaniards brought and that have been preserved intact in Mexico while they have disappeared from common use in Spain. Moreover, the Mexican, particularly in the villages, uses images and stock slang phrases that have become clichés. Quezada utilizes all of these language resources. His characters speak a Castillian that could never be heard outside Mexico, but that in Mexico is both comical and sarcastic in tone.

Despite his use of these resources, Quezada is systematically hostile to folklore; he doubtless considers it a survival from a dead society. He ridicules the *mariachis,* those wandering singing musicians in *charro* costumes who deafen those about them with popular songs; he mocks the old typical cuisine, extolled by Mexicans, that for the cartoonist is a cause of malnutrition.

From time to time Quezada, inspired by the daily news, makes an excursion outside the country to propose burlesque solutions for international problems. . . . Naturally, his criticism of North American intervention and militarism is persistent; but he is not one-sided, for he also satirizes the politics of Moscow.

An example may show how Quezada generally orients his cartoons. . . . Mexico does not suffer from a shortage of water in the capital, but the experts say there will be one in the near future. Quezada satirizes the Mexican inclination to let the next generation face the problem. He concludes that if water is lacking in Mexico, instead of rationing it or looking for solutions, the Mexicans will do "the usual thing: we will wash our hands and blame the government." In passing, he makes a point of deflating a common myth when he writes in the same cartoon, "The happy and unconcerned Mexican, or the sad and unconcerned, which amounts to the same thing . . ." Sometimes he parodies common sayings, as when he writes on the hat of Charro Matías, while making public accusations of favoritism against some organization, "Don't accuse, it may demoralize."

The New Objectives

Examining the cartoons of Quezada and of other contemporary Mexican cartoonists, one can see into the real Mexico. One can understand prevailing customs and mental habits, especially in respect to reactions that had not attracted the attention of sociologists or anthropologists, or even ethnologists. This, incidentally, explains the popularity that Quezada has attained.

One of the most constant preoccupations of the Mexican intellectual in the last twenty or thirty years has been the interpretation of his personality and the search for an answer to the question, "What is a Mexican?" This is understandable if one keeps in mind the history of Mexico, a land of *mestizos*, in which different peoples and cultures have been intermingled. These movements have been nationalist, social, and political: nationalist, due particularly to the proximity of the United States; social, owing to the survival of anachronistic and uneconomical systems of land tenure; and political, originating in the constant fluctuation between democratic and dictatorial regimes.

Quezada and the new style of Mexican cartooning—new in themes and in treatment—respond to this restlessness and at the same time help to allay it. They introduce aspects of the Mexican personality that the people are less ready to recognize, to confess, to study. The fact that this has been done with sarcasm and with humor has undoubtedly helped to make acceptable the description of certain realities that would otherwise have been denied or rejected as un-Mexican. In this sense Quezada and his colleagues have demonstrated a laudable degree of intellectual value and independence.

While the old political cartooning continues, the new style has greater popularity. More important, it constitutes a considerable contribution, although probably without previous reflection on the part of the cartoonist, to what seems to be the essential and ultimate objective of Mexican life—an objective more instinctive than conscious: the formation of a nationality. To the degree that the new cartooning fulfills this function, it can be considered a result of the Mexican Revolution, which has had in its past and present consequences the same aspirations.

22

THE MOST POWERFUL COUNTRY IN THE WORLD: A CARTOON

Abel Quezada

The owners of La Fonda del Refugio, one of Mexico City's best-known restaurants, have covered the walls of one upstairs dining room with framed cartoons by Abel Quezada. This tribute recognizes his popularity beyond such outstanding cartoonists working in Mexico as Rius, José Polomo, and Gabriel Vargas. Quezada's wit often slashes at bantam-rooster machismo and oil-rich displays by sheiks in sombreros. On the other hand, he is a Mexican, and sometimes his cartoons, such as the following selection, become a kind of collective dream for his people.

From *The Dust of Impossible Worlds* by Abel Quezada. © 1963 by Prentice-Hall, Inc. Published by Prentice-Hall, Inc., Englewood Cliffs, NJ 07632.

1

LAST NIGHT I DREAMT THAT **MÉXICO** WAS THE **POWERFUL** COUNTRY AND THE **U.S.** THE **WEAK** ONE...

2

THAT AUTOMOBILES SOLD THE WORLD OVER HAD NAMES LIKE "GONZÁLEZ", "LÓPEZ" AND "RODRIGUEZ"...

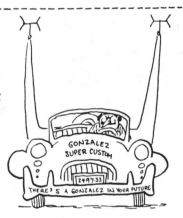

3

I DREAMT WE ORGANIZED COMMITTEES FOR FAIR PLAY AND ELBOW ROOM FOR NORTH AMERICANS BECAUSE SOME MEXICAN RESTAURANTS REFUSED TO SERVE THEM...

4

... THAT WE WENT IN FOR THE GOOD NEIGHBOR POLICY AND HIRED NORTH AMERICAN FIELD HANDS TO HARVEST OUR CORN AND BEAN CROPS.

5

... THAT WE HANDED OUT **PESOS** BY THE BUCKET TO HELP THE **U.S.** AND OTHER UNDERDEVELOPED PEOPLE, CHARGING ONLY A MODEST INTEREST...

6

... AND I WOULD LOVE TO GO ON DREAMING, BUT I WOKE UP.

23

THE CHURCH SINCE 1940

David C. Bailey

David C. Bailey (1930–82), professor of history at Michigan State University, wrote extensively on contemporary Mexico. In addition to articles in the major historical journals, he completed Charles C. Cumberland's Mexican Revolution: The Constitutionalist Years *(1972) and compiled* The Guide to Historical Sources and Archives of Coahuila *(1976). His monograph* ¡Viva Cristo Rey!: The Cristero Rebellion and the Church-State Conflict in Mexico *(1974) remains the standard volume on this subject. The essay that follows was part of a general study of the Roman Catholic Church in Latin America that Bailey had begun shortly before his death.*

Bailey's research revealed that after 1940 both Mexican politicians and prelates increasingly came from the same social class, often the same families. Consequently they shared experiences that would allow cooperation. Nevertheless, he discovered that the Church-state peace since 1940 reflects need rather than goodwill. The Church hierarchy fears confrontation that may bring renewed anticlericalism or might result in the current regime's being deposed, allowing a takeover by a radical leftist government. Secret conversations have arranged Church-state rapprochement on the national textbook question and the government's family-planning programs. Bailey discusses the complex divisions within the Church that make it difficult for any prelate to speak for the Church. These differences have been magnified as priests respond to Vatican II and the Medellín statement of the Latin American bishops. Both these councils urged the Church to work more actively for the social needs of parishioners. In the Mexican episcopate, conservatives, traditionalists, moderates, and radical priests have conflicting views on how this should be accomplished. This selection should be compared with Reading 15, which describes the Church-state conflict before 1940, to understand why both government and Church feel the need for peaceful coexistence. Bailey's essay reveals fascinating information on the selective enforcement of the Constitution's anticlerical laws and demonstrates with this practical example the cooptation and cooperation process used by the PRI in its relations with interest groups as powerful as the Catholic Church.

Miguel Avila Camacho expressed a new mood in the government toward the Roman Catholic Church in his first year in office, when he responded to a journalist's question about his attitude toward the Church. He answered with the simple words, "*Soy creyente*" ("I am a believer"). His statement mirrored the call of Archbishop L. M. Martínez of Mexico City, who asked all Catholics to support the Avila Camacho government. Both leaders stated the desire for an end to the Church-state controversy. This had been affirmed by the public when they attended in huge numbers the last motion picture of the Cárdenas presidency, *Creo en Dios* (*I Believe in God*). The president and the archbishop ushered in a new era in Church-state relations in 1940. The rapproachement became increasingly visible in 1952, when President Miguel Alemán publicly embraced the archbishop.

The years since 1940 can be described as a period of religious peace in Mexico, if compared to the prior thirty years. But this comparison can be misleading, and if it is overemphasized the contrast can too easily distort the situation at present. In reality, the last forty years have been tranquil only in a superficial sense. The modus vivendi between Church and state is actually a standoff, a truce in which both sides continue to harbor deep suspicions of each other. There is a profound lack of trust. The harmony that has existed is grounded in necessity rather than goodwill.

Leaders of both Church and state have been determined to avoid conflict, and they have devised elaborate ways to do this. They have usually been able to anticipate problems and to limit the damage if something happens. Actually, there have been hundreds of incidents during the last forty years, some of which resulted in violence. This was especially true in the 1960s when leading priests and the National Union of Parents Association led demonstrations across the nation to protest the decision of the Adolfo López Mateos government to institute a system of free and compulsory textbooks, the *texto único*. Catholic parents and priests protested the portrait of the Church as an obstacle to modernization and objected to other sections of these national volumes. The schoolbook crisis flared into violence in several provincial towns. These incidents were overwhelmingly local; none of them ran out of control, although there always existed the fear that one might. Leaders on both sides recognized that neither could probably win an open contest of national proportions, or rather, that winning would not be worth the cost. Leaders also realized that an open confrontation would almost certainly cause dangerous divisions in their respective ranks.

The resolution of the *texto único* crisis came through confidential meetings at the highest levels. Without the official approval of either Church or state, cooperation developed that resulted in the revision of some texts by educational leaders from the Church's Secretariado de Educación, which had been established in 1926. In secret meetings they edited certain passages and solved one issue brought to light by a parents' group. One textbook showed pictures of a young girl and boy, both scantily clad, that came together suggestively when the book was closed. Turning the pictures back to back restored decorum, removing the criticism.

There has been a well-honed sense of limits on both sides since 1940. The bishops speak out on social issues; they deplore injustice and substandard living conditions, for example, but they studiously avoid blaming the government for them, or at most, they do it in oblique ways. They counsel obedience to civil authority while at the same time urging Catholics to seek repeal of the offensive religious laws. They condemn violence, but they warn that the denial of rights can lead to it.

The government has maintained the 1917 constitutional provisions that stripped all churches of juridical personality, nationalized all real estate held by religious institutions, empowered the government to decide what Church buildings can be used for worship, restricted the clergy to native-born Mexicans, and prohibited the religious from political activity. (Most of these limitations are contained in Article 130.) The ruling party refuses to change these laws, but it selectively suspends enforcement of them, while leaving the implication that suspension depends on the clergy's good behavior. In 1975 it was estimated that there were 1,400 priests in the Archdiocese of Mexico, of whom 75 to 80 were foreign missionaries. These foreign priests encountered no problems from civil authorities.

When the government undertakes programs that might cause conflict, it first consults Church officials. This has been the case with school textbooks since the mid-1960s, and with Mexico's family planning programs initiated by President Luis Echeverría in the 1970s. This consultation is of course entirely quiet and unpublicized. It has in some cases reached the extent of clearing with local bishops the selection of candidates of the official party.

The balance depends on national stability — on the existence of a strong state that is able to manage this complicated and delicate relationship with the Church. The higher clergy knows this, and most of the bishops would be alarmed at the prospect of the PRI's losing national power. For this reason, the upper clergy have a dislike, bordering on contempt, for the National Action Party (PAN), despite its popular reputation of being proclerical. Churchmen believe they can work more closely with members of the PRI than with the PAN candidates, who seem often to be rather poor political choices. The Church fears a resurgence of anticlericalism and also that any new regime might be a Marxist one. As a result, they support stability, despite their distaste for the political organization that makes stability possible.

This same political stability has helped to maintain unity among the Mexican clergy itself during the last forty years, but it is a unity that cannot be taken for granted, especially during a time of trouble. It may be assumed that most of the bishops, and certainly those in policymaking positions, place a high priority on helping maintain national equilibrium. But there exists a lack of cohesion in the episcopate, much of it due to Mexico's regionalism; most bishops guard their autonomy and believe that they are the best judges of how to handle matters in their own dioceses, whether the issues be education, social action, or political relations. The bishops never issued a joint pastoral letter on sex education in the 1960s because they could not agree on one. More than 250,000 copies of one pamphlet entitled *Educación Sexual*, written by a Church official, were distributed in several dioceses, but the pamphlet was banned by the Archbishop of Durango. Mexico has no prelate of the stature of, say, Cardinal Silva in Chile, who can speak for the Church except in the most general terms.

Other potential causes for disunity among the general clergy include the centuries-old rivalry between the regular priests (members of a religious order) and secular priests (ordained parish fathers). This tension carries into educational questions, since the regulars usually serve in the schools and identify and nurture potential vocations among the young. The native priests feel some annoyance with foreigners, especially Spaniards. This reflects the economic pressures on the priesthood. In the 1970s many priests, especially in rural areas, received barely enough to live on, perhaps 400 pesos (at the old exchange of 12.5 to the dollar) a month. The majority of Mexican priests come from the lower middle class and cannot expect help from their families. This causes intense competition for the parishes with prestigious churches. Money divides the clergy. Another prospective division comes from the conflict between those priests eager for changes, such as the saying of the mass in the vernacular, and those who cling to tradition.

The dominant posture of the Church is one of conservatism and caution, for reasons that are both historical and practical. The Mexican Church stands in sharp contrast to the Church in Brazil, Chile, El Salvador, and other Latin American countries where self-confident, articulate activists criticize the established order and even encourage defiance.

On the other hand, some currents bear watching. Since the early 1960s, a number of clergymen have been impatient with the hierarchy's cautious position. The outstanding example was the recently retired bishop of Cuernavaca, Sergio Méndez Arceo, who repeatedly spoke out against the massacre of Tlatelolco (see Reading 25) and imprisonment of political dissenters. Even more influential is Samuel Ruíz of Chiapas, an outspoken advocate of "Liberation Theology." These two, and one or two others, remain exceptions at this time among the bishops. But a smattering of priests, many of them young, have absorbed the spirit of Vatican II and the Medellín conference of 1968. The Second Vatican Council, convened in 1962, issued statements that summarized the responsibilities of the Church to include concern for education, agrarian reform, social problems, and the poverty associated with over-population. The second conference of Latin American bishops at Medellín affirmed the Church's role in liberating the people from neocolonial and repressive institutions in the hemisphere. The Medellín meeting thus seemed to endorse the "liberation theology" of Helder Câmara, archbishop of Recife, who vowed that when peaceful means had been exhausted, violence was justified. Who these priests are in Mexico and just how many of them there are is not known, but during the last several years priests have been jailed, beaten, and removed from their parishes for alleged subversive activities. Very little of this appears in the press in Mexico, but it sometimes gets reported in Catholic periodicals, both there and in the United States.

The bishops' attitude toward activism is not clear, except on the issue of family planning, although it probably worries most of them.

The Mexicans have at times moved discreetly to dampen activism by establishing such agencies as the Secretariado Social, Christus, founded in 1961 by the Archdiocese of Mexico. It is doubtful that the bishops could quell activism effectively, even if they tried. And to try would give the appearance of being even more conservative than many of them would care to appear. In 1979, at the third meeting of Latin American bishops, held at Puebla, Mexico, conservative churchmen tried to capture the meeting but did not succeed. Pope John Paul II, who visited the meeting in Puebla and other locations, generally supported progressive, activist bishops. The pope's encouragement resulted in a strong statement against Latin American poverty. Although at the present there exists no "Catholic Left" in Mexico in the sense that it exists elsewhere, the encouragement by Pope John Paul II and the Puebla conference may lead to one. At the moment, though, conditions militate against it.

Mexico's family-planning program dramatically demonstrates the situation of the Church today. President Luis Echeverría, the father of eight children, had spoken out against the need for population planning when he first took office in 1970; but within three years his administration had initiated government-sponsored family-planning assistance. This program stressed responsible parentage and also provided information on contraceptives. It ran directly counter to Paul Paul VI's reaffirmation of the traditional Church opposition to artificial birth control. Echeverría's program had been discussed in confidence with Church leaders before being made public. The most common method seems to be the IUD called the loop, distributed through the Centros de Salúd. This practice continues with the connivance of the Church hierarchy. Mexican women find that the Church's response to birth control varies tremendously in the confessionals. Each priest takes a different position on it. The Church does take an unequivocal stand against abortion and sterilization. Since the 1970s, rumors have reported a government program to sterilize poor and unwed mothers, but no proof supports these tales. The Church prelates continue their grudging support of the government.

As for the future of Church-state relations during the *sexenio* of President Miguel de la Madrid, much depends of course on conditions over which the Church has little control. If the political and economic situation remains more or less as it was in 1984—that is, if things do not get markedly worse —then the present arrangement should endure for some time. If economic conditions continue to worsen, with a resulting decline in the already precarious living standard of the disadvantaged classes, then larger numbers of clergy, although probably not a majority, will become more vocal in their criticisms, and perhaps more active as organizers, or mentors, of discontent, particularly in rural areas. Such activity could provoke adverse government reaction. It is even possible that a beleaguered government might attempt to invoke some of the dormant anticlerical laws. To do so would be a clear sign of desperation.

There will be no open break between Church and state unless the state provokes it by taking actions that would violate the modus vivendi —for example, nationalizing Catholic schools. But the Church is in an unenviable, even vulnerable, position. To any potential challengers of the regime, the Church can hardly escape being identified with the present order in Mexico. Even among many Mexicans who would be unsympathetic to a national move leftward, there is a strong, residual antipathy to the clergy. This will surface during any period of disruption.

The Church almost certainly stands to lose in the event of any fundamental political realignment. To cooperate with some sort of rightist, repressive government would hopelessly compromise the clergy and destroy what credibility it has as a force for justice, however weak that image has been. For it to accept accommodation with a frankly leftist regime would be so sharp a reversal of the last half century as to be all but unthinkable. And either of these choices would likely lead to disunity within the Church, which remains perhaps the clergy's most deep-seated fear.

The choices, then, are limited or nonexistent. For the Church, as for certain other interest groups, there are few alternatives to the political order that has provided at least a degree of predictability during the last several decades.

24

SOCIAL CONTROL AND THE MEXICAN POLITICAL SYSTEM

Judith Adler Hellman

Judith Adler Hellman, author of Mexico in Crisis *(1978, 1983), teaches political science at York University, Toronto. In her essay, written for this volume, she explains how the ruling party, the PRI, remains in power by relying on cooptation and repression of individuals and organizations. Few channels for social and economic mobility exist outside the government for university faculty and students, and even fewer for ambitious peasants and workers. Limited opportunity makes them especially susceptible to cooptation. For those too stubborn to accept the party, the government uses different forms of repression, from harassment to assassination. In these two ways, the PRI maintains social control. This essay, moreover, examines how the PRI's worker and peasant sectors have become organizations to control those whom they should represent. The reader should consider how political centralization, particularly the all-powerful president, has contributed to this system.*

The structure of Mexico's ruling party has long intrigued observers. On paper, at least, the Mexican political system provides full democratic expression to every social class. Theoretically, the interests of the Mexican masses are secured through their membership in the peasant and labor sectors of the official party, the Institutional Revolutionary Party (Partido Institucional Revolucionario, or PRI). The National Peasant Confederation (CNC) brings together small-landholding peasants, landless peons, sharecroppers, agricultural wage workers, and the recipients of government land grants in a single organization designed to represent the needs and concerns of the rural poor. The PRI's labor sector, the Confederation of Mexican Workers (CTM), incorporates most organized workers who thus belong to the official party by virtue of their union affiliation. Ostensibly, the central role of these two organizations is to pressure vigorously on behalf of their peasant and working-class constituents in all intraparty debates on policy. Furthermore, the presence of CNC and CTM candidates on the official party's slate in local, state, and federal elections is supposed to guarantee the sounding of an authentic popular voice in every debate at every level of government.

The reality, however, differs greatly from this idealized version of popular representation. Both the peasant and the labor confederations have been plagued by *continuismo,* the tendency of leaders to perpetuate themselves in office. Officers in both organizations have been imposed on the rank and file from above, and the loyalty of these leaders is to their political patrons, not to the base they nominally represent. Members of the two confederations find themselves powerless to remove and replace officers guilty of bad management, dishonesty, or abuse of power.

The lack of internal democracy within the labor sector has been exacerbated by the fact that the old-guard CTM leaders have drawn closer to management and government as they have become a monied elite in their own right. Over the years, as the same group of labor leaders continued in office, many amassed personal fortunes so large that their interests began to coincide more with those of big business than with the working class. The tacit alliance between CTM bosses and management has led to a general decline in the number of strikes and in the militancy of the demands pressed. Furthermore, union officials frequently collaborate with management and with government to speed up the rate of production, hold down wage demands, and quell protest and strike activity. Given the links between the union bureaucrats and big business and government, the official labor movement has gradually lost its independence as an autonomous interest group and the economic and political bargaining power of the workers, organized in the CTM, has declined sharply. Rather than to bargain for concessions to labor, the central role of labor leadership in the official party system has been to ensure labor support for government policy. This is true even when that government calls for wage freezes in the face of rising prices, or other policy that undercuts the basic well-being of the working class.

Likewise, the peasant sector of the party has, over the years, served more effectively as a mechanism to control peasant unrest than as a means through which the relatively powerless rural masses might give expression to their demands. Like the labor officials, CNC officers are appointed rather than elected. Thus the CNC functionary owes his position of power and prestige not to the peasant constituency he, in theory, is chosen to serve, but to a group of powerful state and regional politicians, many of whom are representatives of the landowning class. Furthermore, the CNC depends for its operating expenses on a subsidy paid to the organization by the PRI. Aside from this source of organizational funds, various government agencies pay regular extralegal subsidies to the peasant organization and provide the all-important patronage that further ties the interests of the CNC leader to the government and its agencies.

It might seem that under this system of leadership recruitment, peasants would at least have the leadership services of a group of quick-witted, dynamic individuals who have pushed their way to the head of the patronage queue. Unfortunately, however energetic, efficient, and dedicated aspirant leaders may be in the promotion of their own careers, overenthusiasm in the representation of the peasant constituency is as self-defeating to the rising CNC politician as it is to CTM officials. This is because the CNC is far more involved in maintaining the status quo of land tenure in the countryside than in pushing for the extension of the agrarian reform program or redressing the imbalances of power between the peasant masses and the small elite of commercial landholders.

Thus, the official party sectors originally designed to give voice to workers' and peasants' demands do not, in practice, operate as militant champions of the social classes whom they ostensibly represent. Even less do they pressure to see peasant and working-class interests incorporated into national policy. The main work of these two organizations is to modify or suppress the demands of members and to contain potential unrest among peasants and workers. Their principal responsibility is to deliver peasant and worker support for the PRI (especially at election time) and to gain popular acceptance for government policies, which often run counter to the interests of both peasants and workers.

Discontent

CNC and CTM politicians often organize massive rallies at which banner-waving peasants and workers, carted to the scene by the truckload, shout and cheer for official party candidates. But these carefully orchestrated displays should not be confused with genuine support for the PRI or its programs. When peasants and workers are interviewed privately, there is a striking unanimity of disaffection and disenchantment with the official party. Bitter disillusionment with the PRI can be heard in private conversations in any city, town, or village in Mexico. These feelings of discontent are voiced not only by the peasants, workers, and the majority of Mexicans who are chronically unemployed and bear the heaviest brunt of the economic policies implemented by the regimes in power since 1940. They are also expressed by students, intellectuals, and a sizable sector of middle-class people who feel the bite of taxes and inflation and the stultifying effects of one-party rule and pervasive corruption in government.

The fact that so much discontent is expressed, albeit privately, suggests that Mexicans enjoy a certain freedom to vent their dissatisfaction, so long as their criticism remains incoherent. It is when the discontented attempt to organize and act in unison to give impact to their criticism and demands for change that they run into trouble. For, as we have seen, the CNC and the CTM provide no hope for those who have reason to push for a reordering of the priorities of Mexican development. And the forms of political expression available to people who want to modify the Mexican system and the policies it produces are severely limited. What, precisely, are the options open to Mexicans — above all to the mass of poor Mexicans — who are unhappy with five decades of official party management?

Opposition

Historically, the dominance of the PRI has not been checked by a vigorous opposition party or parties. The Mexican political system has featured a number of minor parties, but these organizations have not played the role normally associated with opposition parties in most democratic systems. Since the founding of the official party in the aftermath of the Revolution, the relationship between the dominant party and its official opposition has been so close that the minor parties were often referred to as a "kept" opposition. The Mexican sociologist Pablo González Casanova has noted that in some cases opposition parties have been financed by the government itself. At election time these parties would either throw their support to the official party candidate from the outset, or they would provisionally oppose the PRI candidate as a means of bargaining with the government for patronage positions, loans, contracts, and other favors for the most prominent opposition party members. Indeed, in the presidential election of 1976, the opposition parties did not even field a candidate to oppose the PRI's José López Portillo.

With their failure to contest the election of 1976, it became clear that the "kept" opposition parties had reached the point where they were not viable enough even to make a seemingly serious, if unsuccessful, bid for office. Between 1961 and 1976, the proportion of abstentions in congressional and presidential elections rose steadily, despite regulations that oblige Mexicans to vote. A survey by the Mexican Institute of Public Opinion indicated in 1977 that 90 percent of respondents in the Federal District felt that even *symbolic* participation in politics was meaningless. Acting to counter this crisis of legitimacy, in 1977 a new Federal Law on Political Organizations and Electoral Processes was enacted by the regime that enhanced the opportunities for new opposition parties to gain legal registration and to participate more fully in the electoral and governmental processes. The application of a complicated formula for the distribution of seats in the Chamber of Deputies gave greater representation to new minor parties in the legislature. Although the political reform guarded the numerical superiority of the PRI, it did open new organizational opportunities to opponents of the regime. A number of small parties of the Left gained official political status, and the Mexican Communist Party emerged from the semiclandestine state in which it had languished since it became the target of anti-Communist repression in the late 1940s and 1950s.

Do the political reform and the activity of the plethora of small parties it has stimulated mean that genuine, as distinct from "kept" opposition groups, currently present an alternative to PRI rule? Or does the participation of right- and left-wing opponents of the PRI serve merely as elaborate window dressing for democracy? Critics of the reform underscore the tokenism implied in having the Board of Elections budget $20 million and a few hours of free broadcast time to be shared among all opposition parties, when the PRI spent an estimated $300 million on the last campaign, and the official party's candidate moved about in a fleet of jets and helicopters accompanied by an entourage that included 150 members of the press. Skeptics point to the persecution suffered by opposition politicians—especially Communists—in the areas in which they have been able to take local elections. Many are dismayed to see that electoral irregularities still occur with the same discouraging regularity as in the days before the political reform.

In the short run, it seems clear that the new opposition parties, like the largely discredited ones of the past, have reinforced the legitimacy of one-party rule. It may be that in the longer run they will be successful in carrying forward the talk of popular mobilization in order to pose an effective opposition to the PRI. This possibility turns on the capacity of organized opposition to avoid being drawn into the center of gravity occupied by the PRI. For the political reform of the late 1970s opens meaningful opportunities for opposition to official party hegemony only insofar as the new parties can resist the pull that has historically been exerted by the PRI and the state acting in combination. This is likely to prove very difficult because the Mexican system has traditionally drawn in and neutralized its opponents through a system of elaborate mechanisms that function to defuse dissidence, protest, and nonconformity of every kind. The PRI system tends to absorb all opposition: organized and unorganized, institutional and spontaneous, urban and rural, individuals as well as groups. For the most part, the PRI has managed to retain political control because of its success in coopting all serious rivals for power. When those methods have failed, as we shall see, brutal repression has been employed.

The Cooptation Process

Cooptation is a term used to describe the process by which individuals or groups independent enough to threaten the ongoing domination of a single group or party (in this case, the PRI) are traded small concessions or favors in exchange for moderating their demands and reducing their challenge to the dominant group's control. This process takes place to some extent in almost every political system. But in Mexico, the process has been refined by the PRI to the point that it has paralyzed almost all potential opposition.

The key to the cooptation process lies in the centralization of power in the hands of a very few people who sit in Mexico City. There is only one way to get things done in Mexico, whether one is a functionary of the PRI, a government bureaucrat, or the leader of an "independent" peasant or labor union—that is, a union that has eschewed affiliation to the official party. In any of these cases one is forced to go to the center, to the government offices in Mexico City, to get action. There is no alternative source of authority. Bureaucratic institutions exist at the local, regional, and state levels, but decisionmaking of all kinds takes place in Mexico City, and nearly all policy directives emanate from the government offices in the capital. In many cases politicians find they must go directly to the president himself for the favors or governmental decisions they seek. Peasant leaders, for example, note that they may spend as much as half the year in government offices in Mexico City; although these agencies all have branch offices at the regional or state level, it is more efficient to travel a thousand kilometers to Mexico City than to labor long hours in the state capital to win a concession from, say, the regional secretary of water resources, only to have that decision overturned in Mexico City.

With all decisionmaking in the hands of the president, his close advisers, and his party, how can would-be independent peasant or labor unions win the concessions they need to retain the support of their membership? How can they win favors without compromising too much, without being absorbed by the centralized system they are attempting to challenge or change? A survey of the fate of independent peasant and labor organizations in Mexico indicates that in most cases they do not retain their autonomy. Generally they are coopted or bought off. They receive policy concessions for their followers only in return for moderating their militancy.

Most would-be independent popular movements in Mexico are eventually coopted because cooperation or collaboration with the PRI is one of the few avenues of social and economic mobility open to many Mexicans, especially lower-class Mexicans. More important, it is virtually the only way that organizations can win the concessions from the state that they need to fulfill their role as peasants' or workers' representatives. Thus, cooptation operates on two levels: individual and institutional. On the individual level, the process can be observed in the careers of opposition leaders who "sell out" either because the personal rewards and opportunities offered by compromising with the system prove too tempting to resist, or because these leaders are genuinely convinced that by "joining the mainstream" or "working within the system" or "burrowing from within" they will be more effective in realizing the goals of the discontented people they seek to represent.

Cooptation for personal mobility is a pattern we can easily trace in the lives and careers of many noted Mexican intellectuals, including some who were, at one point, known for radical oppositionist views. To be sure, some fortunate individuals manage to achieve prestige, power, or wealth without scrambling for a prominent position in the PRI government structure. In some cases an exceptionally talented person may gain an international reputation, which means that he need not depend on the place he can make for himself in the official party or government hierarchy. Some opposition scholars and intellectuals, for example, retain their sense of political independence and personal integrity by finding work with an international organization like the United Nations, by taking positions as visiting professors abroad, or by working in Mexico in institutions funded largely by foreign foundations. But when and if these appointments come to an end, even the most independent intellectual comes face to face with a sad fact: private universities in Mexico tend to be traditional, conservative, and for the most part Catholic. Technical institutes are under direct federal government authority. And among public institutions, only the National University has any claim to independence from direct government control, and even this institution has, in some periods, been subject to the heavy hand of government meddling.

The overlap between government service and university instruction is so great that there are few university teachers who might hope or expect to earn their living from teaching alone. Thus for intellectuals who choose to live in Mexico, some direct or indirect association with the government is almost impossible to avoid, whether they are employed at the university, in a government-funded research center, or carry out intellectual work within the government or party itself. Obviously, not every intellectual in Mexico can earn a living on the staff of the handful of opposition publishing houses and periodicals. Sooner or later all intellectuals who are not independently wealthy must deal with the dilemma of how to earn a living in Mexico and still retain political independence.

And in fact we find that recruitment of university graduates directly into government or official party jobs is a direct and often irresistible process even for students who have a noted history of left-wing politics. Indeed, one of the best ways for a student to assure himself an attractive job offer after graduation is to build a reputation as a militant leftist student leader. Many of the most choice plums in the state and party hierarchy are reserved for buying off the most articulate, charismatic, and hence politically dangerous leftist students. The routine cooptation of militant student leadership has become so institutionalized in Mexico that personally ambitious students have been known to form radical student groups and initiate student strikes specifically to draw the government's attention to themselves so that they might reap the rewards that accrue to a coopted militant.

If the range of alternatives for personal mobility outside of the state and party are constricted for opposition intellectuals, the avenues of upward mobility open to Mexicans of peasant or working-class origins are much narrower. For lower-class Mexicans, the PRI represents one of the few paths for socio-economic advancement. Working with the CNC, for example, a peasant who is ambitious may overcome his disadvantaged background and rise through the ranks to occupy positions that provide considerable power and wealth. With every step up the CNC ladder, the salary grows and so do the opportunities for kickbacks, payoffs, and other illicit gains. Some particularly adept peasants have parlayed their positions as professional peasant representatives into sizable personal fortunes. Some have even acquired enough money and land to take their place in the ranks of large landowners. Because the CNC provides stepping stones for socio-economic advancement on an individual basis, some peasants are drawn into the official peasant organization precisely because it offers opportunities for the extraction of wealth and prestige that are otherwise absent in the world of an uneducated or poorly educated rural Mexican. Obviously, then, the temptation to work within the system is very great for potential peasant leaders.

The same temptations that lure peasant leaders into the official party machine also draw many potential labor leaders into the CTM. Affiliation with the CTM opens to an ambitious worker a wide range of patronage positions and sinecures at salaries well above a laborer's pay If we compare the opportunities for upward mobility that exist in Mexican society for ordinary peasants and workers with the range of economic and social possibilities that are open to peasants and workers who are coopted into the official party family, we must wonder not that so many people are coopted, but rather that many peasants and workers actually chose the rough rocky course of independent political action.

Cooptation of Organizations

As we have noted, the process of cooptation operates on an institutional or organizational level as well as on an individual plane. As such, cooptation also affects peasant and labor organizations that are not affiliated with either the CNC or the CTM. Most of these organizations have developed in response to specific dissatisfaction with the two PRI sectors in terms of their performance as representative organs. Some of these peasant and labor unions are locally or regionally based, while others, at least nominally, blanket the entire republic. Some are affiliated with the Mexican Communist party; others are independent of affiliation with any political party. All face a common dilemma.

Since the leadership of independent organizations is not imposed from above, as with CNC or CTM officials, independent leaders need popular support to stay in office. Indeed, they need popular support if the organizations themselves are to survive. Obviously the leaders of independent organizations cannot maintain the loyalty of their membership if they cannot effectively represent these members' interests. Peasants and workers who choose to affiliate with an independent organization have normally taken a bold step. In most cases the easy road is to register with the appropriate affiliate of the PRI. Opting for membership in an independent union is often a very committed act. But regardless of how committed a peasant or worker may be to certain ideals, he still needs to be represented by an organization that can effectively advance his interests; an organization that can win labor contracts, represent him before an arbitration board, petition the land reform ministry on his behalf, or market his crop at a decent price. Peasant and labor unions that cannot provide these services for their members have great difficulty in surviving as viable organizations.

Unfortunately, independent labor and peasant unions operate at a serious disadvantage. The bureaucracy that administers the land reform program is complex, vast, and totally in the hands of official party politicians. A variety of federal banks, agencies, ministries, and departments exercise a determining control over land distribution, agricultural production, credit, marketing, and the rural economy as a whole. Together these federal agencies decide which and how much land will be distributed to landless petitioners, which peasants will receive irrigation water from national hydraulic projects, how much technical aid, fertilizer, insecticide, and equipment will be made available, and so forth. In many cases independent peasant groups struggle for years to draw official attention to illegal holdings only to find that when the land is expropriated, it is distributed to CNC-affiliated peasants. In other cases independent peasant groups have lobbied vigorously for state investment in the agrarian economy of their region. But when the projects become a reality, the independent peasant organization members are excluded from the program. Thus the more militant a peasant organization is, and the more serious a challenge it presents to PRI control, the greater the difficulty it faces in winning concessions for its members, or in consolidating the concessions won in the past.

Independent labor organizations are likewise in a disadvantaged position with respect to the government bureaucracies with which they deal. In many cases they are denied legal recognition by the Ministry of Labor. If they are not formally registered as labor representatives, the leaders of such independent unions cannot enter arbitration proceedings on behalf of their members, or negotiate labor contracts, or hold positions on the government commissions on wages. So restricted is the role that independent labor unions can legally play that in some industries workers who join these organizations are forced to hold dual union membership; they retain their CTM union cards so that they will be included in the collective work contracts negotiated by the CTM, and at the same time they attend union meetings at the independent federation and bring their grievances to the attention of the independent labor leaders. For their part, all these leaders can do is make extralegal representations to the Ministry of Labor or to management. Yet, often even this extralegal representation yields more satisfactory results for the worker than he gets when he brings his grievance to his CTM representative, who is likely to be in the pay of the factory owner and who, in any event, has nothing to gain from stirring up trouble for the factory owner.

With so many factors working to the disadvantage of independent organizations, the pressure is great to conform, to assume a conciliatory position toward the government, and even to bring the organization into alliance with the CTM or CNC. Careful study of those independent peasant and labor organizations that have survived for a decade or more generally shows a trend away from militant, oppositionist positions in favor of conformity, collaboration, and cooperation with government.

Naturally, not all opposition organizations succumb to the pressure to fall in line with the government. And among those organizations that we might identify as having been coopted, not all have been compromised to the same degree. The line between partial and total cooptation is hazy, but, roughly speaking, we could say that those individuals or organizations who give up an independent political identity to affiliate directly with the official party or consistently support official party candidates in electoral contests have been completely coopted. Those people and organizations who remain outside the PRI but cooperate off and on with the government, occasionally supporting PRI candidates at election time and playing the political game for concessions according to the established rules, could be called partially coopted.

Repression

When oppositionists refuse to modify their demands or to accommodate themselves or their organization to the system, they are repressed. Repression, like cooptation, differs in degree. Like cooptation, it may be more or less complete.

One form of repression is constant harassment. Meetings and demonstrations are broken up, printing presses are destroyed by hired thugs, armed provocateurs are sent in to menace students in their classrooms, and so forth. Individuals may be followed by police agents, and they or their families may be implicitly or explicitly threatened with violence. The crucial point about all these forms of harassment is that they are likely to make it difficult, if not impossible, for an organization or individual to act politically. In such cases so much energy must be devoted to self-defense and — in the case of organizations — to internal security, that the harassed person or organization may become politically paralyzed.

An even more serious stage of repression is reached when movement leaders are summarily arrested and put in prison, frequently at the most crucial moment in the development of their political struggle. The leaders may be held for a year or longer, with or without a trial. But even when their imprisonment is relatively short-term, they may find upon release that their movement has lost momentum.

Further along the scale of repression is the long-term imprisonment of a movement's key leaders. During long-term imprisonment, the health and at times even the spirit of leaders may be broken, while without its leadership the movement may lose momentum and in the long run disintegrate completely. After a lengthy term behind bars, the leaders may be released only to find that they have neither the physical strength nor the remaining political support to resume their activities or rebuild their movement.

Finally, the most serious form of repression is the assassination of principal leaders and slaying of supporters. The cases in which the activists in an opposition organization are wiped out together with the leadership occur, generally speaking, in the countryside. Sometimes the army or the police forces play a direct role in the slaughter, while at other times "private armies" of thugs hired by landowners whose interests are threatened carry out the massacre of peasant families involved in the struggle. It is difficult to know how often either the state or landlords have recourse to this extreme measure, but if we consider only the well-known, well-documented incidents of assassination, we must conclude that it is not infrequently employed. The names of some of the leaders who were killed because they would not compromise are widely recognized. But in most cases we will never know the names or number of people who refused to moderate their political behavior, because these people were eliminated before they reached national or international prominence.

Rural people are most often killed in their local areas and word seldom travels beyond the region, while urban oppositionists "disappear" in a variety of mysterious ways, one being the practice of dropping people out of airplanes into the Gulf of Mexico. Both local and national newspapers carry frequent accounts of violent conflict in the countryside. However, often what is reported as a shootout between rival peasant factions, a simple case of homicide, or a gun battle between police and a bandit gang turns out, upon careful investigation, to have been an instance of armed repression of an opposition movement or leader by hired assassins. Therefore, it would be no exaggeration to say that probably every day in some part of Mexico a dissident peasant, a radical labor leader, or a militant student is killed by either the army, the police, or political opponents on the local scene.

Thus, while we have some idea of how many organizations make an accommodation with the system, we can only guess at the number of people and groups who refuse to be coopted. Accordingly, we can only speculate whether as many Mexicans resist the cooptive pull of the political system (and are eliminated from the political scene as a result) as choose the path of collaboration with their government. But overall, the pattern is clear enough: Some groups are coopted, while those that refuse to cooperate are harassed, repressed, or decapitated through the imprisonment or assassination of their leaders.

And so the party that came to power after the decades of revolutionary struggle continues to perpetuate itself in power. It is not that opposition movements do not develop to challenge the dominance of the ruling party. It is rather that such movements are usually demobilized before they can grow powerful enough to make their impact felt. In this system of social control, both repression and persuasion play a role in the maintenance of order. There is every indication that those in power greatly prefer to coopt a student or labor leader or to buy off a group of troublesome peasants with a grant of marginal land than to mow down dissidents in a hail of bullets — especially if the dissidents present themselves in a plaza in Mexico City, rather than on a lonely mountainside in Guerrero. However, the readiness of those in power to employ force in tight circumstances also works to increase the persuasive power of their cooptive techniques.

25

MASSACRE IN MEXICO

Elena Pointowska

As athletes, journalists, and spectators gathered in Mexico City for the 1968 Olympic Games, they were stunned by the massacre of student demonstrators at the Plaza of Three Cultures (also called Tlatelolco) the night of October 2. Some ten thousand students met in peaceful protest against police repression, illegal arrests, and violations of human rights. Suddenly army and police squads opened fire on the students. The Manchester Guardian's *investigation reported that 325 men and women were killed. More than two thousand reportedly were wounded. More than two thousand were jailed, and five years later more than seventy remained in prison. Elena Pointowska, a well-known Mexican journalist and author of eight fiction and nonfiction volumes, obtained these eyewitness accounts from students, journalists, police, and bystanders. Whether they supported the government or the students, their voices express the author's confusion that the killings could occur and her anguish at the death of her son, a victim of Tlatelolco.*

Student demonstrations have occurred sporadically since before the Revolution and had become increasingly common in Mexico City and the provinces after World War II. The 1968 movement developed to protest the government's use of the granaderos, *or riot police, to break up a fight between students representing rival prep schools in July. Student protests provoked further incidents with the police. Huge demonstrations at the National University (UNAM) and the National Polytechnical Institute resulted in the formation of a National Strike Committee (CNH) and the formulation of demands to end repression. Students attempted to gain the support of workers with rallies, street drama, and speeches. They wanted a mass movement to force the government to reform the official party so as to provide greater opportunity for political participation. To display their commitment and discipline, the leaders organized a silent march that brought an estimated half million people to the Zócalo, the capital's center plaza. President Gustavo Díaz Ordaz refused to negotiate with the students, nor would he chance disruption of the Olympics. His stepped-up repression of the demonstrators climaxed October 2.*

The testimonies that follow reveal much about the demonstrators and their attitudes. The participation of female students and the reactions of their male counterparts offer a striking picture of the status of women in Mexico. Other accounts indicate in personal terms the meaning of torture. Above all, the witnesses interviewed by Pointowska express the confusion, fear, and horror that night in the Plaza of Three Cultures.

I'm from the UNAM, where they talk in a pedantic in-group jargon. If you're a university student, you're one of the elite. I'd hung around with boys whose fathers worked for my father ever since I was a kid, and when I began working in the brigades I could make myself understood, but I soon noticed that when guys from the Faculty of Political Sciences, Paco Taibo for instance, came in contact with working-class people, in the beginning especially, they would talk to them about the class struggle, the means of production in the hands of the bourgeoisie, the class in power, and all that stuff, and nobody understood them. There was no communication. As a matter of fact, there was a wall of mistrust between them. The same thing happened with the students from Humanities. The girls from Philosophy would come back from the brigade meetings looking as cute as hell and with a big smile on their face and say, "Comrades, we went to see the workers today! It was really great, really exciting! We passed out handbills: 'Come on, you workmen, take one, here you are, my good fellow.' " And the workers would say: "What the hell do those girls think they're doing?" The workers looked on us students as clowns of some sort, if not downright asses. Then I noticed that the language began changing, or rather, that we were discovering a common language, and that's what pleased me most about the whole Movement.... Little by little working-class people began to teach us how to talk like them and the way they applauded showed us we understood each other. We began to learn about Mexico and its sad realities. This was an everyday experience in the brigade. Once we went to a market out by Ixtapalapa to pass out handbills. Later it came my turn to speak, and when I finished, a little old lady, a really old one, gave me a couple of pesos tied in a handkerchief or a little rag. I was terribly touched, and gave her money back to her because she needed it more than we did, but I'll remember her little wrinkled hand, that crumpled handkerchief, her withered old lady's face peering up at me for the rest of my life. . . . Another time, those of us from Theoretical Physics and Sciences held a meeting in Xochimilco. All of us were deeply touched by the people's response. We drew a crowd of six thousand!

Salvador Martínez de la Roca (Pino),
of the Action Committee, UNAM

The fact is, workers are very reactionary.

Rebeca Navarro Mendiola, student at the Faculty of
Philosophy and Letters, UNAM

They're so thick between the ears! What a laugh—politicizing workers!

Raquel Núñez Ochoa, student, Iberoamerican University

TO THE PEOPLE:
The National Strike Committee invites all workers, peasants, teachers, students, and the general public to the
GREAT SILENT MARCH
In support of our six-point petition:
1. Freedom for all political prisoners.
2. Revocation of Article 145 of the Federal Penal Code.
3. Disbandment of the corps of granaderos.
4. Dismissal of police officials Luis Cueto, Raúl Mendiolea, and A. Frías.
5. Payment of indemnities to the families of all those killed and injured since the beginning of the conflict.
6. Determination of the responsibility of individual government officials implicated in the bloodshed.
We have called this march to press for the immediate and complete satisfaction of our demands by the Executive Power
We repeat that our Movement has no connection with the Twentieth Olympic Games to be held in our country or with the national holidays commemorating our Independence, and that this

Committee has no intention of interfering with them in any way. We insist, once again, that all negotiations aimed at resolving this conflict must be public.

The march will begin today, Friday the thirteenth, at four p.m. at the National Museum of Anthropology and History and will end with a public meeting in the Plaza de la Constitución.

The day has come when our silence will be more eloquent than our words, which yesterday were stilled by bayonets.

Paid announcement in El Día, *September 13, 1968*

Women were responsible for much of the Movement's fighting spirit. I remember lots of the girl comrades: Marta, from the Wilfredo Massieu School; Tita and Nacha from Law; Bertha from Medicine; Mari Carmen, Evilia, and Betty from Sciences; Consuelito, Maravilia, and Adriana from Preparatory; Marcia, of course — and thousands of others, literally thousands more, and as groups the marvelous girls from the School of Nursing at Poli, the ones from Biological Sciences, from the med school at UNAM, and so on.

The girl comrades from the School of Nursing were real heroines during the attack on the Santo Tomás campus. They did the whole Adelita bit spontaneously, straight from the heart. They willingly risked their lives to care for our wounded, help get them off the campus, and attend to their every need. Because of their courage and their loyalty to the cause all our women comrades came to play a very important role in the Movement.

The girl students once phoned us that right-wing student groups had taken over a University high school. We immediately rounded up a whole bunch of students to go see what was happening. I saw four girls from my school get on the bus from Economics. "You girls get out of there this minute. We men are the only ones who are going this time," I told them.

They were highly indignant, and immediately replied that Che [Guevara] allowed women to fight in *his* brigade, and the hell with me. I insisted, and thought they'd finally agreed to get off the bus. I went back inside for a moment and then climbed back on the bus, and we started off. Some three hundred of us men students arrived at the high school — plus the four girl students sitting way at the back of the bus from Economics, where I wasn't likely to spot them.

Luckily nothing happened there at the high school, and we all got back safe and sound to CU.

In the last speech of the day at the Silent Demonstration, I said something I really regret now. It was a bad mistake, and what's more, entirely unfair of me, to have said at one point in my speech, "Let us not shed tears like women for what we were unable to defend like men." The day after the demonstration, when I got back to my school, I found two brigades of girls waiting there for me. I spent several hours trying to explain, amid angry shouts and quite justifiable protests on their part, that what I had said had merely been a figure of speech. They finally were kind enough to accept my apology, and two days later they brought me a delicious cake, which those of us in the brigade on guard and other comrades devoured on the spot.

Eduardo Valle Espinoza
(Owl-Eyes), of the CNH

The tallest one came over to me and put a hood over my head, one made of some sort of thick cloth, like burlap, but so coarsely woven that I could see light through it. The thing covered my entire head and neck, down to my Adam's apple. Then they grabbed my arms and tied my hands behind my back.

At that moment I heard the same hoarse voice as before, rasping in a threatening tone, "Who's your successor on the National Strike Committee?"

"I don't have any idea," I answered.

"Well then, we'll just have to refresh your memory. Either you talk or we'll kill you. . . . You traitor, you bastard, you! What do you sons of bitches want, anyway? Tell me, what's the point of what you're doing?" he asked then. . . .

More punches then, this time right in the balls. The pain was so intense I doubled up and fell to the floor. They stopped punching me then and instead began kicking me from head to foot as I lay there. . . .

More punches, plus electric shocks in my testicles, my rectum, my mouth. And more questions . . .

"We're going to shoot two others before we shoot you."

I heard two volleys of rifle fire and two *coups de grâce* with a pistol, and then they led me over to touch two bodies lying there. . . .

Then they tied me up again and shot a pistol off just half an inch or
so from my ear. Then after that they said, "Let's not bother killing
him . . . let's just cut his balls off. . . ." After they'd subjected me to
what they called a "warm-up," they injected my testicles with an
anesthetic and pretended they were castrating me—cutting my
scrotum with a razor or a scalpel—I still have a scar there. All this
happened on the night of October 2, 1968, and went on till six the
next morning, the third. . . . All because I refused to sign a statement
denouncing the Popular Student Movement or incriminating
myself—the whole bunch of lies they wanted me to sign my name
to would have betrayed the democratic cause of our people, and I
refused to sign that "confession." At six on the morning of the third,
I was taken to Lecumberri Prison again, where I was held incom-
municado, in the worst possible conditions: they wouldn't even let
me out of my cell to go to the bathroom, and I had to use a five-
gallon bucket that was never cleaned once during the entire twenty-
eight days that I was kept there in solitary. I didn't even see the
guards. I had neither a blanket nor a mattress. They kept me on a
near-starvation diet—the only food they gave me was one glass of
corn gruel in the morning and another in the evening, pushed
through a hole in the door of my cell. . . .

Luis Tomas Cervantes Cabeza
de Vaca, of the CNH

The Army units approached from all directions and encircled the
crowd in a pincers movement, and in just a few moments all the
exits were blocked off. From up there on the fourth floor of the
Chihuahua building, where the speakers' platform had been set up,
we couldn't see what the Army was up to and we couldn't
understand why the crowd was panicking. The two helicopters that
had been hovering over the Plaza almost from the very beginning
of the meeting had suddenly started making very hostile maneuvers, flying lower and lower in tighter and tighter circles just above
the heads of the crowd, and then they had launched two flares, a
green one first and then a red one; when the second one went off the
panic started, and we members of the Committee did our best to
stop it: none of us there on the speakers' stand could see that the
Army troops below us were advancing across the Plaza. When they

found themselves confronted by a wall of bayonets, the crowd halted and immediately drew back; then we saw a great wave of people start running toward the other side of the Plaza too; and as we stood watching from up there on the speakers' stand, we saw the whole crowd head in another direction. That was the last thing we saw down below, for at that moment the fourth floor was taken over by the Olimpia Battalion. Even though we had no idea why the crowd had panicked and was running first in one direction and then in the other, those of us who had remained there at the microphone till the very last found ourselves looking down the barrels of machine guns when we turned around. The balcony had been occupied by the Olimpia Battalion and we were ordered to put our hands up and face the wall, and given strict orders not to turn around in the direction of the Plaza; if we so much as moved a muscle, they hit us over the head or in the ribs with their rifle butts. Once the trap they had set snapped shut, the collective murder began.

Gilberto Guevara Niebla, of the CNH

Perhaps the most tragic sight of all was the blood-stained shoes scattered all over the Plaza, like mute witnesses of the sudden flight of their owners.

José Luis Mejías, in an article entitled "A Meeting That Ended in Tragedy," Diario de la Tarde, *October 3, 1968*

A doctor bandaged me all up, and then he said to me, "Take those stairs over there and get out of here. There's no reason why you should have to make a statement. If you stay here, they may arrest you. . . . Go see a doctor tomorrow and have him take care of you. You're all right for the time being. I've disinfected the wound. . . ." That doctor and lots of the others were furious at the soldiers for having invaded the Red Cross hospital. . . .

My daughter and I went straight home from the Red Cross, and I was indignant when the newspapers reported during the next few days that the students had been armed and had deliberately provoked the Army into attacking them. I'm morally certain that it's a lie that the students had weapons, because among the hundred or

so persons in that shop where we were, not a one of them was
carrying any sort of weapon.

Matilde Rodríguez, mother of a family

At the morgue . . . the autopsies showed that most of the victims
died . . . of bayonet wounds . . . others from gunshot wounds from
weapons fired at close range. The doctors performing the autopsies
were particularly struck by three of the corpses they examined: that
of a youngster of about thirteen years of age who had died of a
bayonet wound in the skull . . . that of an old woman who died from
a bayonet wound in the back . . . and that of a young girl who had
received a bayonet wound in her left side extending from her
armpit to her hip. . . .

*News story entitled "Heartrending Identification of the
Victims," El Universal, October 4, 1968*

Margarita was absolutely beside herself. We spent the entire night
looking for her son, and her fit of hysteria reached its peak, so to
speak, the next day, when they phoned us that he was in one of the
apartments in the Chihuahua building, though they couldn't tell us
exactly which one he was in. Then I witnessed really awful scenes,
because it wasn't only Margarita who was searching, but lots of
other people, lots of other mothers looking for their children, lots of
whom were very young, a couple of them only two years or so old,
though others, like Margarita's boy, were high-school kids.
Margarita was more or less out of her mind by that time and was
going from door to door shouting, "Carlitos, it's me, Mama! Let me
in!" It was all straight out of Kafka. Obviously, her son wouldn't
have opened the door for anyone.

Mercedes Olivera de Vázquez, anthropologist

The next day and during the days that followed, people became
more and more apprehensive. There were thousands of persons
who had suddenly disappeared without a trace. Alarming, contradictory rumors that went the rounds made people even more
enraged and distraught. There were huge throngs at the hospitals

day after day, around the clock: people kept scrutinizing the lists of wounded and making the rounds of all the morgues in the city to see if their friends or relatives were among the dead, and spent endless hours waiting at the gates of the prisons and the various courts for the lists of prisoners to be posted. People were not only grief-stricken and worried; they were also angry at the government's repressive policies, and the situation was further aggravated by the insolent behavior of the police toward those who came to them to inquire after their friends and relatives. After eleven days with absolutely no news as to what had happened to Raúl, my husband and I paid to have a petition addressed to the Attorney General of Mexico inserted in the newspaper.

Manuela Garín de Alvarez, mathematician
and professor at the School of Engineering and
Faculty of Sciences, UNAM

I went to the Franciscan Brothers of the Tlatelolco parish and told them that I had come as a representative of a group of mothers of youngsters who had been killed and wounded on October 2, and that we would like to have a requiem mass said for them there in Tlatelolco.

The reply was, "We're very sorry, but there aren't any priests available to celebrate a requiem mass on the day you've requested. Our list of masses that day is already full up.". . .

"In that case this is doubtless the only church in Mexico that has every minute of its time booked up . . .

"No, the church is entirely booked that day." . . .

Margarita Nolasco, anthropologist

Two helicopters kept circling the church. I saw several green flares go off in the sky. I stood there like a robot, listening to the familiar sound of bullets whizzing past. . . . The gunfire became heavier and heavier, and then Army troops appeared, as though somebody had pushed a button. . . .

Rodolfo Martínez, press photographer,
in "The Gun Battle as the Press Photographers
Saw It," La Prensa, October 3, 1968

Don't be frightened, don't run, they're trying to stir up trouble, don't try to escape, comrades, keep calm, everybody, don't run, keep calm, comrades. . . .

Eduardo Espinoza Valle (Owl-Eyes), of the CNH

They're dead bodies, sir. . . .
A soldier, to José Antonio Campo, reporter for El Día

Not since the military uprising against Madero led by Victoriano Huerta in 1913 had there been anything that had damaged our image as much as Tlatelolco/October 2, that had so defiled us, that had so stunned us, that had filled our mouths with the taste of blood, the blood of our dead.

Isabel Sperry de Barraza, mother of a family

26

MEXICO'S FOOD PROBLEM

Thomas G. Sanders

In the 1970s the American Universities Field Staff initiated a long-term program examining the effects of modernization on value systems, including problems related to population growth. Nothing is more crucial for an increasing population than food. As a field staff member, Thomas G. Sanders, who has published widely on contemporary Brazil, Chile, and Mexico, wrote a series of reports on Mexican agriculture. In the following essay, written during the presidency of Luis Echeverría (1970–76), he discusses the food problem from the perspectives of the nation's nutritional situation, the relationship between the burgeoning population and food production, and increasing food imports. Each of these themes provokes heated debate: Do corn, beans, and tortillas constitute a diet poor in nourishment or simply a nonwestern meal? Can and should the government attempt to control the population? Should small agricultural units (especially the ejidos) be sacrificed to large-scale, mechanized agribusiness to reduce imports? The debate questions revolutionary traditions of indigenism (the diet), secularization (agreement with the Church on population policy), and agrarian reform (distribution in small plots). Sanders examines the clash of revolutionary goals and the reality of the nation's limited arable land and poorly distributed water resources. He provides a valuable discussion of rural classes. These should be compared to the visions of the countryside held by the early revolutionaries. The author also discusses CONASUPO, the agency that regulates prices and that has become the crucial link between the food producers and the hungry, urban poor. Sanders tries to strike a balance between optimism for the Echeverría program and pessimism with Mexico's bureaucratic implementation of reforms.

Since the mid-1970s when Sanders made this appraisal, Mexico's problems have increased. The population has zoomed from 48,225,238 in 1970 to 67,405,700 in 1980, tripling since 1940. Urbanization has intensified the popula-

tion problem, especially in the capital, which experts estimated in 1984 had become the world's largest city, with eighteen million residents. Food imports continued to grow, adding to the other severe difficulties caused by the collapse of the Mexican peso (fluctuating at about 210 to the dollar in 1984) and the world's largest foreign debt. During the administration of José López Portillo (1976–82), the subsidized food program proved incapable of providing sufficient staples to the masses caught between the less and less valuable peso and the more and more costly tortillas, beans, and chiles. Were Sanders to write his essay in the grinding circumstances of the mid-1980s, he would describe a much more somber situation. Among the nation's problems, food remains the most basic.

Although revolutions overthrow the most hated symbols of the past and forge a new sense of national identity, they do not automatically solve problems. Mexico is a good example. It carried out the first great social revolution of the twentieth century and broke up the large landholdings called *haciendas,* but after fifty years of a new social order, the agricultural sector has not been sufficiently reorganized to guarantee a good diet for the Mexican people.

The current Mexican agricultural situation is best interpreted as one of deep concern, though not of disaster. That population is growing faster than food production and the government is importing unprecedented quantities of staples like corn, beans, wheat, milk, and cooking oil has received attention and criticism. To counterbalance these factors, however, Mexico remains an important exporter of such agricultural products as cotton, livestock, sugar, vegetables, fruits, and coffee, which under normal circumstances outweigh import needs.

The Problem

The Mexican food "problem" can be defined within three perspectives: (1) the current nutritional situation of the people, (2) the relationship between population growth and food production, and (3) the rapid increase of food imports since 1970.

The food problem in Mexico is not one of starvation but of deficiency, accentuated by inequitable distribution of available food resources among different classes and regions. Recent studies by the Mexican Institute of Nutrition highlight some of the inadequacies of the national diet. As in most countries, there is a wide spectrum in the quantity of food consumed by Mexicans, but three "typical" diets are common. Diet A, which prevails among peasants and to some extent the lower classes of the cities, is composed of corn and beans, supplemented by a few other products like fruit, sugar, and meat on special occasions. Diet B is slightly more diversified. The corn and bean base is supplemented by coffee, wheat bread, soup of rice or pasta, and meat. Diet B is found in small towns and among the upper lower and middle classes. Diet C, common to the urban upper and middle classes, is similar to the pattern in developed countries. For breakfast it may include juice, eggs, and *café con leche*. The midday meal is large, with corn, beans, meat, salad, rice, and dessert. The evening meal is similar, but with smaller quantities of the different items.

Diet A is the country's chief problem. It is characteristic of perhaps half the population, and it provides an estimated 2,115 calories daily per person, but includes only 56 grams of protein. Some of Mexico's leading anthropologists argue, correctly, I think, that the peasants' diet is better than it appears on the surface, because they eat chile peppers (rich in vitamins) and seasonal fruits, and drink alcoholic beverages like *pulque* (made from *maguey*). They also may eat a wide range of nutritious plants, leaves, roots, insects, birds, and rodents, which are considered unacceptable by more affluent people. And finally, the daily staples are supplemented at fiestas by a variety of special foods, of which meat is the most important nutritionally.

Other studies demonstrate dietary variations between the more developed and the underdeveloped regions of Mexico. The best standards are found in the Northwest and along the border with the United States, where serious malnutrition does not exist, and preschool mortality averages only 4.8 per 1,000 inhabitants. Daily calorie consumption reaches 2,330, including 69 grams of protein. A second region comprises the North in general and both coasts. There people average 2,124 calories and 60 grams of protein. Preschool mortality is 10.2/1,000, and 1 percent of the people suffer from serious nutritional deficiencies. In the center of the country, average calorie levels drop to 2,064 and proteins to 56 grams. Serious malnutrition affects 3.5 percent of the people, and preschool mortality ascends to 16.5/1,000. The region with the most deficient food intake is the Southeast, plus the states of Chiapas, Oaxaca, and Guerrero in the South. Daily averages there are 1,893 calories and 50 grams of protein. Preschool mortality is 25.2/1,000, and 4.1 percent of the population are gravely malnourished.

It is commonly said that Mexicans are not hungry, because they eat large quantities of filling corn dishes such as tortillas, tamales, *pozole* (a soup), and *atole* (a gruel), but rather they are poorly nourished in terms of basic food requirements. Unquestionably, the health and stature of many Mexicans are affected by the following dietary deficiencies. (1) Milk consumption is very low. Although the overwhelming majority of Mexican mothers, especially the poor, nurse their children, people drink little or no milk after weaning. Nutritionist Dr. Adolfo Chávez estimates that of the approximately eleven million children in Mexico under five years of age, three million never drink milk, and another three million do not drink enough. This has serious consequences for physical and mental development. In the poorest states of the Federation, more than 60 percent of the population have never had milk after infancy. (2) Proteins are derived largely from nonanimal foods. Beans, a basic staple, are the Mexicans' salvation because of their high protein content. Animal proteins, which have a more favorable relationship of essential amino acids, are insufficient among the poor because meat, milk, and eggs are at best only occasional food items. The average national meat consumption, for example, is only 7 kilos, 620 grams (approximately 17.5 pounds) annually. (3) Deficiencies in essential vitamins and minerals cause elevated rates of anemia (in 20 percent of preschool children), pellagra, scurvy, and short stature. . . .

From a second perspective on Mexico's food "problem," population growth and consumer demand are putting increasing pressure on agriculture and livestock production. In comparison with other countries, Mexico's performance, measured in terms of percentage increase in agriculture and livestock production since 1935, has been meritorious, but population increase and demand for food during the same period have absorbed increments in production and exceeded them in recent years. . . . Agricultural policy until the 1940s was oriented chiefly to instituting a revised system of land tenure, a slow process because of inadequate personnel and funds. And only in the 1940s and 1950s, and then sporadically, have governments been willing to dedicate significant sums of money to programs for increasing production. Agricultural production grew 5.9 percent annually between 1940 and 1950, 6.0 percent from 1950 to 1960, and 7.2 percent from 1960 to 1965.

Before 1940 agricultural policy focused on land redistribution, culminating in the administration of President Lázaro Cárdenas (1934–40), who transferred more than 20 million hectares to 775,845 beneficiaries. For various reasons, the more conservative administrations that followed Cárdenas gave less emphasis to agrarian reform and more to building infrastructure and introducing new technology. Large sums went into building irrigation dams; a research program utilizing foreign personnel was set up with the help of the Rockefeller Foundation; and by the 1950s some of the more progressive farmers had begun using improved seeds, fertilizer, machinery, and insecticides. This group, a small minority of the Mexican agricultural population, achieved significant increases in production of such crops as wheat, according to a pattern that was later to be called the Green Revolution. In their case, irrigation and the new technological inputs contributed to spectacular increases.

In other cases, growth in production resulted from opening new lands. Substantial expansion also occurred in cultivation of cotton, sugar, and vegetables, which are largely controlled by a small group of sizable producers and exported. Other increases occurred in sorghum and potatoes, which had not been significant Mexican products in the past.

On the other side of the ledger, the vast majority of Mexican farmers, peasants with small holdings, did not participate in these technological changes. Their methods continued to be traditional and their yields low. While all components of the Mexican agricultural system increased their production somewhat during the late 1940s and the 1950s, the more innovative farmers with larger holdings, who had access to irrigation and adopted new technology, made a more than proportional contribution to the expanded output. And in the most common food items, return per hectare grew at a relatively slow pace. In the two decades 1940–50 and 1950–60, corn yields per hectare increased 2.5 and 0.7 percent annually, wheat 2.6 and 3.3 percent, and beans 3.2 and 4.1 percent. . . .

During the past decade, however, Mexico has experienced a crescendo of population growth rates that now average 3.4 percent annually. Agricultural production . . . did not keep up with population, much less with consumer demand. The percentage of public investment allocated to agriculture and livestock, which ranged up to 20 percent in the period from 1940 to 1957, declined to about 9 percent in 1970. In part, this was because the presidential administrations of Adolfo López Mateos (1958–64) and Gustavo Díaz Ordaz (1964–70) were giving central emphasis to industrialization, and in part because earlier productive increases created the illusion that solving the agricultural problem and providing an adequate food supply are easier than they really are.

From the perspective of food imports, the food problem has also worsened, particularly since 1970, as Mexico has imported ever increasing quantities of basic food items. In part, this has resulted from bad weather, which damaged crops and upset plans for self-sufficiency, but most important, demand for food is constantly growing as a correlate of increases in population, consumption, and higher expectations of an inadequate diet. The Echeverría administration is clearly aware of the serious difficulties in the agricultural sector and is allocating unprecedented sums to resolve them.

In the years immediately preceding 1970, Mexico was practically self-sufficient in basic foodstuffs because of the productive increases through 1965. In 1970, the food import bill was a modest 1,760 million pesos (12.5 pesos = US$1).

During the 1970s, however, food imports have risen at an alarming rate. . . . Food exports, on the other hand, have not grown comparably, especially between 1973 and 1974. In fact, the export values of such key rubrics as shrimp, tomatoes, fresh meat, and fresh vegetables went down during this period.

Apart from the fact that importing food that can be produced domestically fails to utilize the country's already excessive rural labor supply, the most disturbing trend in these figures is that in 1974, Mexico's long-time commercial advantage in food and agricultural products has probably disappeared. . . .

Hopefully this is a temporary fluctuation, for its long-range effects could be quite damaging. Mexico has depended immeasurably on the agricultural trade surplus for capital goods, raw materials, and other essentials for its industrialization, as well as for food imports.

The Policy Framework

The policy framework for overcoming the problem of inadequate food production includes the factors of land and water resources, the system of land tenure, and the categories or classes of rural labor. This framework can be interpreted in two ways. On the one hand, it can be viewed as a set of potential factors to be used in increasing production, on the assumption, which is correct, that natural and human resources are not being used to their full potential. On the other hand, they may be considered limiting factors, not only because they are restraints but also because they accentuate the problem that planners face.

Land and Water

Contrary to much popular Mexican belief, the land that can be utilized for agriculture and livestock is restricted in size and poor in quality. . . .

Available water, which comes chiefly from streams, is poorly distributed in relation to patterns of population settlement. The regions of great population, like the center and the border with the United States, already suffer a deficit of water. Although total water possibilities in these areas have not been exploited, agricultural, industrial, hydroelectric, and domestic demands are straining existent supplies. In contrast, most of the water in Mexico is found at low altitudes or in the Southeast, where population is lightly concentrated. Though extensive hydraulic construction over several decades has managed to provide the infrastructure for steady increases in agricultural production, the decades to come will require more concentrated exploitation of surface and sub-surface water resources, the transfer of water from surplus to deficit regions, and a national policy of saving and wise use of water.

The amount of arable land with which Mexican agricultural policy can work is consequently limited. Although analyses of its extent differ, the following can be considered a minimum estimate:

The total irrigated area of Mexico can be estimated at 11 million hectares [27.2 million acres], including three million which can be irrigated with subsoil water. Another 19 million [hectares] can be cultivated by rainfall, in more or less uncertain conditions depending on location, that include two million located in the humid zones, which require dams for control and channeling the rivers as well as for blocking, channeling, and draining the land. To sum up, the agricultural future of Mexico is based on the exploitation of 30 million hectares [74 million acres].

A more sanguine calculation can be based on even more recent affirmations by the Secretariat of Hydraulic Resources that the country can irrigate as many as 16 million hectares. If this is so, the total agricultural resources of Mexico may reach 35 or 40 million hectares. When this total is compared with population projections, it was estimated that in 1980, when Mexico would have 71 million inhabitants, one-half hectare [1.24 acres] would be cultivated for each person. By the year 2000, when the most common population estimate is 135 million, only one-fourth hectare per person will be available to grow crops.

Land Tenure

A second factor some feel the Mexican government must consider in its food policy is the land tenure systems that have evolved since the Revolution. It is common for both Mexicans and outside critics to blame agricultural problems on certain tenure arrangements — usually either minifundism or latifundism. In reality low production stems from a complex legacy of the past, not simply land tenure. Throughout its history Mexican agriculture has been characterized by simple technology, climatic uncertainty, low yields, and a subsistence existence for most producers. The problem of development is precisely to replace traditional procedures by more modern ones. High levels of production have been achieved in only a minority of Mexican landholdings. The objective of policy must be to expand production more widely throughout the entire agricultural system, no matter what the structure of landholding may be. . . .

The heritage of agrarian reform is the land tenure policy that current and future Mexican governments will follow, and if necessary, change. Agrarian reform has given Mexico a dual tenure system, *ejidal* and private. Communal property is similar to *ejidos*, in combining community grazing and forest lands with individual plots. Within the *ejidos*, organization ranges from totally "collective" (or cooperative) to totally individualistic. This has resulted from the incapacity of public authorities, once they determined the boundaries of the *ejidos*, to control the mode of organizing production. And finally, both the *ejidal* and private sectors have wide variations in size of holding, in cultivable land, and in irrigation. . . .

Rural Classes

The allocation and acquisition of land over many decades has resulted in five definable rural classes.

(1) The *ejidatarios.* These are the beneficiaries of agrarian reform and as such are the most closely tied to government. Their lands range from good to bad, from large to small, and the system of production from collective (or cooperative) to individualistic.

From a policy point of view the *ejidatarios* offer certain problems. First, most of them are minifundists, 85 percent having less than 10 hectares of cultivable land. The amount of hectarage in some instances cannot provide a minimum existence at existing. production levels, and in others, it can do so only if yield per hectare is greatly increased. Not surprisingly, many *ejidatarios* rent to others or neglect their land while they work elsewhere. Second, most *ejidatarios* continue to lack definitive title to their land. . . .

Since most *ejidatarios* have no proof of ownership, they cannot utilize such vital government resources as credit. And third, most *ejidatarios* are not organized according to procedures for maximizing production. Once *ejidos* were formed, their members agreed on individual plots and in most cases on individual systems of exploitation that made the *ejidatarios* little different from property-owning minifundists.

(2) Minifundists. This class originated because the *hacienda* owners, faced with eventual expropriation, were willing to sell fractions of their holdings to salaried workers, renters, and other buyers. The buyers often preferred to take advantage of the opportunity to own land rather than face the delays, uncertainty, and bureaucratic entanglements in soliciting participation in an *ejido*. In 1960, Mexico had 929,000 smallholders with less than five hectares. Like the poorer *ejidatarios*, they still produce largely for home consumption and do not enjoy the benefit of government services.

Minifundism is especially common in the heavily populated

central and southern Pacific regions. In the former zone, 81.2 percent of the private holdings are less than five hectares and in the latter, 78 percent.

Extensive government investment in infrastructure and promotion of cooperatives can improve output among some of this group, but basically they do not have promising possibilities. . . .

(3) Medium-sized producers. According to the Agricultural Census of 1960, about 162,000 owners have between 10 and 100 hectares of productive land. Although in the past expansion of this class was perceived as a solution to agricultural needs, it represents only a small minority of the rural population today and probably will not expand, given the current policy of distributing the remaining available land.

This class has diverse origins. In some instances they are the original owners (or their descendants) of the inalienable portion of larger holdings that have been expropriated. Some of them were skilled agricultural personnel such as administrators who acquired land after the Revolution. In other cases enterprising individuals have simply accumulated more land than the average smallholder, or in some instances they acquired land through government colonization programs.

As rural, middle-class owners, their educational level and understanding of agricultural technology are a step above the minifundists, many of whom are illiterate or semiliterate. Because of the size, stability, and productivity of their holdings, they usually have no trouble securing credit and other productive inputs. In many cases they employ hired labor and produce largely for the market.

(4) Large landholders. This small group has been an important contributor to the production of such commercial crops as wheat and soybeans for the domestic market and vegetables, cotton, and sugar for export.

Although the Revolution aimed at destroying latifundios, this class survived principally because of the political influence of their beneficiaries, government recognition of their contribution to the national economy, and generous legal limits to inaffectability of property. Current agrarian reform legislation allows owners to retain up to 100 hectares of irrigated land, 150 hectares dedicated to cotton, or 300 hectares in bananas, sugar cane, coffee, henequin, coconuts, cacao, fruit trees, or certain other products. Anyone who qualifies for these exemptions is automatically a large-scale and probably a prosperous farmer. The law also allows an individual to own 200 hectares of rainfed arable property, 400 hectares of good pastureland, 800 of mountains or pasture in arid zones, or whatever quantity is necessary to maintain 500 head of cattle. . . .

The large landholders in agriculture (though not necessarily in livestock) are modern producers, with access to diversified sources of credit and significant capital investments in machinery, packing facilities, and housing for their employees. Almost universally they use modern inputs and harvest significant returns.

(5) Landless laborers or *jornaleros*. In 1910, when the Revolution broke out, Mexico had about 3.5 million landless peasants. Sixty years later, after three million *ejidatarios* and private owners have acquired plots, nearly four million peasants do not own land. According to development theory, the landless should either have become salaried workers within a productive agricultural system or migrated to the cities. Although some have succeeded in these options, by and large the Mexican economic system has not met the basic needs of the rest.

The explanation is that while the rural population of Mexico has steadily declined in relation to the urban percentage, it has at least doubled in absolute numbers. The individuals who received land had children, but only some of these can inherit their parents' property. There is not enough land for the others to inherit. Being landless, they must either work for daily wages in the countryside or migrate to the cities. The *jornaleros* (from *jornal*—a day's wage) constitute the largest rural class, 54 percent of the agricultural work force, and it is estimated that they increased in absolute numbers by 60 percent between 1960 and 1970. . . .

The *jornaleros* constitute the poorest, most marginalized class in Mexico. Unprotected by the labor laws and unorganized, they earn the lowest daily wage of any group, usually lower than the legal minimums, and they rarely participate in social security. Their low wage levels are compounded by underemployment. According to one estimate, the average number of days *jornaleros* work annually declined from 194 in 1950 to 100 in 1960 and 75 in 1970.

That the landless are anything but happy with their situation is evident in the numerous land invasions that occur every year and in the appearance of a rural guerrilla movement, led until his recent murder by Lucio Cabañas. In discussions with agricultural officials,

I frequently mention the problem of the *jornaleros* and have never found a satisfactory suggestion for incorporating them effectively into the economy, at least in its present capitalist form. Government programs are aimed primarily at those with land. Since urban employment opportunities are not keeping up with the rate of population increase in urban areas, millions of poorly educated and unskilled rural workers have no destiny there. The nation has almost no additional land to bestow on them. And the number of *jornaleros* seems certain to continue increasing.

A Résumé of the Problems

. . . Although the underlying aggravant of the agricultural problems is population increase and the principal symptom of its sickness is inadequate production, a number of other needs have been cited by critics and underlie the government's diagnosis. A few of the more important are the following:

(1) The land tenure structure has not been settled. . . .

(2) Land is fragmented. . . .

(3) Productive practices are largely traditional, and most farmers do not know about or use modern technology.

(4) With only one-fourth of the potentially irrigable land developed, production continues to depend in the rainfed zones on the vagaries of weather.

(5) Although agricultural research is one of the highlights in the otherwise underdeveloped institutional picture, it has achieved the greatest effect in irrigated, productive regions. . . .

(6) Public and private credit serves only a small percentage of producers, perhaps 15 to 20 percent. . . .

(7) Planning and extension services were not effectively institutionalized until after 1970. . . .

(8) Part of the supply of fertilizer and improved seeds has to be imported because national production is not adequate.

(9) Rural income remains low, not only because of the small size of holdings and lack of technology, but because of the multiple intermediaries who buy from the producer cheaply and sell at a high price.

(10) Human resources are not organized to improve production. . . .

The multiplicity of these problems and the total context they

represent support the government judgment that increasing production cannot be considered as an isolated aim. Technically,
production will expand if the farmer uses such inputs as high
yielding and disease resistant seeds, fertilizer, controlled water, and
insecticides. But as a neglected and virtually marginalized sector,
agriculture must undergo other changes as well before it can
effectively absorb these inputs. Consequently, government policy
has other objectives besides production increase.

One of these is redistribution of income to favor the rural
population. Although agriculture, livestock, fishing, and forestry
composed 40 percent of the work force in 1970, they provided little
more than 10 percent of the gross domestic product. This lack of
equilibrium has been aggravated for years by policies of maintaining low food prices to benefit urban consumers and by
transferring foreign exchange earned by the sale of food and raw
materials to the purchase of inputs for industrialization. The
Echeverría administration considers income redistribution one of
its central goals, though no studies are thus far available to indicate
whether government investment, price, and tax policies, plus the
inflationary ambient of the past two years, have indeed redistributed services to the farmers. I am doubtful. Among the
redistributive policies promoted by the government have been
higher support prices for crops, higher proportional investment in
agriculture and livestock, special development programs for
selected rural zones, and tax changes in 1974, which weighed most
heavily on wealthy and urban groups and were justified as
necessary to assure resources for the rural programs.

A second emphasis aims directly at the population factors that
are accentuating rural problems. In addition to the National
Population Policy, which proposes to reduce rural mortality and
fertility by improving educational and health services, including
family planning, development programs in the countryside are
consciously designed to retain people there and provide work for
the excess manpower.

And third, the government would like to improve infrastructure and social services in small villages as a precondition for
greater peasant participation in the changes. A wide range of
programs in various entities of government are concerned with
"capacitación" of individuals and "promoción" of communities, all
of which are trying to change the mentality of peasants and secure

their collaboration. In many instances, this is accompanied by educational, health, and other benefits in the communities.

The administrative structure of Mexican agriculture is a tangled labyrinth that includes more than 100 secretariats, decentralized agencies, banks, commissions, committees, foundations, funds, public companies, and industries. Merely to understand this system and the functions of each component is a major job. Duplicated responsibilities are common. Although overlapping has some benefits (entities active in the countryside for other purposes help promote agricultural objectives), the disadvantages include rivalries, excessive administration, and problems of coordination. . . .

Perhaps the most significant indicator of a changed government attitude toward agriculture is the increase in the budget. Complete figures are difficult to acquire because the responsible institutions are so dispersed, but in presenting the budget for 1975, the secretary of finance said that investments in the sector increased from an annual average of 11.2 percent of the budget between 1965 and 1970, to 17.8 percent in 1974, and more than 20 percent in 1975. In 1970 public investment in agriculture and livestock was about 4 billion pesos, in 1974, about 12 billion, and in 1975, about 15 billion is scheduled. (From 1970 to 1974, inflation was approximately 50 percent.) These increases reflect a belief that in a strict sense the deficiencies of the sector stem from more than a decade of neglect, and the only way to reverse the trend is by channeling more resources and personnel into it. . . .

Along with a fresh flow of money, new policies have been established in the institutions concerned with agriculture and livestock. One of the most important alterations is occurring in the former DAAC, now the Secretariat of Agrarian Reform. Shortly after President Echeverría took office, he submitted a new Agrarian Reform Law, to shift focus from land policies of distributing property and confirming titles to transforming the *ejidos* into more imaginative and effective productive units. As a prerequisite the law is trying to overcome *caciquismo* (personalism) and corruption in the *ejidos* by establishing secret ballots and limiting terms of office.

According to the new law, the General Assembly of the *ejidos* will plan use of their varied resources, which in many instances heretofore have not been rationally exploited. Although the amount of arable land in most *ejidos* is small, they usually have extensive hectarage in pasture, woods, and often coastline. *Ejidos*, for example, own 50 percent of Mexico's forest resources. The aim of the new legislation is to convert the *ejidos* into effective enterprises that will plan and manage their assets. In addition to working their agricultural land in larger units, the *ejidos* are encouraged to develop forestry and fishing, add to and modernize their stock of animals, poultry, and bees, establish processing industries, develop artisanry, and if the potential is there, enter the tourist industry. . . .

In irrigation, more attention is going to smaller dams and to water control projects in the southeastern tropics. This does not mean neglect of the traditional irrigation centers. In fact, major agricultural states like Sonora and Sinaloa in the Northwest also have priority, because they are proven zones of high productivity. It is now recognized, nevertheless, that small projects have many advantages: They are less expensive; they can absorb extensive unskilled manpower; and they benefit some of the poorer areas of the country, where unemployment is high and production low.

Two such programs deserve mention. One is the Program of Irrigation Units for Rural Development, created in 1970. The number of small dams has grown from 189 in 1970 to 2,209 in 1974, servicing 494,678 hectares and 163,283 farmers. The second is the Benito Juarez Plan, administered by SAG. It constructs small dams and watering places for cattle. Begun in 1972, it has spent nearly 400 million pesos a year and by mid-1974 had completed 135 projects.

The tropical regions are also receiving special emphasis, especially in the Southeast, which is the only part of the country with territory for absorbing more population. States like Tabasco, Yucatán, Campeche, and Quintana Roo have considerable agricultural and cattle-raising potential. Though there is no great rush to the tropics now, the role of the Southeast in colonization and production will become more evident. For the moment, the most important dam construction is taking place there, in zones where the principal problem is not lack of water, but controlling the excess. The Secretariat of Agrarian Reform also has a program for establishing the new population nuclei in this region, and experiments in improving agriculture and livestock are in process.

An important instrument for channeling funds into agriculture is the Plan for Rural Development. Organized within the Secretariat of the Presidency, the plan is currently spending 2.5 billion pesos annually on a variety of infrastructural improvements including dams, roads, schools, potable water, and extension services, in approximately sixty regions. By the end of 1975, this program will be influencing 59 percent of the rural population and 100 regions, some of which have been chosen for their productive potential, but most of which are among the most backward parts of the country. The program's emphasis will be on *ejidos* and communal lands.

These investments are designed to improve living conditions and increase production in some of the most underdeveloped regions, and to retain many individuals who would otherwise migrate to the cities. The approach in the Plan for Rural Development is to attend to the prerequisites before directly attacking insufficient production. A road may have to be built to reach the market, educational standards improved to encourage receptivity to new methods, and dams built to guarantee crop stability. Increasing production cannot be a goal by itself when many of the rural communities lack infrastructure and social services. This long and expensive process may not show immediate results, but without it as an initial approach, nothing further can be done.

The government is also trying to improve more direct factors in increasing production, including research, credit, extension, and fertilizer production. . . .

A final institution of major importance for agriculture is the National Company of Popular Commodities (CONASUPO), which regulates prices and acts as an intermediary between producers and consumers. In 1975, it had the largest regular budget of any entity active in agriculture. . . .

CONASUPO is best described as a vast government commercial system, which, by undercutting Mexico's traditionally rapacious intermediaries, guarantees farmers a high price for their crops and sells at low prices to the consumer. It operates through its colorful outlets, which are scattered throughout Mexico, from the capital city down to villages of less than one thousand inhabitants. Founded in 1961, CONASUPO has expanded its capital, activities, and outlets since 1970 as a result of government emphasis on improving rural income, keeping consumer prices down because of inflation, and increasing imports.

It is now recognized that a major reason for low production in the late 1960s was that farmers were discouraged from planting basic staples because official prices were too low and did not change. In 1972, CONASUPO initiated a set of increases with the help of the Secretariat of Industry and Commerce by which purchase prices for corn and wheat have approximately doubled and for beans more than tripled. Other products in demand and needing stimuli have received comparable price rises. CONASUPO also purchases large quantities of basic food items from the farmers at the guaranteed prices. Each year farmers can deliver their crop to one of the CONASUPO purchasing centers and sell it. As a monopolist of food commodities, CONASUPO then sells these same products in its retail outlets at a lower price than other retailers. Items such as corn and milk are listed at less than CONASUPO pays, representing a subsidy to the consumer. In addition, CONASUPO imports items to avoid shortages that would encourage speculation and accentuate inflation.

Mexican agricultural officials believe that if the tempo of investment is maintained and the preceding programs are carried out, Mexico should produce not only enough to feed its people but also to maintain its long-time role as an important agriculture and livestock exporter. The solutions presume a drastic change in the nature of Mexican agriculture and the relationship of government to the sector—in short, a modernization of agriculture that has never been seriously attempted before. Dr. Brauer, the secretary of agriculture and livestock, even believes that by the year 2000, Mexico can produce 100 percent more than the population will consume.

The basis of this hope lies in expanding the areas under irrigation and improving technology in them. In 1972, 35 percent of national production occurred in the irrigation zones under the control of the SRH, which at the time totaled 2,693,355 hectares out of perhaps 12 million planted. If more of the estimated 16 million irrigable hectares can produce at high levels, present food supplies can be multiplied.

The experimental project called Plan Puebla has demonstrated that production can also be increased in the rainfed areas, improving the living standard of small producers through concentrated extension services and local research. Although the rainfed zones would not be as decisive for overall output as the irrigated areas, modernizing cropping practices would achieve another important policy goal—to retain peasants on the land by enabling them to achieve a better standard of living.

Mexico has achieved a high level of technical expertise in the government entities concerned with agriculture, even though political factors continue to impinge on decisions. The technicians have the ability to carry out the programs, provided that agriculture continues to receive priority and funds flow accordingly. Although many of the best personnel are in SRH and INIA, throughout its system Mexico now has a cadre of well-qualified persons, many with doctorates earned abroad. The immediate step must be to scatter this expertise more widely, as current policies are doing, by increasing enrollment in the various agricultural schools and hiring more personnel, especially in key linkages between local research and extension, and between the central administration and peasants.

The setting for new initiatives is good. Two or three decades ago, Mexico did not have the elite of qualified persons to carry out an autonomous agricultural modernization. If modernization had taken place under foreign advice, it would probably have provoked strong political opposition. Now Mexicans can plan and execute their own approach, taking responsibility for the successes and failures they will have.

They will confront many problems.

(1) The most uncertain one is weather. Government spokesmen apparently expected 1974 to start a new era of self-sufficiency, but floods, drought, and frost undermined these hopes. Although weather might have been exceptionally bad, the country's tendency to suffer severe crop losses from weather has to be included among the geographical limitations that policy must take into consideration. It is also possible that Mexico is being affected by long-term weather changes like those that have caused serious crop losses in other parts of the world.

(2) In the coming years unemployment and underemployment will probably become much more serious problems than they already are, perhaps even challenging Mexico's vaunted political stability and capacity to conciliate diverse interest groups. Even though increasing production, initiating public works projects, and encouraging the development of alternative economic activities can absorb some manpower, the country faces a staggering problem of providing work for the landless laborers, who should total more than five million by 1985.

(3) To implement the program currently in process will require

a degree of planning and control by government unprecedented in Mexican history. Like most government programs it will probably move by steps, covering only a part of its intended participants and beneficiaries for many years. But if the Mexican government can bring about a genuine modernization of agricultural production, it will be a far more effective government than it is now.

(4) The dependence on irrigated land for increased production will bring into play the problem of salinization. It is commonly estimated that about 25 percent of the irrigated land is unusable for this reason. Recovery of this land will be complicated and expensive.

(5) In my conversations with agricultural technicians, many emphasized problems of organization and coordination that are currently hindering a more effective implementation of the programs. The agricultural bureaucracy's poor reputation for efficiency will have to be tackled if government plans are to succeed.

(6) Technocratic approaches to agriculture usually look good on paper but often founder when put into practice. The announced goal of organizing peasants to make their own decisions and emphasizing collective modes of production will be difficult to implement, given peasant individualism and traditional government paternalism, to which the peasant adapts when he has to do so. The government is correct in assuming that without more active peasant participation, the program cannot succeed. Unfortunately, the Mexican system has operated to coopt rather than encourage differences, and Mexican officialdom may not know how to proceed other than paternalistically. If so, the peasants may interpret it as one more example of manipulation and unfulfilled promises. Mexico has a long history of peasant organization and struggle, which, if allowed more expression, could turn out to be an important resource for shaping peasant participation.

27

MEXICAN VIEWS OF THE UNITED STATES

Michael C. Meyer

Michael C. Meyer, director of the Latin American Area Center at the University of Arizona, has written ten books on contemporary Mexico and edited the Hispanic American Historical Review. *Most recently he published* Land and Water in the Southwest *(1984) and is best known for his and William Sherman's superb* The Course of Mexican History *(2d ed., 1983). In this essay, he discusses the image that Mexicans have of the United States as one key to understanding foreign policies.*

As the Mexican government shapes its international policies, it is guided by historic ideals and current concerns but is influenced even more by its perceptions of other nations. In no case does a foreign image weigh heavier on these policymakers than in relations with the United States. Having shared a border with the United States since independence helps explain Mexico's development and culture; this relationship is one reason that Mexico is different from other Latin American nations. Examining the image that Mexicans hold will not only make understandable their foreign policy, but also reveal warts that Americans overlook on themselves. Meyer describes different views held by different groups, ranging from the generally favorable impression held by Mexican businessmen to the caustic conspiratorial opinions voiced by intellectuals; in between can be found the attitudes of government officials and the masses. The essay succinctly reviews the historical events that have conditioned these views and demonstrates the reason no Mexican politician can afford to be overfriendly toward the United States.

For the student of Mexican history, this essay raises many questions: If images of the United States shape Mexican foreign policy, what images of Mexico influence United States foreign relations? If Mexico's view is the product of historical factors, what events have shaped images in the United States? How have movies, newspapers, and advertising confirmed these stereotypes of the Mexican? Meyer offers a provocative analysis of the way Mexico's elementary school textbooks present the United States. Mexican stereotypes of Americans should be compared with the characteristics that schoolbooks in the United States ascribe to Mexicans.

An earlier, more abbreviated version of this article appeared under the title "Roots and Realities of Mexican Attitudes Toward the United States," in Richard D.

Erb and Stanley R. Ross, eds., United States Relations with Mexico: Context and Content *(Washington: American Enterprise Institute for Public Policy Research, 1981), pp. 29–38.*

How do the citizens of one country view those of another? Invariably our perceptions of others in the community of nations combine reality and myth, accuracy and fallacy, truth and distortion. One need not subscribe to any one theory to appreciate that vested interests, whether parochial or universal, sometimes promote acceptable systems of national belief or stereotypes. If they are successful over a long period of time, those stereotypes permeate the views that parents pass on to children, that educational systems instill in the youth, that the press and popular culture direct to the adult community, and that politicians too often use for their own purposes. In addition, all judgments about others are, at least to some extent, ethnocentric, conditioned by a unique set of cultural and intellectual values. If such a theory of international perception helps explain the intensity of anti-Communist feeling that periodically surfaces in the United States, it also helps shed light on how Mexicans understand the people and institutions of their northern neighbor.

As citizens of a superpower on the world scene, should we be troubled by what others think? Does our concern simply result in a needless and futile browbeating? The answer to the first question is yes, and to the second no. We citizens of the United States should have less trouble than others with these two questions. At the beginning of the nineteenth century, not long after our war for independence, a young Frenchman, Alexis de Tocqueville, came to our country and in a classic study entitled *Democracy in America* told us much about ourselves, including many things we preferred not to know. Unencumbered by the worldview of the nation in which he found himself, de Tocqueville was able to offer a fresh and imaginative impression of the upstart republic. To be sure, some of what he wrote revealed an imperfect, even contorted, appreciation of the United States; but many of his revelations would not have been perceived by anyone other than an astute foreigner.

It is far from a futile exercise to listen to the views of others. Even the more overdrawn caricatures are generally rooted in some reality, and even the exaggerations that one finds most offensive are important because they are often believed and acted upon. Historians have long been aware that total myths are poignant, as they tend to propel human actions and thus assume an important reality of their own.

Mexico is a country incredibly rich in proverbs, adages, and mottoes. One that crosses all class lines laments, "Poor Mexico! So far from God and so close to the United States!" This refrain capsulizes the ironies of a Catholic country in which anticlericalism has reigned supreme; it echoes as well the frustrations of a poor country on the border of a superpower. Without question, geographical proximity has produced many important Mexican perceptions of the United States. It has certainly been a major determinant in the economic and political interactions between the two countries. These historical processes, in turn, condition many of the attitudes that Mexicans harbor about their more powerful neighbor to the north.

United States–Mexican Relations:
A Brief Historical Sketch

The United States was the first country in the world formally to recognize Mexico's independence from Spain early in the nineteenth century. Having only recently emerged from a similar colonial experience, statesmen in Washington realized that diplomatic recognition was important to Mexico City if independence were to flourish and a healthy nation-state emerge. Recognition was extended, and diplomats were exchanged in December 1822. Within a year, however, the administration in Washington had issued a new, wide-reaching proclamation that theoretically would be the cornerstone of United States relations with the newly emerging republics of Latin America. The 1823 Monroe Doctrine stated that monarchy as a form of government was not compatible with the freedoms recently won by the new nations of the western hemisphere. Therefore, the great monarchies of Europe were warned that the United States would consider any attempt to extend their systems to the western hemisphere as dangerous to our peace and safety. Should Mexico and the rest of Latin America not have been delighted? Was not the Monroe Doctrine a tacit promise of alliance if Spain should try to reconquer her lost territories in America? Did not it express a community of New World interests? The Mexican view was not that positive. The Monroe Doctrine obviously affected the future of all Latin America, yet not one Latin American country had been consulted before its proclamation. The United States was putting Latin America on notice that it was taking charge.

The Monroe Doctrine resulted in the birth of two Mexican attitudes toward the United States. First, if a partnership were to be established in the nineteenth century, it was not to be an even affair. The United States clearly planned to be the dominant partner. More important, when the monarchies of Europe began to violate the terms of the Monroe Doctrine, the United States showed no inclination to back up its haughty words with action. Spain invaded Mexico in 1829 in an attempt to reconquer its recently lost Mexican province. The United States did nothing. Nine years later France invaded the port of Veracruz to collect past debts. Again the United States stood mute. Mexicans began to wonder if the words of the United States were to be trusted. The doctrine seemed to be nothing more than self-serving bombast.

By far the most important event in nineteenth-century relations between the United States and Mexico was the war fought between the two countries from 1846 to 1848. Without examining the intricacies of the cause, we can say that the most careful scholars of the conflict, in both the United States and Mexico, have labeled it as a war of aggression by the United States, at the end of which the United States appropriated almost half of Mexico's national territory. The early fears of Mexican skeptics now seemed well founded. Since the sixteenth century Mexico had been searching in the north for the elusive El Dorado, an alluring source of great wealth. Almost as if to rub salt in the wound of Mexico's defeat, it was finally found at Sutter's Fort in California just a year after the Mexican War ended. The tremendous mineral wealth uncovered on the heels of the California gold rush would finance much of the United States' industrial revolution—not Mexico's. To the extent that historical legacies precipitated Yankeephobia in Mexico, the Mexican War must be held largely accountable.

Relations between the United States and Mexico improved markedly during the last quarter of the nineteenth century and the first decade of the twentieth. Porfirio Díaz, during a regime that lasted thirty-four years, stabilized the country, put Mexico's eco-

nomic house in order, and set Mexico on the path of modernization. To accomplish the latter he invited foreign capital, particularly
from the United States, and offered protections and guarantees
sufficiently inviting to attract millions of dollars of American
investment. This capital made a major contribution toward building the vast Mexican railroad network and reviving the nation's
economy, but some Mexicans began to argue that their country was
becoming too lucrative as an investment field. They saw the
absurdities of the Spanish colonial period repeating themselves.
Few of the profits from investment were being redirected into the
Mexican economy. The Spanish treasure ships, the famous gal-
leons, were again departing Mexican shores laden with the country's wealth and leaving behind an impoverished populace.

It was not surprising, then, that when the great Mexican
Revolution erupted in 1910, the issue of foreign investment figured
prominently in revolutionary rhetoric. Díaz, another adage holds,
had allowed his country to become the "mother of foreigners and
the step-mother of Mexicans." And when the revolutionaries began
to consolidate their victory, they provided that in the future foreign
investment must always be kept within the framework of national
interests. Most important, in the new Mexican Constitution of 1917,
the state was given the express right to expropriate property
(including but not limited to that owned by foreigners) if a different
ownership pattern better suited the social needs of the Mexican
community.

The chaos of the early revolutionary period (1910–20) severely
tested diplomatic relations between the United States and Mexico.
The harmonious relationship fostered by Díaz fell easy victim to the
rancor of the day. On two occasions the United States intervened in
Mexico with military force: once in Veracruz in 1914 and again in
northern Mexico following Pancho Villa's attack on Columbus,
New Mexico, in 1916. Tensions remained high in the 1920s as
United States investors, especially the oil interests, were threatened
by the implementation of the Constitution of 1917 and sought to
garner promises of protection from the White House and Congress.
When the long-expected oil nationalization did come in 1938, the
reaction in the United States was tumultuous. President Lázaro
Cárdenas's nationalization decree threatened to set the two coun-
tries on a collision course. That it did not do so was a tribute to
Franklin D. Roosevelt's Good Neighbor Policy and the good-faith

negotiations of the Mexican government and the oil companies concerning the issue of equitable compensation. Ironically, the nationalization of the oil companies ultimately fostered better, not worse, relations. Mexicans expected another military intervention. When it did not come they were noticeably relieved.

The cleared diplomatic atmosphere reflected itself graphically during World War II. It was never the intention of the United States that Mexico should make a major military contribution to the Allied war effort. Mexico was assigned a supporting role, and it performed that role admirably. Mexican strategic raw materials, kept by the government at reasonable prices, were directed to war-related industries in the United States. Mexican agricultural products helped feed the Allied armies, and Mexican workers (the beginning of the *bracero* program) came to the United States to help fill the labor shortage created in this country by the draft.

The cordial relationship carried over into the postwar era. Most outstanding issues were resolved amicably, even a century-old boundary dispute known as the Chamizal controversy. The one problem that defied easy solution and, in fact, grew in intensity throughout the 1960s, 1970s, and early 1980s, was that of the undocumented worker. Pressures in both Washington and Mexico militated against the resolution of this issue.

The historical realities outlined above have conditioned much of the Mexican view of the United States. As one begins to probe in greater depth, however, it becomes readily apparent that there really is no one Mexican view of the United States; there are a number of different worlds in the Mexican universe of opinions.

The Government View

In many ways the Mexican government finds itself in the position of any government living in the shadow of a much more powerful neighbor. It is careful not to offend overtly but must be mindful of various domestic constituencies. Although Mexico has been governed for decades by a single political party, and policy decisions are in no way dependent upon election results, the press is relatively free and does not hesitate to assail those officials with whose policies it disagrees.

It is in the best Mexican political tradition that even the most specific policy can be wrapped within an all-encompassing philosophical cloak. The Revolution in general, and Mexico's relations with the United States in particular, provided the successive governments of the twentieth century with one such philosophical stance. On the heels of interventions by the United States in 1914 and 1916, Venustiano Carranza proclaimed a nonintervention doctrine. Mexico would not tolerate any foreign intervention in her own domestic affairs and would not support the policies of other governments that intervened in the internal affairs of any other country.

Under the cloak of nonintervention, Mexico could oppose the efforts of the United States to unseat Fidel Castro in the early 1960s and to wage war in Vietnam in the late 1960s and early 1970s. In the latter case, when U.S. policy was criticized, it was not because the United States was devastating Southeast Asia and, in the process, claiming many innocent lives. Mexico's critique was rather on the basis that no country should intervene in the internal affairs of another sovereign nation. (It is interesting, and perhaps even instructive, that little was said about Cuban intervention in Africa or the Soviet invasion of Afghanistan.) The United States is consequently viewed as a country that will withstand criticism if some moral or philosophical justification can be mustered in support of it. Mexico's failure to support President Jimmy Carter's boycott of the Moscow Olympics thus fell into its tradition of ignoring the policies of other nations that the Mexicans call universalism.

In its international pronouncements, especially those that concern the United States, the Mexican government is sensitive to public stances that might seem to compromise the country's sense of independence and national dignity. A corollary is that the issues that enhance independence and national dignity are given extensive coverage in the press. For example, when Presidents Lyndon B. Johnson and Adolfo López Mateos signed the Chamizal Treaty, resolving the boundary dispute in the El Paso – Ciudad Juárez area, the Mexican president and the press said that Mexico's honor had been redeemed as a powerful country admitted a past wrong. Similarly, when Presidents Luis Echeverría and Gerald Ford met on the Sonora-Arizona border a decade later, the Mexican president announced that his country's sense of national independence would not permit it to sell its newly discovered petroleum to the United States at anything resembling a special price. When President Carter visited President José López Portillo in Mexico City, he was lectured, in terms that some considered offensive, on the meaning of Mexican independence.

Because of the history of relations between the United States and Mexico and the type of nationalism that grew out of the Mexican Revolution, government officials, no matter what personal views they might hold, cannot appear to be overfriendly to the United States and on occasion must assume an anti–United States posture. Their failure to engage in these exercises might mean a loss of credibility within the Mexican political community. It is a tightrope that Mexican politicians, seemingly by osmosis, learn to walk.

The Intellectuals' View

Many Mexican intellectuals are eminently reasonable in their views of the United States; but no matter how distinguished they may be in their own fields of endeavor, they find themselves in a minority among their colleagues. The more common pattern is for the intelligentsia to be vituperative and rather conspiratorial with respect to the United States, the country they love to hate. The Mexican Left (and most intellectuals are found somewhere within the Left) has traditionally been critical not only of United States foreign policy but also of the values that the United States public holds dear.

Throughout most of the twentieth century, the treatment of ethnic minorities, especially Mexican Americans, by the United States has been subject to attack; but as undeniable progress has been made in the areas of civil rights and equal opportunity, the focus has shifted. The targets of the intellectual assault are now dependency, multinational corporations, and the Central Intelligence Agency. Their theory is that the world is composed of independent and dependent states; it serves the interests of the strong to keep the weak countries, such as Mexico, in a perpetual state of dependence. The institutions that assume this responsibility are, from the private sector, the multinational corporations and, from the public sector, the CIA. Possibly by accident but probably by design, they work together in Latin America to foster dependence upon the United States.

Dependency theory stated in these terms sounds simplistic, but like its Marxist precursor, the doctrine has been developed with amazing sophistication. Without question it has opened our eyes to new perceptions, provided a theoretical handle with which to grasp a wide spectrum of internationally related events, and made us more aware than ever of undeniable abuses by the most powerful nations in the world. It has no doubt been nurtured, given strength, and made palatable to many by recent revelations of covert CIA activity in Chile, Cuba, and Nicaragua and multinational bribery of officials in half a dozen Latin American countries. But it is not without its problems. When distorted and misused, dependency theory holds the United States accountable for all of Mexico's chronic ills.

The roots of intellectual Yankeephobia, if not its passion, can be partially explained in terms of the stark contrasts between the two countries. Whereas the United States is sufficiently affluent to place men on the moon and launch space shuttles, millions of Mexicans live in abject poverty. Whereas scholars in the United States win Nobel Prizes in the hard sciences, the Mexican school system cannot educate all of the country's children. Whereas United States physicians regularly record startling medical breakthroughs, even do prenatal blood tests, tens of thousands of Mexican babies die at birth for want of the most elementary medical care.

In addition, the pervasive cultural presence of the United States appears at times to overwhelm Mexican society. This phenomenon is called, somewhat theoretically, *cultural imperialism*. Whatever one wants to call it, the phenomenon is real. Thousands of anglicisms invade the Spanish language. Billboards advertise United States products. Few middle-and upper-class Mexican women seem to manage without cosmetics manufactured in the United States. Newspapers rely on the wire services of the Associated Press and United Press International. Programs produced in the United States dominate television screens, and motion pictures made in Hollywood draw long lines at movie theaters. American-style restaurants cater to tourists, and loud American music blares from bars and discothèques. Certainly it can be argued that none of these phenomena is intended. Yet the cumulative impact produces a resentment that, when mixed with other ingredients, easily transforms into overt hostility.

The Businessmen's View

Of all groups in Mexican society, the well-educated business community undoubtedly holds the most favorable view of the United States. Leading Mexican businessmen, Roman Catholics for the most part, have even been known to praise openly the hard work, discipline, and thrift so often associated with the Protestant ethic. They often send their children to the United States for higher education, and in spite of the vagaries of the peso, they continue to come themselves, combining business and pleasure.

These businessmen have a positive view of United States society in general, but they most admire their North American counterparts. Interestingly, American businessmen are viewed less as competitors than as examples. Whenever practical, the Mexican business community emulates the latest merchandising, packaging, and advertising practices that have been successful north of the Rio Grande. Like their North American counterparts, they call for less state intervention and a diminished state regulatory role in the economy, especially in joint investment ventures with United States businessmen.

Because the Mexican economy is so closely tied to that of the United States, Mexican government policies considered unfavorable toward the United States, or those that might dampen the highly important tourist trade, are opposed by an increasingly strong business lobby. The businessman sees clearly that the economic wealth generated by the U.S. business community has brought it not only comfort but also power and influence; if this can be accomplished in the United States, it might well be accomplished in Mexico, too. In short, unlike the Mexican intellectual, the Mexican businessman does not view United States society as grossly materialistic.

The Popular View

Because of the relative absence of careful social science research on mass attitudes toward the United States, an assessment of mass views must be more impressionistic than empirical. It is obvious that millions of uneducated and unskilled Mexican workers view the United States as a country that affords them hope for a better future. Were this not true, the influx of undocumented workers into the United States would not be a problem of such far-reaching proportions. At the same time, they come to the United States with mixed emotions. Not only is their fear of apprehension realistic, but they have learned in various ways that once they are in the United States they are likely to suffer the humiliations of exploitation and racial prejudice.

Mass views of the United States are conditioned by whatever exposure to the educational system the population may have received and by the bombardment of popular culture. In 1959 the Mexican government passed legislation making primary-school textbooks uniform, free, and obligatory throughout the country. As a result, the same texts are used in every Mexican school for grades one through six. For the many Mexicans whose education does not go beyond the sixth grade, concepts of nationalism and views of the United States are based, in part, on the foundations of these *textos gratuitos.*

The volume used in the fourth grade for history and civics is an especially important contributor to the development of Mexican nationalism. As is true in all countries, nationalism in Mexico is conditioned by the heroes and antiheroes of history and is also rooted in its views of the outside world. Xenophobia — and, in this particular case, Yankeephobia — is definitely one of the factors that binds the country together. The volume used in the second grade teaches children the national anthem, and below a picture of civilians defending the country against the United States' invasion at Veracruz the students are asked to fill in the missing lines from the anthem. With the missing lines filled, the stanza reads:

> But if a foreign enemy dares
> To profane with his footprint your soil
> Just remember, Beloved Fatherland, that the heavens
> Have given you a soldier in each of your sons.

In the fourth-grade volume, the Mexican War is used to teach a basic lesson in patriotism: "It is an experience that we should never forget. The unity of all Mexicans is essential because with internal harmony comes progress and with progress comes the ability to put an end to such deceptions and injustices." It is obvious that the United States does not emerge in a favorable light in the primary texts. What comes through clearly is the picture of a bully and an aggressor.

The views of the United States presented in the *textos gratuitos* are reinforced by other elements of popular culture. The Mexican *corrido*, the folksong of the masses, theoretically incorporates lessons of "history" but in practice often misinterprets historical reality to reinforce many negative stereotypes about the United States. These folk ballads, expressing dislike of the United States at best and hatred at worst, are sung in cantinas and fiestas, played on the radio, and reproduced for mass distribution on record albums and cassette tapes.

Corridos in translation cannot convey the intensity of meaning and sentimentality they have in the original Spanish. The few examples cited, therefore, have only loose translations with only brief introductory remarks.

Not surprisingly, many *corridos* damn the United States for the Mexican War, especially the opinion voiced in Washington shortly after its conclusion that the United States should have taken all of Mexico, rather than only half.

> Los yankis malvados
> No cesan de hablar
> Que habrían de acabar
> Con esta nación.

> The vicious Yankees never
> stop saying that they probably
> should have finished off this nation.

The North American invasion of Veracruz, and the accompanying loss of life, provoked a number of condemnations of the United States. One of the most popular is entitled "La heróica acción del Capitán Azueta."

> En una Guerra Espantosa
> El gran Puerto se envolvió
> Por los Yankis maldecidos
> Que han traído la invasión.

> Hubo muertos y hubo heridos
> Grandes prejuicios y horrores

Han causado en Veracruz
Los bandidos invasores.

In a horrible war,
the great port was enveloped
by the wicked Yankees
who had invaded.

There were dead and wounded.
The bandit invaders
brought prejudice and horrors.

Most common in the *corridos* is the treatment that Mexican workers receive at the hands of North Americans, whether they are working for them in Mexico or in the United States.

Insultan a los Mexicanos
Y los corren de los campos
Para ocupar a sus paisanos
Que llegan como lagartos.

They insult Mexicans
and run them from the fields
to employ their countrymen
who arrive like reptiles.

But the special plight of the undocumented worker in the United States prompts indignation and compassion.

Mas hoy con la nueva ley
Del Gobierno Americano
Por donde quiera es malvisto
Todo pobre Mexicano.

Porque los Americanos
No nos tienen compasión
Y hombres, niños y mujeres
Los llevan a la prisión.

Yet today with the new law
of the American government
everywhere they view badly
the poor Mexican.

Because the Americans
don't have compassion,
they take men, women, and children
to prison.

The picture of the United States that emerges from the *corridos* and other elements of popular culture (such as the murals that adorn public buildings throughout Mexico and satirical comic books such as *Los Agachados* and *Los Supermachos*) is sometimes so unfavorable as to constitute a caricature. But its impact on the popular imagination is telling.

Synopsis of the Mexican View

Dissected into parts, the Mexican view of the United States emerges as rather more negative than it actually is. A fragmented analysis does not take into account, for example, that in each representative group there are many who deviate from the norm. In addition, in each group one can detect an ambivalent attitude that in effect constitutes a love-hate perspective. Even the most strident Mexican Yankeephobe often finds certain things to admire in United States society. Finally, the most discerning Mexican critics make that important distinction between the United States people and United States policy pronouncements with which they disagree.

Policy decisions concerning relations between the two countries should take into account that the United States is not universally esteemed in Mexico. Criticisms of the United States are often exaggerated and distorted, but many are rooted in readily understandable historical fact. Educated Mexicans are more historically oriented than their North American counterparts, and they frequently point out that we in the United States find it convenient to have short memories.

Mexican policymakers, though not concerned about being turned out of office in the next election, are nevertheless mindful of their constituents' interests and are inevitably guided by the nationalistic ideology that grew out of the Mexican Revolution.

BIBLIOGRAPHICAL NOTE

The discussion of Mexican textbooks was based on Josefina Vázquez de Knauth, *Nacionalismo y educación en México* (Mexico: El Colegio de México, 1975). The *corrido* extracts reproduced here are taken from Merle E. Simmons, *The Mexican Corrido as a Source for Interpretive Study of Modern Mexico, 1870–1950* (Bloomington: Indiana University Press, 1957).

APPENDIX
MEXICO'S PRESIDENTS SINCE 1876

1876	Porfirio Díaz
1880	Manuel González
1884–1911	Porfirio Díaz
1911	Francisco León de la Barra (interim)
1911–13	Francisco I. Madero
1913	Pedro Lascurain (interim)
1913–14	Victoriano Huerta (interim)
1914	Francisco S. Carbajal (interim)
1914, 1915–20	Venustiano Carranza
1914	Eulalio Gutiérrez (interim, named by Convention)
1914	Roque González Garza
1915	Francisco Lagos Cházaro
1920	Adolfo de la Huerta (interim)
1920–24	Alvaro Obregón
1924–28	Plutarco Elías Calles
1928–30	Emilio Portes Gil (interim)
1930–32	Pascual Ortiz Rubio
1932–34	Abelardo L. Rodríguez (interim)
1934–40	Lázaro Cárdenas
1940–46	Manuel Avila Camacho
1946–52	Miguel Alemán Valdés
1952–58	Adolfo Ruiz Cortines
1958–64	Adolfo López Mateos
1964–70	Gustavo Díaz Ordaz
1970–76	Luis Echeverría Alvarez
1976–82	José López Portillo
1982–	Miguel de la Madrid Hurtado

FOR FURTHER STUDY

The items suggested here are limited to recent publications. Individuals who desire a more complete list of works should refer to one of the standard histories of Mexico, the best-researched and most complete to date being that of Michael C. Meyer and William L. Sherman entitled *The Course of Mexican History* (New York: Oxford University Press, 1979; 1983). Another help for researchers is the bibliographical aid. W. Dirk Raat's *The Mexican Revolution: An Annotated Guide to Recent Scholarship* (Boston: G. K. Hall & Co., 1982) contains an historiographical and bibliographical survey of books and articles on contemporary Mexico that were published between 1960 and 1980.

On historiography see Thomas Benjamin and Marcial Ocasio, "Organizing the Memory of Modern Mexico: Porfirian Historiography in Perspective, 1880s–1980s," *Hispanic American Historical Review* 64 (May 1984): 323–64. This surveys the literature of the late Porfiriato and the early revolutionary years. It is complemented by David C. Bailey's fine essay, "Revisionism and the Recent Historiography of the Mexican Revolution," *Hispanic American Historical Review* 58 (Feb. 1978): 62–79. An important aid to research is Richard E. Greenleaf and Michael C. Meyer, *Research in Mexican History* (Lincoln: University of Nebraska Press, 1973).

For interdisciplinary studies on twentieth-century Mexico see *Contemporary Mexico: Papers of the Fourth International Congress of Mexican History,* ed. by James W. Wilkie, Michael C. Meyer, and Edna Monzón de Wilkie (Mexico and Los Angeles: El Colegio de México and UCLA Latin American Center, 1976). A multivolume monograph series of the history of the Mexican Revolution is *Historia de la Revolución Mexicana 1911–1960,* 25 vols. (Mexico: El Colegio de

México, 1977–). For historical biographies of leading "revolutionary" caudillos see *Essays on the Mexican Revolution: Revisionist Views of the Leaders*, ed. by George Wolfskill and Douglas W. Richmond (Austin: University of Texas Press, 1979). An indispensable source of printed documents for the early revolutionary era is *Documentos históricos de la Revolución Mexicana*, 27 vols., ed. by Isidro and Josefina E. de Fabela (Mexico: Fondo de Cultura Económica, vols. 1–5, 1960–64; Editorial Jus, vols. 6–27 plus index, 1965–73 and 1976).

A lively narrative history for the 1910–40 period is William Weber Johnson's *Heroic Mexico: The Violent Emergence of a Modern Nation* (Garden City, N.Y.: Doubleday, 1968). A competent survey history is Jan Bazant's *A Concise History of Mexico From Hidalgo to Cárdenas, 1805–1940* (Cambridge, Eng.: At the University Press, 1977).

A challenging theoretical and interpretive work is Donald Hodges and Ross Gandy, *Mexico 1910–1983: Reform or Revolution?* (London: Zed Press, 1983). These authors survey a variety of Marxist and non-Marxist interpretations and present their own independent Marxist evaluation, which distinguishes social from political revolution and highlights the central role of a new bureaucratic class. The best Trotskyist interpretation of the Mexican Revolution is Adolfo Gilly's *La revolución interrumpida* (Mexico: Ediciones El Caballito, 1972), a work that argues that the socialist revolution was interrupted by a "petit-bourgeois" transitional regime. (The English version is *The Mexican Revolution* [London: Verso Editions, 1983].) The main liberal interpretation of the Mexican Revolution as an unfinished bourgeois political and social revolution is Pablo González Casanova, *Democracy in Mexico* (New York: Oxford University Press, 1970). A New Left view is developed by James D. Cockcroft in *Mexico: Class Formation, Capital Accumulation, and the State* (New York: Monthly Review, 1983) and by Arnaldo Córdova in *La formación del poder político en México* (Mexico: Ediciones Era, 1975) and *La ideología de la Revolución Mexicana* (Mexico: Ediciones Era, 1973).

For specific twentieth-century themes see the following: On agrarian reform, Steven E. Sanderson, *Agrarian Populism and the Mexican State: The Struggle for Land in Sonora* (Berkeley: University of California Press, 1981); David F. Ronfeldt, *Atencingo: The Politics of Agrarian Struggle in a Mexican Ejido* (Stanford: Stanford University

Press, 1973); Gerrit Huizer, "Peasant Organization and Agrarian Reform in Mexico," in *Masses in Latin America,* ed. by I. L. Horowitz (New York: Oxford University Press, 1970); Frans J. Schryer, *The Rancheros of Pisaflores* (Toronto: University of Toronto Press, 1980); Arturo Warman, *Y venimos a contradecir: Los campesinos de Morelos y el estado nacional* (Mexico: Ediciones de la Casa Chata, 1976). For urban labor history see Howard Handelman, "Organized Labor in Mexico: Oligarchy and Dissent," *American Universities Field Staff Reports,* no. 18, 1979; Evelyn P. Stevens, *Protest and Response in Mexico* (Cambridge, Mass.: MIT Press, 1974).

On the cooptation process see Susan Eckstein, *The Poverty of Revolution: The State and the Urban Poor in Mexico* (Princeton: Princeton University Press, 1977); and Judith Adler Hellman, *Mexico in Crisis* (New York: Holmes & Meier, 1983). For the political system see the compilation of articles edited by José Luis Reyna and Richard Weinert entitled *Authoritarianism in Mexico* (Philadelphia: Institute for the Study of Human Issues, 1977). Also see Peter H. Smith, *Labyrinths of Power: Political Recruitment in Twentieth-Century Mexico* (Princeton: Princeton University Press, 1979). On diplomacy the best single volume in English is Karl M. Schmitt, *Mexico and the United States, 1821–1973: Conflict and Coexistence* (New York: John Wiley & Sons, 1974). An interesting study of the impact of international business and global capitalism on Mexico's economy from 1821 to 1969 is José Luis Ceceña, *México en la órbita imperial: Las empresas transnacionales* (Mexico: Ediciones El Caballito, 1975).

For cultural, intellectual, and social history see the following: John S. Brushwood, *Mexico in Its Novel* (Austin: University of Texas Press, 1966); Merle E. Simmons, *The Mexican Corrido as a Source for Interpretative Study of Modern Mexico, 1870–1950* (New York: Krause Reprint Co., 1969; reprint of 1957 ed.); Henry C. Schmidt, *The Roots of Lo Mexicano* (College Station: Texas A&M University Press, 1978); Octavio Paz, *The Other Mexico: Critique of the Pyramid* (New York: Grove Press, 1972); Donald J. Mabry, *The Mexican University and the State: Student Conflicts, 1910–1971* (College Station: Texas A&M University Press, 1982). On women and the suffrage movement see Donna M. Wolf, "Women in Modern Mexico," *Studies in History and Society* 1 (1976): 28–53. Also see María Mendieta Alatorre, *La mujer en la Revolución Mexicana* (Mexico: Instituto Nacional de Estudios Históricos de la Revolución Mexicana, 1961); and Anna Macias, *Against All Odds: The Feminist Movement in Mexico to 1940* (Westport, Conn.: Greenwood, 1982). And for the best down-to-earth description of the joys and trials of everyday life in Mexico see Carl Franz and Lorna Havens, *The People's Guide to Mexico: Wherever You Go . . . There You Are!* 5th ed. (Santa Fe: John Muir Publications, 1979).

Readings on popular culture include Carl J. Mora, *Mexican Cinema: Reflections of a Society 1896–1980* (Berkeley: University of California Press, 1982); Guy Bensusan, "Mexican Popular Music: Some Viewpoints," *Studies in Latin American Popular Culture* II (1982): 213–19; Philip L. Barbour, "Commercial and Cultural Broadcasting in Mexico," *American Academy of Political and Social Science* 208 (March 1940): 94–102; William H. Beezley, "The Porfirian Persuasion: Sport and Recreation in Mexico of the 1890s," *Proceedings* of the Rocky Mountain Council on Latin American Studies (Las Cruces: New Mexico State University, 1983): 136–45. Those who read Spanish should consult Jorge Mejía Prieto, *Historia de la radio y la televisión en México* (Mexico: O. Colmenares, 1972); Salvador Pruneda, *La caricatura como arma política* (Mexico: Instituto Nacional de Estudios Históricos de la Revolución Mexicana, 1958); and Rafael Carrasco Puente, ed., *La caricatura en Mexico* (Mexico: Imprenta Universitaria, 1953).

On the era of the Great Rebellion, 1900–1923, see the following: The most recent overall study is Ramón Eduardo Ruíz's prizewinning book, *The Great Rebellion, 1905–1924* (New York: W. W. Norton & Co., 1980). An indispensable work that supplants many previous studies, also a prizewinning book, is *The Secret War in Mexico: Europe, the United States, and the Mexican Revolution* by Chicago historian Friedrich Katz (Chicago: University of Chicago Press, 1981). A vital reference work for the 1913–20 period remains Charles Cumberland's *Mexican Revolution: The Constitutionalist Years* (a sequel to his work on Madero), published by the University of Texas Press in 1972. For the earlier period, also published by the University of Texas Press, see James D. Cockcroft, *Intellectual Precursors of the Mexican Revolution, 1900–1913* (1968).

For the topic of urban labor during the Great Rebellion era see John M. Hart, *Anarchism and the Mexican Working Class, 1860–1931* (Austin: University of Texas Press, 1978), and Ramón Eduardo Ruíz, *Labor and the Ambivalent Revolutionaries: Mexico, 1911–1923* (Baltimore: Johns Hopkins University Press, 1976). For diplomacy of the borderlands see W. Dirk Raat, *Revoltosos! Mexico's Rebels in the*

United States, 1903–1923 (College Station: Texas A&M University Press, 1981), and for Woodrow Wilson's diplomatic initiatives between 1915 and 1921 see Mark T. Gilderhus, *Diplomacy and Revolution* (Tucson: University of Arizona Press, 1977).

For biographical-historical studies of the leading political figures of the Great Rebellion see the following: William H. Beezley, *Insurgent Governor: Abraham González and the Mexican Revolution in Chihuahua* (Lincoln: University of Nebraska Press, 1973); Martín Luis Guzmán, *Memoirs of Pancho Villa*, trans. by Virginia H. Taylor (Austin: University of Texas Press, 1975); Michael C. Meyer, *Huerta: A Political Portrait* (Lincoln: University of Nebraska Press, 1972); John Womack, Jr., *Zapata and the Mexican Revolution* (New York: Vintage Books, 1968); Linda B. Hall, *Álvaro Obregón* (College Station: Texas A&M University Press, 1981).

A political narrative of the Calles-Cárdenas era is John W. F. Dulles, *Yesterday in Mexico: A Chronicle of the Revolution, 1919–1936* (Austin: University of Texas Press, 1967). For a detailed Marxist interpretation of the Cárdenas era see Arnaldo Córdova, *La política de masas del cardenismo* (Mexico: Ediciones Era, 1974). On the Cristeros see both Jean A. Meyer, *The Cristero Rebellion*, trans. by Richard Southern (New York and London: Cambridge University Press, 1976), and David C. Bailey, ¡*Viva Cristo Rey! The Cristero Rebellion and the Church-State Conflict in Mexico* (Austin: University of Texas Press, 1974). On agrarianism see Heather Fowler Salamini, *Agrarian Radicalism in Veracruz, 1920–38* (Lincoln: University of Nebraska Press, 1978). Finally, James W. Wilkie and Edna Monzón de Wilkie have compiled *México visto en el siglo XX* (Mexico: Instituto Mexicano de Investigaciones Económicas, 1969), which is composed of oral history memoirs of leaders who figured prominently in Mexico's public life in the 1920s and 1930s.

On current history see *Mexico Today*, ed. by Tommie Sue Montgomery (Philadelphia: Institute for the Study of Human Issues, 1982), a collection of fourteen timely essays by prominent Mexican academics and politicians. Also see the several stimulating essays in "Mexico in the Eighties" in *Latin American Perspectives* 32 (Winter 1982). For the topic of public health see James J. Horn, "The Mexican Revolution and Health Care, or the Health of the Mexican Revolution," *Latin American Perspectives* 39 (Fall 1983). For agricultural policy see Cynthia Hewitt de Alcántara, *La modernización de la agricultura mexicana, 1940–1970* (Mexico: Siglo XXI Editores,

1978). George W. Grayson's *The Politics of Mexican Oil* (Pittsburgh: University of Pittsburgh Press, 1980) is an important study on the role and impact of the oil industry, especially during the José López Portillo years. On repression in the Mexican political system see Arturo Warman, *"We Come to Object": The Peasants of Morelos and the National State* (Baltimore: Johns Hopkins University Press, 1981), and Fernando Carmona, et al., *El Milagro Mexicano* (Mexico: Editorial Nuestro Tiempo, 1970). Also see the reports of the International League of Human Rights, as well as Amnesty International. On covert activity see Manuel Buendia, *La CIA en México* (Mexico: Ediciones Oceano, 1983).

Because of current interest in audiovisual materials, a few words about films are in order. The best guide to Latin American instructional and feature films is Jane M. Loy's *Latin America: Sights and Sounds, A Guide to Motion Pictures and Music for College Courses,* Consortium of Latin American Studies Program Publication No. 5 (Gainesville, Fla., 1973). Two of the better-known periodicals in this area are *Film and History* and the *Film Quarterly.* See also J. A. S. Grenville, *Film as History: The Nature of Film Evidence* (Birmingham, Eng.: University of Birmingham, 1970).

Films available for classroom use include *North from Mexico* (Mass Communications, Inc.); *Memorias de un mexicano,* a documentary based solely on Mexican archival film footage available at ten North American universities (Tulane, Texas-Austin, Texas – El Paso, Connecticut, SUNY-Buffalo, Iowa, Nebraska, California – Los Angeles, Massachusetts-Amherst, Princeton); *The Forgotten Village,* based on a story by John Steinbeck (Audio-Brandon); *Viva Zapata,* another Steinbeck classic starring Marlon Brando (Audio-Brandon); Luis Buñuel's classic *Los olvidados* (*The Young and the Damned*) (Audio-Brandon) and *Mexican Bus Ride* (Swank); *Mexico: The Frozen Revolution,* based on archival film footage (Tricontinental Film Center); *The Ragged Revolution: The Romance and the Reality of the Mexican Revolution, 1910–1920,* also based on rare photos and recently discovered film footage (Document Associates); *Octavio Paz: Uncommon Poet* (Films for the Humanities, Princeton); and *The Ballad of Gregorio Cortez* (Embassy Pictures, 1983). A cross-cultural and comparative history of Mexico and the United States available on videotape for classroom use only, in English and Spanish, is *Mexican Maize: An Historical Labyrinth* (W. Dirk Raat, producer; Instructional Resources Center, State University of New York at Fredonia, 1983).

INDEX